CW00369196

Welcome to the 2008 edition of our Great Britain & Ireland Hotels & Spas Guide, which after 25 years of being published in a 'coffee table' style has undergone some significant and refreshing changes. This new compact size remains highly visual and features easier to read entries, clearer maps and more informed text. Using less paper, the reduced weight also helps us to be more environmentally friendly as we distribute worldwide, currently stretching from Chile to China.

The Guide has been designed to help you make the right choice. Our Recommendations offer a breadth of variety and value as we understand that today's traveller often seeks out different experiences: a romantic anniversary break, a tranquil and informal environment, a contemporary city base or classic gourmet sophistication.

Our collection is made up of six Guides, representing over 1,300 annually inspected and recommended hotels, resorts, spas and meeting venues throughout 67 countries. You can read about the other guides on page 343 or see the whole collection online at www.johansens.com

This 2008 edition includes many new Recommendations as well as consummate favourites for you to try, and you can be certain that our team of Inspectors has been busy ensuring that only the best places are recommended and those that don't reach our exacting standards are not.

If you have a chance we would love to hear about your experience by completing a Guest Survey Report at the back of this Guide or online. Feedback is an influencing factor when we compile nominations for our Annual Awards for Excellence.

Above all, we hope you enjoy your stay and please remember to mention 'Condé Nast Johansens' when you make an enquiry or reservation.

Andrew Warren
Managing Director

# BEYOND COMPARE...

Image from britainonview.com

# About this Guide

### To find a hotel by location:

- Use the **county maps** at the front of the Guide to obtain a page number for the area of the country you wish to search.
- Turn to the **indexes** at the back of the book, which start on page 324.
- Alternatively, use the **maps** at the rear of the Guide where each hotel is marked.

If you cannot find a suitable hotel you may decide to choose one of the properties within the *Condé Nast Johansens Recommended Small Hotels, Inns & Restaurants Guide.* These more intimate establishments are listed on pages 291–292.

Once you have made your choice please contact the hotel directly. Rates are per room, including VAT and breakfast (unless stated otherwise) and are correct at the time of going to press but you should always check with the hotel before you make your reservation. **When making a booking please mention that Condé Nast Johansens is your source of reference.**

We occasionally receive letters from guests who have been charged for accommodation booked in advance but later cancelled. Readers should be aware that by making a reservation with a hotel, either by telephone, e-mail or in writing, they are entering into a legal contract. A hotelier under certain circumstances is entitled to make a charge for accommodation when guests fail to arrive, even if notice of the cancellation is given.

Higland p263

Aberdeenshire p256

Perth & Kinross
p270

Argyll &
Bute p257

Glasgow
p262

Edinburgh
p261
Midlothian
p269

SCOTLAND

South
Ayrshire
p272

Dumfries & Galloway p259

Donegal
p234

N. IRELAND

Mayo
p248

Monaghan
p250

Cavan
p232

Galway
p236

Dublin
p235

Kildare
p246

IRELAND

Kilkenny
p247

Wexford
p252

Kerry
p240

Cork p233

ENGLAND

WALES

SCOTLAND

N. IRELAND

IRELAND

Northumberland p157

Tyne & Wear p197

Cumbria p61

Durham p96

North Yorkshire p217

Lancashire p131

West Yorkshire p229

South Yorkshire p228

Isle of Anglesey p282

Conwy p277

Cheshire p46

Derbyshire p75

Lincolnshire p135

Gwynedd p279

Satffordshire p172

Nottinghamshire p158

ENGLAND

WALES

Shropshire p165

Leicestershire p134

Rutland p164

Norfolk p153

Ceredigion p275

Birmingham p38

Powys p287

Worcestershire p210

Warwickshire p198

Northamptonshire p154

Cambridgeshire p44

Pembrokeshire p286

Herefordshire p125

Suffolk p173

Bedfordshire p27

Monmouthshire p284

Gloucestershire p97

Buckinghamshire p39

Hertfordshire p126

Vale of Glamorgan p290

Cardiff p274

Newport p285

South Gloucestershire p114

Oxfordshire p161

London p136

Bath & NE Somerset p20

Berkshire p29

Wiltshire p204

Somerset p166

Hampshire p115

Surrey p180

Kent p129

Devon p78

West Sussex p192

East Sussex p183

Dorset p91

Cornwall p50

**Channel Islands**

Jersey p16

5

# Key to Symbols

23 Total number of bedrooms

Owner managed

CC Credit cards not accepted

Quiet location

Wheelchair Access. We recommend that you contact the hotel to determine the level of accessibility for wheelchair users.

Chef-patron

M 23 Meeting/conference facilities with maximum number of delegates

8 Children welcome, with minimum age where applicable

Dogs welcome in rooms or kennels

At least 1 bedroom has a four-poster bed

Cable/satellite TV in all bedrooms

CD player in bedrooms

DVD/video player in bedrooms

ISDN/modem point in all bedrooms

WiFi Wireless Internet connection available in part or all rooms

Non-smoking bedrooms available

Lift available for guests' use

Air conditioning in all bedrooms

Gym/fitness facilities on-site

SPA A dedicated spa offering extensive health, beauty and fitness treatments together with water treatments

Indoor swimming pool

Outdoor swimming pool

Tennis court on-site

Walking – details of local walking routes and packed lunches can be provided and an overnight drying room for clothes is available.

Fishing on-site

Fishing can be arranged

Golf course on-site

Golf course nearby, which has an arrangement with the property allowing guests to play

Shooting on-site

Shooting can be arranged

Horse riding can be arranged

Property has a helicopter landing pad

Licensed for wedding ceremonies

View of the lake at Sharrow Bay, Cumbria

the perfect end to every day.

Sleepeezee Contract Beds
1-8 Hulbert Industrial Estate
Cinder Bank, Dudley,
West Midlands. DY2 9AD
T: +44 (0) 1384 455515
F: +44 (0) 1384 246179
email: contractservices@sleepeezee.co.uk
online: www.sleepeezee.co.uk

BY APPOINTMENT TO
H.M. THE QUEEN
BEDDING MANUFACTURERS
SLEEPEEZEE LIMITED, ROCHESTER

BY APPOINTMENT TO
H.R.H. THE PRINCE OF WALES
BEDDING MANUFACTURERS
SLEEPEEZEE LIMITED, ROCHESTER

# Sleepeezee

## CONTRACT BEDS DIVISION

Image from britainonview.com

# Condé Nast Johansens

Condé Nast Johansens Ltd, 6-8 Old Bond Street, London W1S 4PH
Tel: +44 (0)20 7499 9080  Fax: +44 (0)20 7152 3565
E-mail: info@johansens.com
**www.johansens.com**

| | |
|---|---|
| **Publishing Director:** | Patricia Greenwood |
| **PA to Publishing Director:** | Clare Freeman |
| **Hotel Inspectors:** | Jean Branham |
| | Peter Bridgham |
| | Geraldine Bromley |
| | Robert Bromley |
| | Audrey Fenton |
| | Henrietta Fergusson |
| | Pat Gillson |
| | Marie Iversen |
| | Pauline Mason |
| | John Morison |
| | John O'Neill |
| | Mary O'Neill |
| | Fiona Patrick |
| | Liza Reeves |
| | Leonora Sandwell |
| | Nevill Swanson |
| **Production Manager:** | Kevin Bradbrook |
| **Production Editor:** | Laura Kerry |
| **Senior Designer:** | Michael Tompsett |
| **Copywriters:** | Sophie Cliffe-Roberts |
| | Norman Flack |
| | Debra O'Sullivan |
| | Rozanne Paragon |
| | Leonora Sandwell |
| **Marketing & Sales Promotions Executive:** | Charlie Bibby |
| **Client Services Director:** | Fiona Patrick |
| **Managing Director:** | Andrew Warren |

Copyright © 2007 Condé Nast Johansens Ltd.
Condé Nast Johansens Ltd. is part of The Condé Nast Publications Ltd.
ISBN 978-1-903665-33-6
Printed in England by St Ives plc
Distributed in the UK and Europe by Portfolio, Greenford (bookstores).
In North America by Casemate Publishing, Pennsylvania (bookstores).
Front cover picture: Cowley Manor, Gloucestershire

# Awards for Excellence

The Condé Nast Johansens 2007 Awards for Excellence were presented at our Awards Dinner held at Jumeirah Carlton Tower, London, on 6th November, 2006. Awards were received by properties from all over the world that represented the finest standards and best value for money in luxury independent travel. An important source of information for these awards was the feedback provided by guests who completed Condé Nast Johansens Guest Survey Reports. Forms can be found on page 344.

**2007 Winners appearing in this Guide:**

Most Excellent Service
- THE ATLANTIC HOTEL AND OCEAN RESTAURANT
– Jersey, Channel Islands, p16

Most Excellent Coastal Hotel Award
- THE NARE HOTEL – Carne Beach, Cornwall, p50

Most Excellent City Hotel Award
- LACE MARKET HOTEL – Nottingham, Nottinghamshire, p158

Most Excellent Country Hotel
- LINTHWAITE HOUSE HOTEL – Windermere, Cumbria, p73

Most Excellent Country Hotel Award
- BODYSGALLEN HALL & SPA – Llandudno, Conwy, p277

Condé Nast Johansens Readers' Award
- KILLASHEE HOUSE HOTEL & VILLA SPA
– Killashee, Kildare, p246

Most Excellent Meeting Venue
- CALCOT MANOR HOTEL & SPA – Tetbury, Gloucestershire, p111

Champagne Taittinger Wine List of the Year Award
Overall Winner
- HOLBECK GHYLL COUNTRY HOUSE HOTEL
– Ambleside, Cumbria, p62

Knight Frank Award for
Outstanding Excellence & Innovation
- ANDREW DAVIS – Owner, von Essen Hotels

'Life is to be enjoyed, let us do the hard work for you'.

Personal | Insurance | Solutions
Preferred insurance partner of Condé Nast Johansens

# 0800 230 0833
Johansens@jltgroup.com

Personal | Insurance | Solutions
Preferred insurance partner of Condé Nast Johansens

JARDINE LLOYD THOMPSON
Personal Risks

# The Perfect Combination...

## Condé Nast Johansens Gift Vouchers

Condé Nast Johansens Gift Vouchers make a unique and much valued present for birthdays, weddings, anniversaries, special occasions and as a corporate incentive.

Vouchers are available in denominations of £100, £50, €140, €70, $150, $75 and may be used as payment or part payment for your stay or a meal at any Condé Nast Johansens 2008 recommended property.

**To order Gift Vouchers call +44 (0)207 152 3558 or purchase direct at www.johansens.com**

## Condé Nast Johansens Guides

As well as this Guide, Condé Nast Johansens also publish the following titles:

Recommended Small Hotels, Inns & Restaurants, Great Britain & Ireland 2008
Recommended Hotels & Spas, Europe & The Mediterranean 2008
Recommended Hotels, Inns, Resorts & Spas, The Americas, Atlantic, Caribbean & Pacific 2008
Luxury Spas Worldwide 2008
Recommended International Venues for Meetings & Special Events 2008

**To purchase Guides please call FREEPHONE 0800 269 397 or visit our Bookshop at www.johansens.com**

# Channel Islands

For further information on the Channel Islands, please contact:

**Visit Guernsey**
PO Box 23, St Peter Port, Guernsey GY1 3AN
Tel: +44 (0)1481 723552
Internet: www.visitguernsey.com

**Jersey Tourism**
Liberation Square, St Helier, Jersey JE1 1BB
Tel: +44 (0)1534 448800
E-mail: info@jersey.com
Internet: www.jersey.com

**Sark Tourism**
The Visitors Centre, The Avenue, Sark, GY9 0SA
Tel: +44 (0)1481 832345
E-mail: contact@sark.com
Internet: www.sark.info

**Herm Tourist Office**
Administration Office, Herm Island, Guernsey GY1 3HR
Tel: +44 (0)1481 722377
E-mail: admin@herm-island.com
Internet: www.herm-island.com

or see **pages 293-296** for details of local historic houses, castles and gardens to visit during your stay.

For additional places to stay in the Channel Islands, turn to **pages 291-292** where a listing of our Recommended Small Hotels, Inns & Restaurant Guide can be found.

# The Atlantic Hotel and Ocean Restaurant

LE MONT DE LA PULENTE, ST BRELADE, JERSEY, JE3 8HE
**Tel:** 0845 365 2395 **International:** +44 (0)1534 744101 **Fax:** 01534 744102
**Web:** www.johansens.com/atlantic **E-mail:** info@theatlantichotel.com

***Our inspector loved:*** *The view of the ocean from the Michelin-Starred restaurant.*

**Price Guide:**
single £150–£190
double/twin £205–£325
suite/deluxe £325–£565

**Awards/Recognition:** Condé Nast Johansens Most Excellent Service 2007; 1 Star Michelin 2007

**Location:** A13, 0.5 miles; St Helier, 5 miles; Jersey Airport, 3 miles

**Attractions:** Jersey War Tunnels; Jersey Zoo; Orchid Farm; La Mare Vineyards

This stunning hotel is the object of continuous and thoughtful investment by its owner who places the needs of his guests first. Be spoiled by superb service and contemporary interiors that are decorated with vibrant island art. The Atlantic stands in 6 acres of private grounds alongside La Moye Golf Course with sympathetic cliff-top landscaping that has opened a new vista, allowing an uninterrupted view of the ocean across a 5-mile sweep of St Ouen's Bay. Enjoy a special treat and stay in the prestigious Atlantic Suite with its own entrance hall, living room, guest cloakroom and service pantry. Gaining a much deserved Michelin Star, the restaurant showcases modern British cuisine, with an emphasis on seafood and fresh local produce. Be sure to book in advance.

# The Club Hotel & Spa, Bohemia Restaurant

GREEN STREET, ST HELIER, JERSEY JE2 4UH
**Tel:** 0845 365 2419 **International:** +44 (0)1534 876500 **Fax:** 01534 720371
**Web:** www.johansens.com/theclubjersey **E-mail:** reservations@theclubjersey.com

**Our inspector loved:** *The wonderfully welcoming bedrooms.*

**Price Guide:**
double/twin from £195
suite from £350

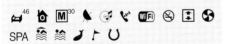
SPA 🌊 🌊 ♪ ⏲ ↻

**Awards/Recognition:** 1 Star Michelin 2007;
4 AA Rosettes 2007-2008

**Location:** A15, 0.25 miles; Jersey Airport, 5 miles

**Attractions:** Shopping in St Helier; Maritime Museum; Jersey Pottery; Elizabeth Castle and Harbour

The Club Hotel and Spa reflects the real buzz that exudes from St Helier itself. Designed with contemporary elegance and understated luxury in mind, bedrooms and suites are furnished to a standard you'll love - LCD TVs and CD players feature - while sleek bathrooms have granite surfaces, power showers and all-enveloping sumptuous bathrobes. The sophisticated Bohemia Restaurant has rapidly gained an enviable reputation and the place to be seen and be seen in is the hotel's chic, popular bar. At the Club Spa, you're encouraged to savour a slower pace of life to maximise the treatments and benefits on offer and once refreshed take a walk along the sandy beaches, surf, sail, or explore the secret places of this beautiful island.

# LONGUEVILLE MANOR

ST SAVIOUR, JERSEY, CHANNEL ISLANDS JE2 7WF
**Tel:** 0845 365 2038 **International:** +44 (0)1534 725501 **Fax:** 01534 731613
**Web:** www.johansens.com/longuevillemanor **E-mail:** info@longuevillemanor.com

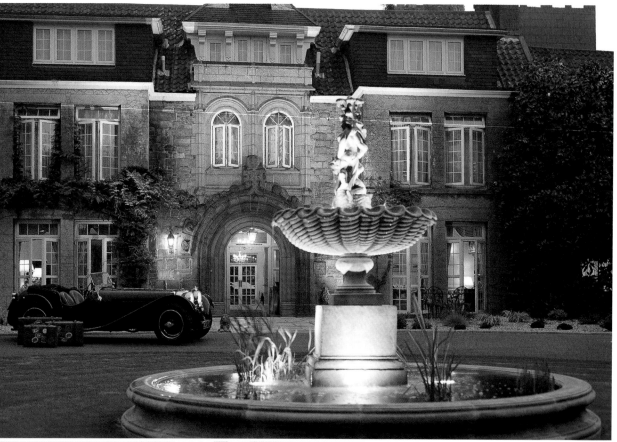

**Our inspector loved:** The honeymoon suite with four poster bed and hand-painted bath for two.

**Price Guide:**
single from £175
double/twin £230–£480
suite £500–£800

**Awards/Recognition:** Relais & Châteaux; 3 AA Rosettes 2007-2008

**Location:** Just off A3; St Helier, 1.25 miles; Jersey Airport, 7 miles

**Attractions:** Jersey Pottery; Durrell Wildlife Conservation Trust; Jersey War Tunnels; La Mare Vineyards

Upon arrival at this restored 13th-century Norman manor house you're greeted in your room or suite by Champagne and homemade shortbread. All rooms are decorated in warm tones with carefully chosen antiques, beautiful fabrics, digital widescreen TVs and DVD/CD players. Honeymooners are in for a real treat in their secluded suite complete with four-poster bed and hand-painted bath for two. Credited with numerous awards the Oak Room restaurant offers fine food and an extensive selection of old and new world wines for which first hand advice may be sought from the Master Sommelier. The Oak Room is also licensed to hold civil wedding ceremonies and with its beautiful setting of pretty gardens and lake, Longueville Manor makes a dreamy wedding location.

Image from britainonview.com

# England

For further information on England, please contact:

**Cumbria Tourist Board**
Tel: +44 (0)1539 822222
Web: www.golakes.co.uk

**East of England Tourist Board**
Tel: +44 (0)1284 727470
E-mail: info@eet.org.uk
Web: www.visiteastofengland.com

**Heart of England Tourism**
Tel: +44 (0)1905 761100
Web: www.visitheartofengland.com

**Visit London**
Tel: 0870 156 6366
Web: www.visitlondon.com

**North East England Tourism Team**
Tel: +44 (0)906 683 3000
Web: www.visitnortheastengland.com

**North West Tourist Board**
Tel: +44 (0)1942 821 222
Web: www.visitnorthwest.com

**Tourism South East**
Tel: +44 (0)23 8062 5400
Web: www.visitsoutheastengland.com

**South West Tourism**
Tel: 0870 442 0880
Web: www.visitsouthwest.co.uk

**Yorkshire Tourist Board**
Tel: +44 (0)1904 707961
Web: www.ytb.org.uk

**English Heritage**
Tel: +44 (0) 870 333 1181
Web: www.english-heritage.org.uk

**Historic Houses Association**
Tel: +44 (0)20 7259 5688
Web: www.hha.org.uk

**The National Trust**
Tel: 0870 458 4000
Web: www.nationaltrust.org.uk

or see **pages 293-296** for details of local historic houses, castles and gardens to visit during your stay.

For additional places to stay in England, turn to **pages 291-292** where a listing of our Recommended Small Hotels, Inns & Restaurant Guide can be found.

# THE BATH PRIORY HOTEL AND RESTAURANT

WESTON ROAD, BATH, SOMERSET BA1 2XT
**Tel:** 0845 365 2397 **International:** +44 (0)1225 331922 **Fax:** 01225 448276
**Web:** www.johansens.com/bathpriory **E-mail:** mail@thebathpriory.co.uk

*Our inspector loved:* The large outdoor terrace for alfresco lunches overlooking the lovely gardens.

**Price Guide:** (incl. full English breakfast) double/twin from £245

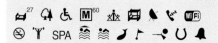

**Awards/Recognition:** 1 Star Michelin 2007; 3 AA Rosettes 2005-2006

**Location:** Bath, 1 mile; M4 jct 18, 7.5 miles; Bristol Airport, 14 miles

**Attractions:** Roman Baths; Theatre Royal; The Cotswolds; Thermae Bath Spa

Standing close to some of England's most famous and finest architecture, The Bath Priory Hotel is very easy on the eye, this Georgian mellow stone building dating from 1835 formed part of a row of fashionable residences on the west side of the city. You will sense this history as you enter the hotel - antique furniture, oil paintings and objets d'art greet you - and well-defined colour schemes uplift throughout. Experience Michelin-Star, modern European cuisine in the charming restaurant, under the watchful eye of Deputy General Manager Vito Scaduto MCA where wines are well chosen. You can arrange private parties in the terrace, pavilion and orangery. Bath, of course, has so much to offer - The Pump Rooms, Museum of Costume and wonderful bijou shops.

# The Bath Spa Hotel

SYDNEY ROAD, BATH, SOMERSET BA2 6JF
**Tel:** 0845 365 2398 **International:** +44 (0)1225 444424 **Fax:** 01225 444006
**Web:** www.johansens.com/bathspa **E-mail:** sales.bathspa@macdonald-hotels.co.uk

***Our inspector loved:*** *The beautiful new Imperial Suites offering a full butler service.*

**Price Guide:**
double/twin £149–£378
4-poster £279–£498
imperial suites £219-£778

**Awards/Recognition:** 2 AA Rosettes 2006-2007

**Location:** A36, 0.5 miles; A4, 2 miles; M4 jct 18, 8 miles; Bristol Airport, 20 miles

**Attractions:** Thermae Bath Spa; Roman Baths; Longleat; Stonehenge

The Bath Spa's mature grounds dotted with ancient cedars, fountains and an elegant Georgian façade merely hint at the warmth, style and service within, and you only have to settle amidst rich colours in the elegant bedrooms or mahogany and marble-clad bathrooms to enjoy a sense of luxurious well-being. All the amenities of a 5-star hotel are here, along with the character of a homely country house, and you can be confident that Chef Andrew Hamer will take particular care of the award-winning contemporary cuisine created for your pleasure. The leisure spa features an indoor pool, gym, whirlpool, outdoor hydrotherapy pool, Thermal Suite, treatment rooms and croquet lawn. You can explore Bath, motor racing at Castle Combe, or go up and away in a hot air balloon !

# DUKES HOTEL

GREAT PULTENEY STREET, BATH, SOMERSET BA2 4DN
**Tel:** 0845 365 3274 **International:** +44 (0)1225 787960 **Fax:** 01225 787961
**Web:** www.johansens.com/dukesbath **E-mail:** info@dukesbath.co.uk

*Our inspector loved:* The wonderfully friendly welcome and blazing open fire in the reception area.

**Price Guide:**
single £100
double/twin £135–£155
suite £195–£215

**Awards/Recognition:** 3 AA Rosettes 2007-2008

**Location:** A36, 0.5 miles; M4 jct 18, 8 miles; Bristol Airport, 15.5 miles; London, 90-min train

**Attractions:** Roman Baths & Pump Room; Museums & Galleries; Theatre Royal; Bath Abbey

Dukes Hotel introduces itself as charming, full of character and style as soon as you walk through the elegant entrance below half-moon shaped decorative glass and edged by slim, black, wrought-iron railings. Grade I listed and built from Bath stone, the hotel is a former Palladian mansion, and today basks in a sense of understated luxury. Most guest rooms and suites have original intricate plasterwork and large sash windows, and from front rooms you can see more Palladio-inspired façades, while those at the back look out to rolling hills. Recently refurbished, the Cavendish Restaurant is light, airy and relaxing, and you can enjoy the best organic and free-range British ingredients, including Cornish lamb, Angus beef and seafood delivered daily from Devon.

# THE ROYAL CRESCENT HOTEL

16 ROYAL CRESCENT, BATH, SOMERSET BA1 2LS
**Tel:** 0845 365 2679  **International:** +44 (0)1225 823333  **Fax:** 01225 339401
**Web:** www.johansens.com/royalcrescent  **E-mail:** info@royalcrescent.co.uk

*Our inspector loved:* The stunning newly decorated Dower House Restaurant and Bar.

**Price Guide:**
double/twin from £245
suite from £435

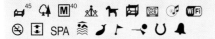

**Awards/Recognition:** 3 AA Rosettes 2006-2007

**Location:** City Centre; A4, 1.5 miles; M4 jct 18, 10 miles; Bath Spa Station, 1 mile

**Attractions:** The Roman Baths; Stourhead; Longleat; Cotswolds

Built in 1775 The Royal Crescent Hotel already had a head start when it came to beauty - as it occupies the 2 central houses of one of Europe's finest masterpieces, a sweep of 30 houses with identical façades stretching in a 500ft curve - a total refurbishment restored many of its classical Georgian features and facilitated essential modern conveniences you would expect today. Each room has been lovingly restored to its original splendour with infinite care for recreating the authentic period details, while the relaxed, informal atmosphere of Dower House restaurant offers you a contemporary menu. You can use the hotel exclusively for special occasions or corporate events. The Bath House is a unique spa, in which to enjoy complementary therapies and holistic massage. You can also take a private cruise in the hotel's vintage river launch.

# Homewood Park

HINTON CHARTERHOUSE, BATH, SOMERSET BA2 7TB
**Tel:** 0845 365 1875 **International:** +44 (0)1225 723731 **Fax:** 01225 723820
**Web:** www.johansens.com/homewoodpark **E-mail:** info@homewoodpark.co.uk

*Our inspector loved:* The comfortable hospitality of this traditional country house.

**Price Guide:**
single from £140
double/twin from £165
suite from £245

**Awards/Recognition:** 2 AA Rosettes 2007-2008;

**Location:** On the A36; Bath 6 miles; M4 jct 18, 15 miles; Bristol Airport, 20 miles

**Attractions:** Longleat; Stonehenge; Stourhead; Roman Baths

First recommended by Condé Nast Johansens in 1983 Homewood Park is situated in a designated area of outstanding natural beauty amid acres of grounds and woodland on the edge of Limpley Stoke Valley. If you really enjoy small country house hotels Homewood is for you, with its elegant interiors, antiques, Oriental rugs and oil paintings. The lavishly furnished bedrooms offer comfort, style and privacy with views over the Victorian garden. Both the bar and drawing rooms feature blazing log fires during the cooler months. Carefully selected wines, stored in the original medieval cellars accompany lunches and dinners that have built an enviable reputation for the hotel, and feature local produce whenever possible.

# HUNSTRETE HOUSE

HUNSTRETE, NR BATH, SOMERSET BS39 4NS
**Tel:** 0845 365 1906 **International:** +44 (0)1761 490490 **Fax:** 01761 490732
**Web:** www.johansens.com/hunstretehouse **E-mail:** reception@hunstretehouse.co.uk

**Our inspector loved:** *The perfect location in beautiful surroundings yet a short drive from both Bath & Bristol*

**Price Guide:**
single from £135
double/twin from £170
suite from £265

**Awards/Recognition:** 2 AA Rosettes 2006-2007

**Location:** A368, 0.1 miles; A37, 1.8 miles; Bath, 8 miles; Brsitol Airport, 15.5 miles

**Attractions:** Roman Baths; Bristol; Wells Cathedral; Cheddar Caves & Gorge

On the edge of the Mendip Hills stands Hunstrete House, largely built in the 18th century and surrounded by lovely gardens. Bedrooms are individually decorated and furnished, many offer uninterrupted views over fields and woodlands. The reception areas feature beautiful antiques and log fires burn in the hall, library and drawing room through the winter. The Terrace dining room overlooks an Italianate, flower-filled courtyard. A highly skilled head chef prepares light, elegant dishes using produce from the extensive garden, including organic meat and vegetables. The menu changes regularly and the the wine list has an excellent reputation. The hotel is also available for exclusive use wedding and corporate events with a marquee to seat up to 120 people.

# THE PARK

WICK, NEAR BATH BS30 5RN
**Tel:** 0845 365 2619 **International:** +44 (0)117 937 1800 **Fax:** 0117 937 1813
**Web:** www.johansens.com/thepark **E-mail:** info@tpresort.com

**Our inspector loved:** *The beautifully decorated Manor House and surrounding views.*

**Price Guide:**
single from £135
double/twin from £185
luxury from £280

**Awards/Recognition:** 2 AA Rosettes 2007-2008

**Location:** Off the A420; A46, 2.3 miles; M4 jct 18, 7 miles; Bath, 4 miles

**Attractions:** Stonehenge; Bristol; Thermae Bath Spa; Cotswolds

If you're a golfer you'll be in 18th heaven at this hotel with its 2 championship golf courses filled with mature trees, lakes and modern specification greens, if you're not, you'll love it anyway for its beauty, stylish bedrooms and glorious natural parkland. The Park's restaurant, Oakwood, was originally an old stone Masonic lodge, and has an open-plan kitchen under the instruction of Chef Mark Treasure. Menus specialise in the simple treatment of roasted meats and fish cooked in a wood burning oven. There are 7 conference and syndicate rooms accommodating up to 150 delegates, and the attractive Park Room, with views over the golf course, seats up to 130 for a private banquet or wedding reception. You're conveniently located between Bristol and Bath. Take the park & ride, just 2 miles from the hotel and enjoy a fabulous day out in the beautiful, Georgian city of Bath

# LUTON HOO HOTEL, GOLF & SPA

THE MANSION HOUSE, LUTON HOO, LUTON, BEDFORDSHIRE LU1 3TQ
**Tel:** 0845 365 3458 **International:** +44 (0)1582 734437 **Fax:** +44 (0)1582 485438
**Web:** www.johansens.com/lutonhoo **E-mail:** reservations@lutonhoo.co.uk

***Our inspector loved:*** *The elegantly beautiful sweeping staircase.*

**Price Guide:**
single £235-£810
double £275-£850
suite £360-£850

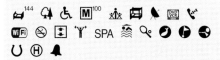

**Location:** A1081, 1 mile; M1 jct 10, 3 miles; Luton Airport, 10-min drive; London, 30-min train

**Attractions:** London; St.Albans; Hatfield House; Woburn Abbey

Newly opened in Autumn 2007, this Grade 1 listed historic country mansion has been restored to its original splendor. As you reach the top of the drive the house comes into view and you can only be impressed. It's majestic. Overlooking over 1000 acres of parkland and formal gardens that Capability Brown once so carefully orchestrated and which now includes a spa, swimming pool, golf course and tennis courts. In the main house there is a perfusion of marble, silks, paneling and marquetry. The sweeping staircase is a masterpiece in itself and the master bedrooms luxuriously elegant. More bedrooms are to be found in the Parklands and in the Historic Flower Garden Wood. Take tea in the Italianate drawing room or experience fine cuisine in the former state dining room, now the Wernher Restaurant. An outstanding retreat.

# MOORE PLACE HOTEL

THE SQUARE, ASPLEY GUISE, MILTON KEYNES, BEDFORDSHIRE MK17 8DW
**Tel:** 0845 365 2075 **International:** +44 (0)1908 282000 **Fax:** 01908 281888
**Web:** www.johansens.com/mooreplace **E-mail:** manager@mooreplace.com

***Our inspector loved:*** *The Cottage bedrooms and watergarden.*

**Price Guide:**
single £59–£130
double/twin £89–£130
suite £150–£195

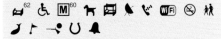

**Awards/Recognition:** 2 AA Rosettes 2006-2007

**Location:** M1 jct 13, 1.65 miles; Milton Keynes Railway Station, 8 miles; Luton Airport, 19 miles

**Attractions:** Woburn Abbey; Whipsnade Zoo; Waddesdon Manor; Bletchley Park

Situated in the village of Aspley Guise just 1.5 miles from the M1 this delightful country house hotel has been sympathetically restored to suit the original 1786 building. Relax and enjoy the attractive patio courtyard, rock garden and waterfall. 62 comfortably appointed bedrooms offer lots of little extras including a welcoming drink and large toweling bathrobes. 10 bedrooms with individual character are to be found in the converted, listed cottage. The highly acclaimed Greenhouse Restaurant, rated amongst the best in the area, is housed in the Victorian-style conservatory, and serves traditional English menus with a European twist. As well as being perfect for private dinners, conferences and special occasions, Moore Place is ideally situated for you to explore places of interest nearby.

# THE BEAR HOTEL

41 CHARNHAM STREET, HUNGERFORD, BERKSHIRE RG17 0EL
**Tel:** 0845 365 2401 **International:** +44 (0)1488 682512 **Fax:** 01488 684357
**Web:** www.johansens.com/bearhotelhungerford **E-mail:** info@thebearhotelhungerford.co.uk

*Our inspector loved: The smart contemporary rooms and restaurant in a welcoming relaxing atmosphere*

**Price Guide:**
standard £136
deluxe £170
suite £206

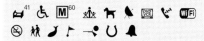

**Location:** On the A4; M4 jct 14, 4 miles; Hungerford Railway Station, 2-min walk; Heathrow, 80 miles

**Attractions:** Kennet & Avon Canal; Newbury Racecourse; Berkshire Downs; Avebury Stone Circle

King Henry VIII gave this attractive 13th-century inn to Anne of Cleeves in 1540, then to Katherine Parr a year later! Throughout the years it's seen many changes, but thankfully hangs onto its traditional feel, and is just a short walk from the picturesque Kennet and Avon Canal. For a weekend or longer stay The Bear is hard to beat, with bedrooms in the main building or around a waterside courtyard. Ideal for business visitors, you can request a room with broadband and WiFi, or avoid them like the plague and go for a more homely choice. The comfy bar is perfect for lunch or informal suppers, while award-winning chef, Phil Wild, presides over the smarter restaurant.

# FREDRICK'S – HOTEL RESTAURANT SPA

SHOPPENHANGERS ROAD, MAIDENHEAD, BERKSHIRE SL6 2PZ
**Tel:** 0845 365 1758 **International:** +44 (0)1628 581000 **Fax:** 01628 771054
**Web:** www.johansens.com/fredricks **E-mail:** reservations@fredricks–hotel.co.uk

*Our inspector loved: The attention to detail, peaceful gardens and wonderful welcome.*

**Price Guide:**
single from £245
double/twin from £325
suite from £450

**Awards/Recognition:** 3 AA Rosettes 2007-2008

**Location:** A4, 1 mile; M4 jct 8/9, 1 mile; Windsor, 6 miles; Heathrow, 17 miles

**Attractions:** Windsor Castle; Henley; Royal Ascot; Legoland

'Putting people first' is the guiding philosophy behind this superb second generation family-run hotel. Extensive landscaped gardens furnished with contemporary artwork overlook a broad swathe of Maidenhead Golf Club. Fredrick's exclusive Spa offers the ultimate in relaxation and was the first in the UK equipped with its own private flotation suite. You can indulge in restorative treatments such as Rasul or LaStone therapies. An experienced eye for detail is evident in the luxurious bedrooms, all with gleaming, marble bathrooms, some with their own patio or balcony. Highly acclaimed Gourmet cuisine, is served in elegant surroundings enhanced by a collection of fine art and sculpture. As well as being suitable for relaxation, leisurely spa breaks, romantic escapes and fine dining, Fredrick's is perfectly located for conferences and corporate hospitality.

# CLIVEDEN

TAPLOW, BERKSHIRE SL6 0JF
**Tel:** 0845 365 3236 **International:** +44 (0)1628 668561 **Fax:** 01628 661837
**Web:** www.johansens.com/cliveden **E-mail:** Reservations@clivedenhouse.co.uk

***Our inspector loved:*** *The approach up the long gravel drive and the wonderful welcome - pure indulgence!*

**Price Guide:** (room only, excluding VAT)
double/twin from £310
suites from £500

**Awards/Recognition:** 1 Star Michelin 2007; 2 AA Rosettes 2007-2008; Best Hotel for Food Condé Nast Traveller Gold List 2007

**Location:** A4, 3 miles; M4 jct 7, 4 miles; Maidenhead, 3 miles; Heathrow Airport, 12 miles

**Attractions:** Windsor Castle / Windsor Great Park; Ascot Racecourse; Wentworth Golf Club; Legoland

Overlooking the Thames in 376 acres Cliveden has been home to a Prince of Wales, 3 dukes, an earl and the Astor family and has been at the centre of Britain's social and political life for over 300 years. With such a 'wow' factor it's hard to know where to begin. Perhaps with the stunning 18th-century Rococo French Dining Room, or the award-winning restaurants, Michelin-starred Waldo's and The Terrace, overlooking the Parterre. Exquisitely furnished, original artworks and antiques feature strongly and if you long for privacy stay at Spring Cottage on the edge of the River Thames. Pamper yourself with treatments in the Spa, roam the estate or cruise the river on a vintage launch.

# DONNINGTON VALLEY HOTEL AND SPA

OLD OXFORD ROAD, DONNINGTON, NEWBURY, BERKSHIRE RG14 3AG
**Tel:** 0845 365 3267 **International:** +44 (0)1635 551199 **Fax:** 01635 551123
**Web:** www.johansens.com/donningtonvalley **E-mail:** general@donningtonvalley.co.uk

*Our inspector loved:* The new spa, spacious bedrooms and wonderful welcome.

**Price Guide:**
single from £180
double/twin £180
suite from £260

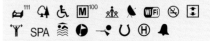

Experience England's most exciting Spa at this highly acclaimed 4 star hotel with it's 111 elegantly designed bedrooms and suites, an award-winning WinePress restaurant and challenging 18 hole golf course. Classic features such as an open log fire, wood beamed bar and lounge area create a friendly, warm and intimate ambience. Donnington Valley Health Club and Spa has everything you could wish for , from an 18m pool, Signature Lifefitness Gym, Jacuzzi, sauna, steam room, aromatherapy room and monsoon shower to seven treatment suites. There are a variety of Spa and Leisure Breaks for families and friends seeking a peaceful, rural setting in the heart of Berkshire. A great location just minutes from junction 13 of the M4.

**Awards/Recognition:** 2 AA Rosettes 2007-2008

**Location:** A34, 3 miles; M4 jct 13, 3 miles; Newbury, 2 miles; Heathrow Airport, 45 miles

**Attractions:** Donnington Castle; Newbury Racecourse; Highclere Castle; Lambourn Downs

# THE VINEYARD AT STOCKCROSS

NEWBURY, BERKSHIRE RG20 8JU

**Tel:** 0845 365 2716 **International:** +44 (0)1635 528770 **Fax:** 01635 528398
**Web:** www.johansens.com/vineyardstockcross **E-mail:** general@the-vineyard.co.uk

***Our inspector loved:*** *The pure indulgence of the rooms, the special atmosphere and wonderful staff.*

**Price Guide:** (room only)
classic £210
luxury £335
suite £430-£645

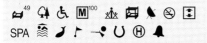

**Awards/Recognition:** 2 Star Michelin 2007; Relais & Châteaux; 4 AA Rosettes 2006-2007

**Location:** A4, 500 metres; M4 jct 13, 2.5 miles; Newbury, 2.5 miles; Heathrow, 45 miles

**Attractions:** Highclere Castle; Newbury Racecourse; Kennet & Avon Canal, Stonehenge

Sir Peter Michael's "restaurant-with-suites" showcases 600 top Californian wines, including those from the Peter Michael Winery. The Head Sommelier has a wide and innovative list with 2000 wines to complement the modern British cuisine created by Executive Chef, John Campbell. Dishes combine a unique blend of flavours and textures creating an unforgettable multi-sensory feast! Awards include 5 Red Stars and 4 AA Rosettes. An arresting collection of paintings and sculptures including the keynote piece "Fire and Water" by William Pye FRBS will inspire you further. The 49 bedrooms include 31 suites which provide stylish comfort. The Vineyard Spa features an indoor pool, spa bath, sauna, steam room and gym. The treatment rooms offer a range of ESPA and Choco, Vino and TruffleTherapy treatments.

# THE CRAB AT CHIEVELEY

WANTAGE ROAD, NEWBURY, BERKSHIRE RG20 8UE
**Tel:** 0845 365 2437 **International:** +44 (0)1635 247550 **Fax:** 01635 247440
**Web:** www.johansens.com/crabatchieveley **E-mail:** info@crabatchieveley.com

***Our inspector loved:*** *The quirkiness, the wonderful location and fabulous rooms.*

**Price Guide:**
single from £110
double £160-£210

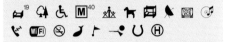

**Awards/Recognition:** 2 AA Rosettes 2007-2008

**Location:** A34, 4 miles; M4 jct 13, 6 miles; Newbury, 2 miles; Heathrow Airport, 45 miles

**Attractions:** Newbury Racecourse; Highclere Castle; Antique town of Hungerford; Walking on the Downs.

David and Jackie Barnard are as passionate as ever in ensuring their boutique hotel and outstanding restaurant are a destination in their own right. Filled with an eclectic mix of maritime and equestrian paraphernalia you immediately get drawn in. Romantics will just adore the bedrooms – inspired by the Barnard's visits to some of the worlds best hotels and each has its own way of indulging the senses. Bora Bora in stunning magenta and white comes with its own secret and very private hot tub garden, Cipriani, with luxurious Venetian fabrics and La Mamounia, evocative and atmospheric with a private tropical garden and an eight seater hot tub! A highly experienced and enthusiastic team are behind the acclaimed Fish and Seafood Restaurant; vegetables from their own garden and fish brought directly from the markets at Newlyn, Brixham and Looe.

# THE GREAT HOUSE

THAMES STREET, SONNING-ON-THAMES, NEAR READING, BERKSHIRE RG4 6UT
**Tel:** 0845 365 2513 **International:** +44 (0)118 9692277 **Fax:** 0118 9441296
**Web:** www.johansens.com/greathouse **E-mail:** greathouse@btconnect.com

***Our inspector loved:*** *The pretty riverside location and mix of facilities.*

**Price Guide:**
single £69.50–£149
double £119–£169
suite £149–£189

**Location:** A4, 1 mile; M4, 5 miles; Reading, 5 miles; Heathrow, 25 miles

**Attractions:** Windsor; Henley; River Thames; Ascot

The Great House has a fantastic "something for everyone" attitude which has proved popular for weddings, parties and corporate events. Bedrooms are located either in the original White Hart Hotel, 16th century Palace Yard & Hideaway Buildings, 17th century Coach House, 19th century Manor House or the brand new Clocktower Building. One room has a four-poster bed and some larger rooms accommodate families and have river views. The Regatta Bar and Restaurant is contemporary, serving Mediterranean and Pacific Rim-inspired dishes, while The Ferrymans Bar embraces tradition. You are also very welcome to travel here by river - there are moorings for up to 4 boats - and you'll be pleasantly surprised at how accessible Sonning, one of the oldest villages in England - is from London, Heathrow and the West Country.

# THE FRENCH HORN

SONNING-ON-THAMES, BERKSHIRE RG4 6TN
**Tel:** 0845 365 2496 **International:** +44 (0)1189 692204 **Fax:** 01189 442210
**Web:** www.johansens.com/frenchhorn **E-mail:** info@thefrenchhorn.co.uk

*Our inspector loved: The exceptionally warm welcome, superb service and riverside location.*

**Price Guide:**
single £125–£170
double/twin £160–£215

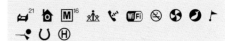

**Awards/Recognition:** 2 AA Rosettes 2007-2008

**Location:** A4, 1 mile; M4 jct 10, 3 miles; Reading, 3 miles; Heathrow Airport, 20 miles

**Attractions:** Henley; Windsor Castle; Stratfield Saye; The Mill Theatre

For over 150 years The French Horn has provided a charming riverside retreat. Today, it continues that fine tradition of comfortable accommodation and outstanding cuisine in a beautiful setting. The bedrooms and suites are traditional and comfortable, many have river views. The old panelled bar provides an intimate scene for pre-dinner drinks in the award winning restaurant with its' speciality of locally reared duck, spit roasted here over an open fire. The restaurant is a lovely setting for lunch, while at night diners can enjoy the floodlit view of the graceful weeping willows which fringe the river. Dinner is served by candlelight and the cuisine is a mixture of French and English cooking using the freshest ingredients, complemented by The French Horn's fine and extensive wine list.

# OAKLEY COURT HOTEL

WINDSOR ROAD, WATER OAKLEY, WINDSOR, BERKSHIRE SL4 5UR
**Tel:** 0845 365 2092  **International:** +44 (0)1753 609988  **Fax:** 01628 637011
**Web:** www.johansens.com/oakleycourt  **E-mail:** reservations@oakleycourt.com

***Our inspector loved:*** *The riverside setting and range of facilities.*

**Price Guide:**
single from £124
double from £134
suite from £224

**Location:** A308; M4 jdt 6, 4 miles; Windsor, 4 miles; Heathrow Airport, 12 miles

**Attractions:** Windsor Castle; Ascot Racecourse; Legoland; Henley

It is difficult to imagine that this impressive, gothic mansion set amidst 35 acres of beautiful grounds by the river Thames could be in such close proximity to London. Oakley Court was built in classic Victorian gothic style, and its impressive architecture and sweeping lawns have been used as the setting for Hammer horror films and a production of Dracula! Abandoning its spooky past the house was converted into a hotel in 1981 and today retains an English country-house style. Bedrooms include the Mansion Bedrooms with their imposing four-poster beds and the River Suites, overlooking the Thames. Fine wines accompany dining in the elegant Oakleaf Restaurant, and its accompanying bar with a winter log fire. The sitting room and conservatory are available for private hire.

# NEW HALL

WALMLEY ROAD, ROYAL SUTTON COLDFIELD, WEST MIDLANDS B76 1QX
**Tel:** 0845 365 2083 **International:** +44 (0)121 378 2442 **Fax:** 0121 378 4637
**Web:** www.johansens.com/newhall **E-mail:** info@newhalluk.com

*Our inspector loved: The friendly unobtrusive attention of the staff.*

**Price Guide:**
single from £120
double/twin from £135
suite from £205

**Awards/Recognition:** 2 AA Rosettes 2006-2007

**Location:** Off the B4148, 1 mile; M42 jct 9, 6 miles; Birmingham NEC, 12.7 miles

**Attractions:** Belfry Golf Course; Drayton Manor Park; Cadbury World; The Black Country Living Museum

Royal intrigue and forbidden passion spanning 900 years, envelop this the oldest inhabited moated manor house in England. Here aristocratic tradition meets modern living with the single objective to help you feel at home. "Special occasion" suites, include the Princess Elizabeth Suite, room for Queen Elizabeth I shortly before her coronation in 1559, features a four-poster bed, sitting room and fireplace, and the open-plan Krug Room, with a luxurious marble bathroom, designed for Luciano Pavarotti.The Bridge Restaurant and less formal Terrace Room offer delicious menus created from local produce complemented by an extensive, wine list. The cocktail bar features record players and you can choose from the extensive collection of vinyl or bring your own LP's! The Spa offers a wide range of relaxing and restorative therapies.

# Hartwell House Hotel, Restaurant & Spa

OXFORD ROAD, NEAR AYLESBURY, BUCKINGHAMSHIRE HP17 8NR
**Tel:** 0845 365 1824 **International:** +44 (0)1296 747444 **Fax:** 01296 747450
**Web:** www.johansens.com/hartwellhouse **E-mail:** info@hartwell-house.com

***Our inspector loved:*** *This grand old house full of charm and welcome.*

**Price Guide:** (including continental breakfast)
single from £160
double/twin from £290
suites from £390

**Awards/Recognition:** 3 AA Rosettes 2007-2008

**Location:** A418, 0.2 miles; M40, 10 miles; Luton Airport, 29 miles; Heathrow, 40 miles

**Attractions:** Waddesdon Manor (NT); Stowe Landscaped Gardens; Oxford; Bicester Village

Standing in 90 acres, landscaped by a contemporary of Capability Brown, Hartwell House is a beautiful Grade 1 listed building with Jacobean and Georgian facades - the residence in exile of King Louis XVIII of France from 1809 to 1814. The large ground floor reception rooms, with oak panelling and decorated ceilings, have antique furniture and fine paintings. There are 46 individually designed bedrooms and suites, 30 in the main house and 16 in the Hartwell Court, where dogs are permitted. The dining room at Hartwell is the setting for award winning cuisine, there are also 2 private dining rooms. The Old Rectory, provides superb private accommodation and swimming pool. The Hartwell Spa is the perfect place to be pampered. Owned and restored by Historic House Hotels Limited

# THE KINGS HOTEL

OXFORD ROAD, STOKENCHURCH, HIGH WYCOMBE, BUCKINGHAMSHIRE HP14 3TA
**Tel:** 0845 365 2841 **International:** +44 (0)1494 609 090 **Fax:** 01494 484582
**Web:** www.johansens.com/kingsbucks **E-mail:** reservations@kingshoteluk.com

*Our inspector loved:* Its contemporary interior with both striking colours and neutral tones as well as the modern facilities and buzzy atmosphere.

**Price Guide:**
single £85-£119
double £105-£139
suite £105-£145

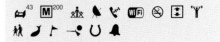

Formerly a busy 16th-century coaching inn, this imposing hotel has been completely refurbished to create a space that is both comfortable and modern. The interior is fresh and attractive with a fashionable twist, a surprising complement to the original façade. There is a pleasing variety of traditionally smart and strikingly trendy bedrooms and suites to appeal to individual tastes and a selection of attractive meeting and conference rooms complete the diverse range of facilities on offer. The atmospheric, convivial restaurant and bar is stylishly appointed and offers simple, freshly prepared and innovative dishes. The hotel is situated near the village green, and suits the business executive and weekend guest alike looking for an excellent location and base from which to explore the glorious countryside.

**Location:** On the A40; M40 jct 5, 0.5 miles; High Wycombe, 7 miles; Heathrow Airport, 29 miles

**Attractions:** Marlow; Henley; Oxford; Royal Ascot

# DANESFIELD HOUSE HOTEL AND SPA

HENLEY ROAD, MARLOW-ON-THAMES, BUCKINGHAMSHIRE SL7 2EY
**Tel:** 0845 365 3261 **International:** +44 (0)1628 891010 **Fax:** 01628 890408
**Web:** www.johansens.com/danesfieldhouse **E-mail:** sales@danesfieldhouse.co.uk

*Our inspector loved:* The first impressive glimpse of the house from the grand sweeping drive and the far reaching views.

**Price Guide:**
single from £240
double/twin from £275
suites from £300

**Awards/Recognition:** 2 AA Rosettes 2007-2008

**Location:** A4155, 0.2 miles; M40 jct 4, 7 miles; Marlow, 3 miles; Heathrow airport, 23 miles

**Attractions:** Henley; Windsor; Ascot; River Walks

Danesfield House Hotel and Spa is set within 65 acres overlooking the River Thames, with panoramic views across the Chiltern Hills. It is the third house on this site since 1664 and was built in sumptuous Victorian style at the end of the 19th century. The newly refurbished executive bedrooms are richly decorated and furnished. Guests may relax in the magnificent Grand Hall, with its minstrels' gallery, in the sun-lit atrium or comfortable bar before taking dinner in one of the 2 restaurants. The Oak Room features the delicious cuisine of award-winning chef Adam Simmonds and the Orangery Brasserie offers a traditional menu created by Andrew West-Letford, the hotel chef. Leisure facilities include the award-winning spa with 20-meter pool, sauna, steam room, gymnasium and superb treatment rooms. There are also 10 private banqueting and conference rooms.

# STOKE PLACE

STOKE GREEN, STOKE POGES, BUCKINGHAMSHIRE SL2 4HT
**Tel:** 0845 365 2843  **International:** +44 (0)1753 534 790  **Fax:** 01753 560 209
**Web:** www.johansens.com/stokeplace  **E-mail:** enquiries@stokeplace.co.uk

***Our inspector loved:*** *The tranquil setting in lovely grounds and spacious, well designed contemporary bedrooms.*

**Price Guide:**
double from £225
suite £275-£350

This beautiful 17th-century Queen Anne mansion is sure to impress you with its beautifully refurbished, contemporary interior that is both elegant and incredibly comfortable. Quirky touches and individuality has been encouraged here which helps create the warm atmosphere that is enhanced by the friendly staff. All the bedrooms have views over the hotel's grounds and some of the spacious suites benefit from giant bay windows and fireplaces. Someone once said, "a garden is solace for the soul," and this pretty parkland within the Stoke Green conservation area is no exception. Capability Brown once lent his hand in creating this haven. The Garden Restaurant produces a contemporary seasonal English menu. For total indulgence there is an in-room spa service.

**Location:** A4, 2.5 miles; M4, 4 miles; Heathrow Airport, 10 miles; Central London, 20-min train

**Attractions:** Windsor and Windsor Castle; Legoland; Henley

# STOKE PARK CLUB

PARK ROAD, STOKE POGES, BUCKINGHAMSHIRE SL2 4PG
**Tel:** 0845 365 2374 **International:** +44 (0)1753 717171 **Fax:** 01753 717181
**Web:** www.johansens.com/stokepark **E-mail:** info@stokeparkclub.com

**Our inspector loved:** *The impressive approach, sumptious yet comfortable rooms and a super spa.*

**Price Guide:**
single from £285
double from £285
suite from £595

**Location:** Off the B416; M4 jct 6, 4.5 miles; Windsor, 5 miles; Heathrow Airport, 7 miles

**Attractions:** Windsor Castle; Ascot; Henley; Legoland

Stoke Park Club set amidst 350 acres of parkland has for more than 900 years been at the heart of English heritage, playing host to royalty and the aristocracy. The magnificence of the Palladian mansion is echoed by the beautifully decorated interior, enhanced by antiques, exquisite fabrics and original paintings. All 21 individually furnished bedrooms and suites have marble bathrooms some with terraces. A further 28 contemporary rooms will open during 2008 adjoining the luxury spa. The Park Restaurant, and 8 function rooms are perfect for entertaining. Since 1908 the hotel has been home to one of the finest 27-hole championship parkland golf courses in the world. An all indulging spa, health and racquet pavilion re-affirms the hotel's position as one of the country's leading sporting venues.

# CAMBRIDGE GARDEN HOUSE

GRANTA PLACE, MILL LANE, CAMBRIDGE, CAMBRIDGESHIRE CB2 1RT
**Tel:** 0845 365 2879 **International:** +44 (0)1223 259988 **Fax:** 01223 316605
**Web:** www.johansens.com/cambridgegarden **E-mail:** info@cambridgegardenhouse.com

***Our inspector loved:*** *The huge Penthouse Suite with its total privacy.*

**Price Guide:**
single from £159
double from £169
suite from £309

**Location:** Just off A603; M11 jct 13, 3 miles; Cambridge Rail Station, 1 mile; Stansted Airport, 28 miles

**Attractions:** Fitzwilliam Museum; Newmarket Racecourse; Cambridge Colleges; Imperial War Museum Duxford

On the banks of the River Cam the Cambridge Garden House is a great base from which to explore one of Britain's most alluring cities. The bedrooms have recently been refurbished in a bold, contemporary style . The larger Executive & Junior Suites have marvellous views of the river and the hotels private gardens from their balconies whilst the stunning new Penthouse boasts inspirational views of Cambridge's elegant spires and celebrated attractions. The Riverside Brasserie, Bar and Lounge offers plenty of choice for dining throughout the day and on warm days lunches and afternoon teas can be taken on the patio. Chauffered punts are available near by for those a bit nervous of trying it for themselves – either way its a memorable way to experience the stunning facades of the world-famous colleges.

# HOTEL FELIX

WHITEHOUSE LANE, HUNTINGDON ROAD, CAMBRIDGE CB3 0LX
**Tel:** 0845 365 1897  **International:** +44 (0)1223 277977  **Fax:** 01223 277973
**Web:** www.johansens.com/felix  **E-mail:** help@hotelfelix.co.uk

***Our inspector loved:*** *The bold splashes of colour and contemporary artworks.*

**Price Guide:**
single £140–£195
double/twin £175–£285

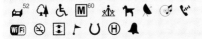

**Awards/Recognition:** 2 AA Rosettes 2007-2008

**Location:** A1307, 1 miles; A.14, 2 miles; M11 jct 13, 3 miles; Stansted Airport, 31 miles

**Attractions:** Cambridge; Imperial War Museum, Duxford; Ely; Newmarket Racecourse

A clever mix of Victorian and modern, Hotel Felix sits in peaceful surroundings within minutes' reach of Cambridge. Bespoke furniture and neutral décor with bold splashes of colour, sculpture and artwork decorate the public spaces.The restaurant and adjacent Café Bar act as focal points where you can enjoy modern cuisine with a strong European influence, fine teas, continental coffees and pastries and wine or champagne by the glass. The impeccable taste and style extends into the bedrooms, all light and airy with king-size beds, high ceilings and views over the gardens. Hotel Felix specialises in private dining and corporate events, accommodating 34 boardroom and 60 theatre style. Stretch you mind by visiting Kings College, the Botanical Gardens or go punting on the River Cam.

# GREEN BOUGH HOTEL

60 HOOLE ROAD, CHESTER, CHESHIRE CH2 3NL
**Tel:** 0845 365 1796 **International:** +44 (0)1244 326241 **Fax:** 01244 326265
**Web:** www.johansens.com/greenbough **E-mail:** luxury@greenbough.co.uk

**Our inspector loved:** *The Roman theme prevalent throughout the hotel.*

**Price Guide:**
single from £125
double/twin from £195
suites from £255

**Location:** on the A56, M53 jct 12, 1 miles; Chester, 1 miles; Manchester Airport, 32 miles

**Attractions:** Chester Super Zoo; Erdigg (NT); Cheshire Plains; Chester Racecourse

Proprietors Janice and Philip Martin have worked ceaselessly to make this place what it is, a friendly and relaxing haven, whilst collecting a fistful of awards in the process, including the Condé Nast Johansens Most Excellent City Hotel in 2004. Arguably Chester's premier small luxury hotel, the 15 bedrooms and suites have been refurbished using Italian wall coverings and fabrics in keeping with the Roman theme throughout the hotel. Original oil paintings depict scenes from a bygone era in Pompeii and antique cast-iron beds, four-posters and Jacuzzi baths add extra drama. You will certainly be tempted into The Olive Tree restaurant by an eclectic mix of aromas and flavours, complemented by a wine list from an extensive cellar. The hotel is within walking distance of historic Chester, and centrally placed for Snowdonia, Cumbria and Manchester.

# NUNSMERE HALL

TARPORLEY ROAD, OAKMERE, NORTHWICH, CHESHIRE CW8 2ES
**Tel:** 0845 365 2089 **International:** +44 (0)1606 889100 **Fax:** 01606 889055
**Web:** www.johansens.com/nunsmerehall **E-mail:** reservations@nunsmere.co.uk

***Our inspector loved:*** *The attentive service in this luxurious Cheshire country house.*

**Price Guide:**
single £150–£175
double/twin £205–£240
junior suites £260–£360

**Awards/Recognition:** 2 AA Rosettes 2007-2008

**Location:** A49, 500yds; A556, 1 mile; M6 jct 18/19, 12 miles; Chester, 12 miles

**Attractions:** Chester Zoo; Tatton Park; Beeston Castle; Blue Planet Aquarium

How often do you get to be surrounded by a lake on 3 sides! Here it's a peaceful dream come true, and the AA 4 Red Star, Nunsmere Hall epitomises the elegant country manor, complete with wood panelling, antique furniture, exclusive fabrics and magnificent chandeliers. Unsurprisingly, most of the rooms and junior suites have spectacular views of the lake and garden, and are well appointed with king-size beds and marble bathrooms. Twice County Restaurant of the Year in the Good Food Guide, the restaurant builds on its reputation by using only fresh seasonal produce. Dust off your cue for snooker, and disappear to several championship golf courses nearby. Oulton Park racing circuit and the Cheshire Polo Club are next door, and although Nunsmere is secluded it's convenient for major towns and routes.

# ROWTON HALL HOTEL, HEALTH CLUB & SPA

WHITCHURCH ROAD, ROWTON, CHESTER, CHESHIRE CH3 6AD
**Tel:** 0845 365 2308 **International:** +44 (0)1244 335262 **Fax:** 01244 335464
**Web:** www.johansens.com/rowtonhall **E-mail:** reception@rowtonhallhotelandspa.co.uk

**Our inspector loved:** *The new spa above the swimming pool, health club and gym.*

**Price Guide:**
single from £145
double/twin £170–£205
suites £380–£525

**Awards/Recognition:** 1 AA Rosette 2007-2008

**Location:** A41, 0.5 miles; M53 jct 12, 2 miles; Chester, 2 miles

**Attractions:** Chester Zoo; Chester Racecourse; Cheshire Oaks Outlet Village; Blue Planet Aquarium

There is so much to say about this hotel that it's difficult to know where start - its original oak panelling, self-supporting hand-carved staircase, inglenook and elegant Robert Adam fireplaces, or the comfortable bedrooms with every contemporary amenity from satellite TV to broadband and voicemail, and even a goodies tray! Just enjoy it all, especially eating great food in Langdale Restaurant - created from local market and hotel garden ingredients - knowing you can exercise to make up for it in the new Health Club. Work out in the gym, on 2 floodlit all-weather tennis courts, or the dance studio, then relax in the pool, Jacuzzi and sauna. Rowton Hall is perfect for corporate events as 4 main conference and banqueting suites hold up to 150 people.

# MERE COURT HOTEL

WARRINGTON ROAD, MERE, KNUTSFORD, CHESHIRE WA16 0RW
**Tel:** 0845 365 2058 **International:** +44 (0)1565 831000 **Fax:** 01565 831001
**Web:** www.johansens.com/merecourt **E-mail:** sales@merecourt.co.uk

***Our inspector loved:*** *The oak-panelled restaurant overlooking the ornamental lake.*

**Price Guide:**
single £130–£152
double/twin £154–£220

**Location:** A50, 50yds; A556, 1 mile; M6 jct 19 / 20, 3 miles; Manchester, 17 miles

**Attractions:** Chester; Various National Trust Properties; Tatton Park; Blue Planet Aquarium

This Edwardian house stands in 7 acres of mature gardens in one of the loveliest parts of Cheshire. Maintained as a family home since 1903, Mere Court has been skilfully restored into a fine country house hotel offering visitors peace and quiet amidst beautiful surroundings. The individually decorated bedrooms have views over the grounds or ornamental lake and a number of them have a Jacuzzi spa bath. Beams, oak panelling and waterside views are features of the Aboreum Restaurant, which serves the best of traditional English and Mediterranean cuisine. Lighter meals can be enjoyed in the Lounge Bar. The original coach house has been converted into a designated conference centre with state-of-the-art conference suites and syndicate rooms accommodating up to 120 delegates.

# THE NARE HOTEL

CARNE BEACH, VERYAN-IN-ROSELAND, TRURO, CORNWALL TR2 5PF

**Tel:** 0845 365 2603 **International:** +44 (0)1872 501111 **Fax:** 01872 501856
**Web:** www.johansens.com/nare **E-mail:** office@narehotel.co.uk

***Our inspector loved:*** *The panoramic sea views and country house comfort.*

**Price Guide:**
single £100-£206
double/twin £190-£380
suite £348-£584

**Awards/Recognition:** Condé Nast Johansens Most Excellent Coastal Hotel 2006; 2 AA Rosettes 2007-2008

**Location:** A3078, 3.8 miles; A390, 10 miles; A391, 15.6 miles; A30, 24 miles

**Attractions:** Eden Project; Lost Gardens of Helligan; Private Cornish Gardens; National Maritime Museum Falmouth

This absolute gem is superbly positioned overlooking the fine sandy beach of Gerrans Bay. A family-run hotel, it has carefully evolved over the years and now has bedrooms overlooking the sea with patios and balconies that are the best vantage point for spectacular views. The main dining room overlooks the sea, where local seafood dishes include lobster and followed by delicious homemade puddings served with generous helpings of Cornish cream. The relaxed Quarterdeck Restaurant is open all day, enticing you for a leisurely pot of tea or a quick coffee before exploring the glorious Roseland Peninsula's coastline and villages, not forgetting Cornwall's beautiful houses and gardens.

# St Michael's Hotel & Spa

GYLLYNGVASE BEACH, FALMOUTH, CORNWALL TR11 4NB
**Tel:** 0845 365 2358  **International:** +44 (0)1326 312707  **Fax:** 01326 211772
**Web:** www.johansens.com/stmichaelsfalmouth  **E-mail:** info@stmichaelshotel.co.uk

**Our inspector loved:** *The Location and relaxed atmosphere.*

**Price Guide:**
single £50–£125
double/twin £95–£195
suite £160–£240

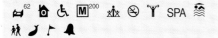

**Awards/Recognition:** 1 AA Rosette 2007-2008

**Location:** Just off A39; Truro, 11.7 miles; Newquay Airport, 25 miles

**Attractions:** National Maritime Museum; Land's End; Eden Project; Coastal walks

St Michael's Hotel & Spa has been carefully and extensively refurbished, resulting in a state-of-the-art health club, spa, award-winning restaurant, and contemporary bedrooms, bars and conference suites. The Flying Fish Restaurant, overlooking the sea and gardens, changes menus regularly so you can sample Cornwall's best fresh fish, seafood and seasonal produce. The sun terrace is the perfect spot for alfresco dining. Surrounded by sub-tropical gardens, the newly created Spa offers an impressive range of health and relaxation treatments, and you can also take a dip in the indoor pool and work out in the large fitness suite. Feel the sand between your toes on the blue flag beach, directly opposite the hotel, or visit the Eden Project within an hour's drive.

# Budock Vean - The Hotel on the River

NEAR HELFORD PASSAGE, MAWNAN SMITH, FALMOUTH, CORNWALL TR11 5LG
**Tel:** 0845 365 3212 **International:** +44 (0)1326 252100 **Fax:** 01326 250892
**Web:** www.johansens.com/budockvean **E-mail:** relax@budockvean.co.uk

*Our inspector loved:* The location, hospitality, ambience and all-year-round facilities.

**Price Guide:** (including dinner)
single £74–£123
double/twin £148–£246
suite £244–£316

A destination in itself, recommended by Condé Nast Johansens since 1983, this family-run hotel is set in 65 acres in an area of outstanding natural beauty with award-winning gardens and a private foreshore on the Helford River. It's all about relaxation and pampering here. Amenities include a large indoor pool, outdoor hot tub, sauna, tennis courts, a billiard room, boating, fishing, and the Natural Health Spa. A local ferry will take you from the hotel's jetty to waterside pubs and Frenchman's Creek and you can even enjoy a trip on the hotel's own river boat. Imaginative 5-course dinners specialise in fresh seafood, which can be walked off on a magnificent myriad of local country and coastal walks.

**Location:** M5 jct 30, 100 miles; A39, 12 miles; Falmouth, 6 miles; Newquay Airport, 30 miles

**Attractions:** Trebah Gardens; Glendurgan Gardens; National Maritime Museum Falmouth; Eden Project

# MEUDON HOTEL

MAWNAN SMITH, NEAR FALMOUTH, CORNWALL TR11 5HT
**Tel:** 0845 365 2059 **International:** +44 (0)1326 250541 **Fax:** 01326 250543
**Web:** www.johansens.com/meudon **E-mail:** wecare@meudon.co.uk

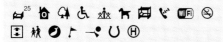

***Our inspector loved:*** *The beautiful location and peaceful gardens leading to their own beach.*

**Price Guide:** (including dinner)
single £120
double/twin £240
suite £330

**Awards/Recognition:** 1 AA Rosette 2006-2007

**Location:** A39, 5 miles; Falmouth, 4 miles; A30, 13 miles

**Attractions:** National Maritime Museum Falmouth; Trebah Gardens; Pendennis Castle; Eden Project

The French name originates from a nearby farmhouse built by Napoleonic prisoners of war and called after their longed-for home village. Comfortable bedrooms enjoy spectacular views over the hotels sub-tropical gardens which tend to be coaxed into early bloom by the Gulf Stream and mild Cornish climate. Local fishermen and farmers supply the kitchen with ingredients to allow a changing seasonal menu. The Pilgrim's are 5th generation hoteliers and it shows in the attention, care and enthusiasm they put into running the place. There are plenty of watersports and outdoor pursuits to indulge in, you can play golf free at nearby Falmouth Golf Club, sail aboard the hotel's skippered 34-foot yacht or just laze on the private beach.

# FOWEY HALL HOTEL & RESTAURANT

HANSON DRIVE, FOWEY, CORNWALL PL23 1ET
**Tel:** 0845 365 1754 **International:** +44 (0)1726 833866 **Fax:** 01726 834100
**Web:** www.johansens.com/foweyhall **E-mail:** info@foweyhallhotel.co.uk

***Our inspector loved:*** *The informal and relaxed atmosphere to suit all ages.*

**Price Guide:** (min 2 nights incl dinner)
double/twin £170–£300 per night
suite £210–£500 per night

**Awards/Recognition:** 2 AA Rosettes 2006-2007

**Location:** A3082, 0.3 miles; A390, 5.7 miles; Newquay Airport, 23.3 miles

**Attractions:** Eden Project; Newquay Zoo; Lost Gardens of Helegan; Readymoney Cove

Situated in five acres overlooking the Estuary, Fowey Hall Hotel is a superb Victorian mansion renowned for its excellent service and comfortable accommodation. Fine panelling and superb ceilings decorate the spacious public rooms. Located in either the main house or the Court, the 36 well proportioned bedrooms include 12 suites and 10 sets of interconnecting rooms. Guests can enjoy local dishes using the best of regional produce including seafood and fish specialities. The hotel offers a fully complimentary crèche service and older children have not been forgotten as "The Beach Hut" in the courtyard is well-equipped with table tennis, table football and many other games. There is also a cinema with a 42" plasma screen showing the latest childrens films.

# HELL BAY

BRYHER, ISLES OF SCILLY, CORNWALL TR23 0PR
**Tel:** 0845 365 1837  **International:** +44 (0)1720 422947  **Fax:** 01720 423004
**Web:** www.johansens.com/hellbay  **E-mail:** contactus@hellbay.co.uk

***Our inspector loved:*** *The exciting menus created by award winning new master chef*

**Price Guide:** (including dinner)
suites £260–£580

**Awards/Recognition:** 3 Red Stars; 2 AA Rosettes 2007-2008;

**Location:** Lands End, 30 miles; Exeter Airport, 1 hour; Penzance Heliport, 20 mins; Penzance Ferry Terminal, 2.5 hours

**Attractions:** Tresco Abbey Garden; Water Sports; Boat Excursions; Fishing

You should visit the magical Isles of Scilly at least once in your life. Hell Bay stands on the rugged West Coast of Bryher – the smallest of the island communities where the local transport network relies on bicycles and colourful boats. This is a spectacular getaway-from-it-all destination. Warm winds of the gulf stream, empty beaches and crystal clear water. We love it. Most of the suites have dazzling sea views. The restaurant serves up dawn fresh crab, lobster and fish hand picked from the local boats. On hand is an outdoor heated swimming pool, gym, sauna, spa bath, children's playground, games room and par 3 golf course. Though you should venture out & explore; fishing trips, diving expeditions, inter-island hops and evening gig races. Fly by helicopter or sail from Penzance or by plane from Bristol, Southampton, Exeter, Newquay and Land's End.

# TALLAND BAY HOTEL

PORTHALLOW, CORNWALL PL13 2JB
**Tel:** 0845 365 2386 **International:** +44 (0)1503 272667 **Fax:** 01503 272940
**Web:** www.johansens.com/tallandbay **E-mail:** info@tallandbayhotel.co.uk

***Our inspector loved:*** *The wonderful relaxing atmosphere and fine dining.*

**Price Guide:**
single £75–£105
double/twin £95–£225

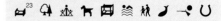

**Awards/Recognition:** 3 AA Rosettes 2006-2007

**Location:** A387, 1 mile; A38, 9.5 miles; Looe, 3.2 miles

**Attractions:** St Ives; National Maritime Museum, Falmouth; Eden Project; Lost Gardens of Heligan

In this wild and romantic location on the Cornish coastline you will find all the ingredients you need to unwind. Exuding a relaxed country house atmosphere, this Old Cornish Manor overlooks the dramatic Talland Bay and where, when the tide is out you can walk amongst the rock pools or take a picnic to the beach. Fully deserving of their 3 AA Rosettes the charming wood panelled restaurant serves delectable dishes influenced by the catch of the day at Looe, seasonally grown vegetables and local organically reared beef and lamb. Each bedroom has its own character, and in particular the suites and balcony rooms have an added touch of luxury. Friendly service is always at hand to help plan your day exploring this stunning area. A great place for Christmas & New Year with it's wonderful house party ambience. Well-behaved dogs welcome.

# THE POLURRIAN HOTEL

POLURRIAN COVE, MULLION, HELSTON, CORNWALL TR12 7EN
**Tel:** 0845 365 2849 **International:** +44 (0)1326 240421 **Fax:** 01326 240083
**Web:** www.johansens.com/polurrian **E-mail:** relax@polurrianhotel.com

*Our inspector loved:* The majestic location, warm welcome and feeling of not wanting to leave.

**Price Guide:** (including dinner)
single £56-£88
double £112-£210
suite £196-£270

**Location:** B3296 Mullion,1 mile; A394 Helston, 7 miles

**Attractions:** Flambards Theme Park; Gweek Seal Sanctuary; Goonhilly Downs Earth Station; Trenance Chocolate Factory

A stay in this incredibly beautiful Edwardian hotel will certainly be a breathtaking and romantic experience. Perched proudly atop a 300-foot cliff with awe-inspiring views of Mounts Bay and the Atlantic Ocean beyond, you will be hard pressed to ever leave! Top-class service is guaranteed, which together with gorgeous décor that is comfortable and inviting, creates a relaxed and informal environment perfect for adults and children alike. The dining room offers fantastic views across the ocean; a truly memorable experience accompanied by unforgettable fine cuisine. The hotel's magnificent gardens lead to a path that gently meanders down to a quiet cove and a pristine sandy beach.

# THE ROSEVINE HOTEL

PORTHCURNICK BEACH, PORTSCATHO, ST MAWES, TRURO, CORNWALL TR2 5EW
**Tel:** 0845 365 2678 **International:** +44 (0)1872 580206 **Fax:** 01872 580230
**Web:** www.johansens.com/rosevinehotel **E-mail:** info@rosevine.co.uk

*Our inspector loved: The location, warm welcome and superb cuisine.*

**Price Guide:**
single £90–£190
double/twin £175–£250
suite £250–£360

**Awards/Recognition:** 1 AA Rosettes 2007-2008

**Location:** A3078, 0.7 miles; St Mawes, 6 miles; A390, 11 miles; Newquay Airport 28 miles

**Attractions:** Roseland Peninsula; Falmouth Maritime Museum; St Mawes; Lost Gardens of Heligan

If you find yourself on the golden sands of National Trust maintained Porthcurnick Beach on a sunny day, you may well think you're in heaven! This late Georgian hotel looks across the beach and Portscatho Harbour and will undoubtedly make you feel both calm and inspired. Many of the bedrooms enjoy spectacular sea views, and making the most of the great outdoors, you can savour the award-winning restaurant's fresh seafood and locally grown produce al fresco. Families are especially well catered for with so much to do nearby such as exploring the area's charming villages, walking along the coastal paths and sandy beaches, riding, sailing and visiting the Eden Project and Truro's cathedral. On rainy days you can swim in the hotel's indoor pool or curl up with a good read in the library.

# THE GARRACK HOTEL & RESTAURANT

BURTHALLAN LANE, ST IVES, CORNWALL TR26 3AA
**Tel:** 0845 365 2497 **International:** +44 (0)1736 796199 **Fax:** 01736 798955
**Web:** www.johansens.com/garrack **E-mail:** djenquiry@garrack.com

*Our inspector loved: The wonderful relaxing atmosphere - Location - Fine dining*

**Price Guide:**
single £75–£105
double/twin £134–£210

**Awards/Recognition:** 1 AA Rosette 2006-2007

**Location:** B3306, 0.65 mile; A3074, 1 mile; A30, 5 miles; Newquay Airport, 27 miles

**Attractions:** Porthmeor Beach; St Ives; St Ives Tate Gallery; Coastal Paths

Perfect for a family holiday, this family-run hotel is set in 2 acres of gardens with fabulous sea views. You can wander down the hill to Porthmeor beach and its excellent surf, St Ives' old town and the new St Ives Tate Gallery, then back up, for a steep, but scenic walk. Bedrooms in the original house maintain the style of the building, while additional rooms are modern in design. A ground floor room has been equipped for guests with disabilities. Lounges have open fires, and a bijou leisure centre contains a small pool, sauna and fitness area. Service is informal yet professional, and the restaurant specialises in seafood, especially fresh lobster.With 70 selected wines. Gateway to wonderful coastal walks, dogs are welcome by prior arrangement.

# ALVERTON MANOR

TREGOLLS ROAD, TRURO, CORNWALL TR1 1ZQ
**Tel:** 0845 365 3609 **International:** +44 (0)1872 276633 **Fax:** 01872 222989
**Web:** www.johansens.com/alverton **E-mail:** reception@alvertonmanor.co.uk

**Our inspector loved:** *The wonderful atmosphere of this former convent.*

**Price Guide:**
single from £75
double £125-£140
suite from £160

**Awards/Recognition:** 2 AA Rosettes 2006-2007

**Location:** On the A39; A30, 12 miles; M5 jct 30, 80 miles

**Attractions:** Lands End; Eden Project; Roseland Peninsular

Standing proudly in the cathedral city of Truro, Alverton Manor is the epitome of a mid-19th-century family home, with handsome sandstone walls, mullioned windows and a superb Cornish Delabole slate roof. Today, owner Michael Sagin and his team maintain a welcoming and relaxed ambience. Bedrooms vary in size and are light and comfortable. The restaurant makes the most of local seasonal produce and supporting this now rear their own Devon Red cattle as well as investing in their own bee hives. This is a wonderful part of the world to discover whatever the season and in the Winter months you can enjoy the warmth of the open fires at Alverton and indulge in a Cornish cream tea.

# LOVELADY SHIELD COUNTRY HOUSE HOTEL

NENTHEAD ROAD, ALSTON, CUMBRIA CA9 3LF
**Tel:** 0845 365 2042 **International:** +44 (0)1434 381203 **Fax:** 01434 381515
**Web:** www.johansens.com/loveladyshield **E-mail:** enquiries@lovelady.co.uk

***Our inspector loved:*** *This informal relaxing hotel set in a picturesque valley.*

**Price Guide:**
single £100–£160
double/twin £200–£320

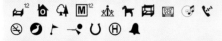

**Awards/Recognition:** 1 AA Rosette 2006-2007

**Location:** A689, 0.3 mile; Alston, 2 miles; M6 jct 40, 22 miles

**Attractions:** High Force - Englands highest waterfall; Hadrians Wall; Penine Way; North Lakes

It's not often we recommend a driving route as well as hotel, but the A686 which leads to Lovelady Shield is officially one of the world's 10 best drives. Bright log fires welcome you on cooler days and owners Peter and Marie Haynes take care to create a relaxed atmosphere in this riverside haven. 5-course dinners prepared by master chef Barrie Garton and rounded off by homemade puddings and a selection of English farmhouse cheeses, have consistently been awarded AA Rosettes for the past 10 years. Many people discover this place en route to Scotland then return to explore the beautiful, unspoilt area properly. For equestrian lovers, pony-trekking and riding can be arranged. The Pennine Way, Hadrian's Wall and the Lake District are within easy reach.

# HOLBECK GHYLL COUNTRY HOUSE HOTEL

HOLBECK LANE, WINDERMERE, CUMBRIA LA23 1LU
**Tel:** 0845 365 1872 **International:** +44 (0)15394 32375 **Fax:** 015394 34743
**Web:** www.johansens.com/holbeckghyll **E-mail:** stay@holbeckghyll.com

*Our inspector loved:* The delicious dinner in the oak panelled restaurant with views over Lake Windermere

**Price Guide:** (including 4 course dinner)
single from £150
double/twin £230–£370
suite £300–£550

Holbeck Ghyll was built in the early days of the 19th century and has a prime position overlooking Lake Windermere and the Langdale Fells. Today, its outstanding award winning reputation is due to proprietors, David and Patricia Nicholson. The majority of bedrooms are large and have spectacular lake views. All are refurbished to a very high standard and include decanters of sherry, fresh flowers, fluffy bathrobes and more. There are 6 rooms in the Lodge and both Madison House and the Miss Potter Suite opened during 2006. The oak-panelled restaurant, awarded a coveted Michelin star and 3 AA Rosettes, is a delightful setting for memorable dining and meals are classically prepared, with the focus on flavours and presentation, while an extensive wine list reflects quality and variety. Health Spa on site.

**Awards/Recognition:** 3 AA Rosettes 2007-2008; 1 Star Michelin 2007; Condé Nast Johansens / Taittinger Wine List Award 2007

**Location:** A591, 0.5 mile; M6 jct 36, 20 miles; Windermere, 3 miles; Ambleside, 1 mile

**Attractions:** Lake Windermere; Lake District National Park; Dove Cottage & Rydal Mount; Brockhole Visitors Centre

# ROTHAY MANOR

ROTHAY BRIDGE, AMBLESIDE, CUMBRIA LA22 0EH
**Tel:** 0845 365 2307 **International:** +44 (0)15394 33605 **Fax:** 015394 33607
**Web:** www.johansens.com/rothaymanor **E-mail:** hotel@rothaymanor.co.uk

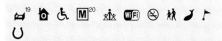

*Our inspector loved:* The attentive service at this relaxing oasis.

**Price Guide:**
single £100–£140
double/twin £160–£185
suite £215

**Location:** A593, 100yds; M6 Jct 36, 18 miles; Ambleside, 0.25 miles; Windermere, 4 miles

**Attractions:** Ambleside; Windermere; Beatrix Potter Museum and Hill Top; Lake District National Park

Take a short walk from the centre of Ambleside to this Regency country house hotel, which, thanks to the Nixon family, has provided a relaxed, comfortable and friendly atmosphere for 40 years. Choose from a variety of bedrooms, some with balconies, and 3 spacious, private suites, 2 of which are situated in the grounds. Some rooms are suitable for families, while others have been designed keeping in mind those with disabilities. Varied menus use local produce whenever possible, and it's worth keeping your eye out for special interest holidays run from October to May - gardening, antiques, bridge, painting and Lake District heritage, are just tasters. Otherwise, there's plenty to do in the area, from walking to cycling, sailing, horse-riding, golf and fishing (permits available).

# TUFTON ARMS HOTEL

MARKET SQUARE, APPLEBY-IN-WESTMORLAND, CUMBRIA CA16 6XA
**Tel:** 0845 365 2766  **International:** +44 (0)17683 51593  **Fax:** 017683 52761
**Web:** www.johansens.com/tuftonarms  **E-mail:** info@tuftonarmshotel.co.uk

***Our inspector loved:*** *The Ian Oats sporting paintings for sale in the bar.*

**Price Guide:**
single £80–£110
double/twin £110–£150
suite £190

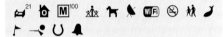

This distinguished Victorian coaching inn, is owned and run by the Milsom family, who also run the The Royal Hotel in Comrie. The bedrooms evoke the style of the 19th century, reflecting the Tufton Arms past Victorian grandeur. The kitchen is run under the auspices of David Milsom and Lee Braithwaite, who spoil guests for choice with a gourmet dinner menu as well as a grill menu, the restaurant is renowned for its fish dishes. Complementing the cuisine is an extensive wine list. This is an ideal base for touring the Lakes, Yorkshire Dales and Pennines. It is also a convenient stop-over en route to Scotland. Superb fishing for wild brown trout or salmon can be arranged. Shooting parties for grouse, duck and pheasant are a speciality.

**Location:** A66, 1 miles; M6 Jct 38, 12 mile; Penrith, 13 miles miles

**Attractions:** Eden Valley; Penine Way; Appleby Golf Course; Lake District National Park

# FARLAM HALL HOTEL

BRAMPTON, CUMBRIA CA8 2NG
**Tel:** 0845 365 3289 **International:** +44 (0)16977 46234 **Fax:** 016977 46683
**Web:** www.johansens.com/farlamhall **E-mail:** farlam@relaischateaux.com

*Our inspector loved:* The luxurious elegance of this borders Hotel.

**Price Guide:** (including dinner)
single £150–£180
double/twin £280–£340

**Awards/Recognition:** Relais & Châteaux; 2 AA Rosettes 2007-2008

**Location:** A689, 500yds; Brampton, 2.5 miles; M6 jct 43 or 44, 10 miles; Carlisle, 12 miles

**Attractions:** Hadrians Wall & the Border Country; Lanercost Priory; Carlisle

Farlam Hall was opened in 1975 by the Quinion and Stevenson families who over the years have achieved consistently high standards of food, service and comfort. This old border house, dating in parts from the 17th century, is set in mature gardens, which can be seen from the elegant lounges and dining room, creating a relaxed and pleasing environment. The fine silver and crystal in the dining room complement the quality of the English country house cooking produced by Barry Quinion and his team of chefs. There are 12 individually decorated bedrooms varying in size and shape, some having Jacuzzi baths, one an antique four-poster bed and there are 2 ground floor bedrooms. Winter and spring breaks are available but the hall is closed for Christmas.

# NETHERWOOD HOTEL

LINDALE ROAD, GRANGE-OVER-SANDS, CUMBRIA LA11 6ET
**Tel:** 0845 365 2082 **International:** +44 (0)15395 32552 **Fax:** 015395 34121
**Web:** www.johansens.com/netherwood **E-mail:** enquiries@netherwood-hotel.co.uk

***Our inspector loved:*** *The oak panelling in the hall and lounge and the stunning views over Morecambe Bay.*

**Price Guide:**
single £80–£115
double £120–£190

**Location:** B5277, 500yds; A590, 3 miles; M6 jct 36, 5 miles

**Attractions:** Morcombe Bay; Holker Hall; Lake District National Park

Dramatic and stately in appearance, Netherwood was built as a family house in the 19th century, and still exudes a warm, family atmosphere thanks to the care of its longstanding owners, the Fallowfields. Impressive oak panelling is a key feature, and provides a fitting backdrop to roaring log fires in the public areas. Bedrooms come with views of the sea, woodlands and gardens. The light and airy restaurant is housed in the first floor conservatory and maximises dramatic views over Morecambe Bay. If you're a family you'll probably spend the lion's share of your time in the indoor pool and fitness centre - the pool even has toys for our younger friends - while an extensive range of treatments are available at "Equilibrium", the hotel's health spa.

# ARMATHWAITE HALL HOTEL

BASSENTHWAITE LAKE, KESWICK, CUMBRIA CA12 4RE
**Tel:** 0845 365 3617 **International:** +44 (0)17687 76551 **Fax:** 017687 76220
**Web:** www.johansens.com/armathwaite **E-mail:** reservations@armathwaite-hall.com

***Our inspector loved:*** *Dining in the new terrace Restaurant with views across Bassenthwaite Lake.*

**Price Guide:**
single £135–£225
double/twin £210–£360

**Awards/Recognition:** 1 AA Rosette 2007-2008

**Location:** A591, 0.25 miles; A66, 1 mile; M6 jct 40, 25 miles; Keswick, 7 miles

**Attractions:** Trotters World of Animals; Bassenthwaite Lake; Lake District National Park; Wordsworth and Beatrix Potter

If you have a passion for boating, walking and climbing, or to simply relax, this 4-star hotel is a peaceful hideaway. On the shores of Bassenthwaite Lake and with a backdrop of Skiddaw Mountain and Lakeland Fells it provides old-fashioned hospitality, as you would expect of a family-owned hotel. Wood panelling, impressive stonework, art and antiques remain, and you can arrange champagne, chocolates and flowers in your room upon arrival. Master Chef Kevin Dowling creates local, seasonal menus in the Rosette restaurant, and the hotel is family-friendly, with a programme of activities for mini guests. Get in touch with your inner child and visit the estate's Trotters World of Animals, home to traditional favourites and endangered species.

# THE LODORE FALLS HOTEL

BORROWDALE, KESWICK, CUMBRIA CA12 5UX
**Tel:** 0845 365 2581 **International:** +44 (0)17687 77285 **Fax:** 017687 77343
**Web:** www.johansens.com/lodorefalls **E-mail:** lodorefalls@lakedistricthotels.net

***Our inspector loved:*** *Having a stroll up to the Lodore Falls and a swim in the open air pool.*

**Price Guide:**
single from £84
double from £142
suite from £264

Close your eyes and imagine stunning lake and mountain views, a waterfall in landscaped gardens warm hospitality and good food and service. Open your eyes and see The Lodore Falls Hotel in the picturesque Borrowdale Valley. The 69 en-suite Fell and Lake View Rooms, include family rooms, internet access and luxurious suites, some with balconies. Light meals and coffee can be enjoyed in the comfortable lounges, whilst the cocktail bar is the ideal venue for a pre-dinner drink. The Lake View restaurant serves the best in English and Continental cuisine accompanied by fine wines. The new Beauty Salon with its 3 beautiful treatment rooms use the famous Elemis beauty products in its treatments and offers pamper days, luxury days and a very special Waterfall treatment day. For children an activity programme is also available for 2 hours daily during school holidays.

**Location:** B5289, 10yds; A66, 4 miles; M6 jct 40, 22 miles; Keswick, 3.5 miles

**Attractions:** Derwentwater Launch; Keswick Golf Club; Trotters world of animals; Honistor Slate Mine with its new Via Ferrata walk/climb

# SHARROW BAY COUNTRY HOUSE HOTEL

HOWTOWN, LAKE ULLSWATER, PENRITH, CUMBRIA CA10 2LZ
**Tel:** 0845 365 2346 **International:** +44 (0)17684 86301/86483 **Fax:** 017684 86349
**Web:** www.johansens.com/sharrowbaycountryhouse **E-mail:** info@sharrowbay.co.uk

***Our inspector loved:*** *The unique dining experience in the Lakeside Restaurant with lovely views of Ullswater.*

**Price Guide:** (including 6-course dinner)
single £160–£280
double/twin £350–£480
suite from £460

**Awards/Recognition:** Relais & Châteaux; 1 Star Michelin 2007; 2 AA Rosettes 2007-2008

**Location:** B592, 2 miles; A66, 6 miles; M6 jct 40, 7 miles; Penrith, 8 miles

**Attractions:** Overlooking Lake Ullswater; Lake District National Park

There's no doubt about it, Sharrow Bay is legendary: a founding British member of Relais & Chateaux, and reputedly the world's first ever country house hotel. Its tranquil setting, in 12 acres of private gardens on the shore of Lake Ullswater is simply magical. You will instantly feel the weight of the world fall from your shoulders as you gaze upon the unrivalled and ever-changing scenes of the spectacular landscape. Bedrooms are individual, very comfortable and elegant. Dining with lake views is an experience to be savoured whether it's breakfast, afternoon tea or dinner in the Michelin starred restaurant. The Bank House, Garden Rooms & Gatehouse Lodge all offer rooms & suites away from the main house and are a great idea for small groups of friends

# THE INN ON THE LAKE

LAKE ULLSWATER, GLENRIDDING, CUMBRIA CA11 0PE
**Tel:** 0845 365 2548 **International:** +44 (0)17684 82444 **Fax:** 017684 82303
**Web:** www.johansens.com/innonthelake **E-mail:** innonthelake@lakedistricthotels.net

*Our inspector loved: The lake-view four poster rooms.*

**Price Guide:**
single from £75
double from £134

**Awards/Recognition:** 1 AA Rosette 2007-2008

**Location:** A592, 100yds; M6 jct 40, 12 miles; Penrith, 12 miles

**Attractions:** Lake Ullswater; Ullswater Steamers; Rheged Centre; Dalemain Stately Home

This 19th century hotel enjoys one of the most spectacular settings in the Lake District. 15 acres of lawn sweep down to the shore of Lake Ullswater, where you can sail from the private jetty and take trips aboard the Ullswater steamers. Relax with a drink in the comfort of one of the lounges or stroll to The Rambler's Bar in the grounds for a proper Lakeland pub atmosphere. Superb food is served in the Lake View restaurant and most bedrooms have stunning views across the lake, ask for a lake-view four poster room. There is a small leisure suite with sauna, solarium, Jacuzzi and a gym. The hotel makes a particularly romantic wedding venue for civil ceremonies and celebrations. The list of local activities is endless, from rock climbing to pony trekking, canoeing, windsurfing and fishing.

# RAMPSBECK COUNTRY HOUSE HOTEL

WATERMILLOCK, LAKE ULLSWATER, NR PENRITH, CUMBRIA CA11 0LP
**Tel:** 0845 365 2138 **International:** +44 (0)17684 86442 **Fax:** 017684 86688
**Web:** www.johansens.com/rampsbeckcountryhouse **E-mail:** enquiries@rampsbeck.fsnet.co.uk

**Our inspector loved:** *Enjoying a delicious Dinner in the restaurant with its views across Lake Ullswater.*

**Price Guide:**
single £80–£165
double/twin £130–£270
suite £270

**Awards/Recognition:** 3 AA Rosettes 2007-2008

**Location:** A592, 0.25 miles; M6 jct 40, 5.25 miles; Penrith, 5.5 miles

**Attractions:** Lake Ullswater; Lake District National Park; Dalemain

Rampsbeck Country House stands in 18 acres of landscaped gardens leading to the shores of Lake Ullswater. Built in 1714 its present owners acquired it in 1983. Thomas and Marion Gibb, with the help of Marion's mother, Marguerite MacDowall, completely refurbished Rampsbeck maintaining its character and adding only to its comfort. Most of the bedrooms have lake and garden views. Three have a private balcony and the suite overlooks the lake. Guests and non-residents are welcome to dine in the candle-lit restaurant. Imaginative menus offer a choice of delicious dishes, prepared by Master Chef Andrew McGeorge and his team. A good bar lunch menu offers light snacks as well as hot food. Guest can stroll through the gardens, play croquet or fish from the lake shore. Closed January to mid-February. Dogs by arrangement only.

# GILPIN LODGE

CROOK ROAD, WINDERMERE, CUMBRIA LA23 3NE
**Tel:** 0845 365 1762 **International:** +44 (0)15394 88818 **Fax:** 015394 88058
**Web:** www.johansens.com/gilpinlodge **E-mail:** hotel@gilpinlodge.co.uk

*Our inspector loved: The garden suites, each with a private patio and Canadian hot tub.*

**Price Guide:** (including 5-course dinner)
single £175
double/twin £250–£360

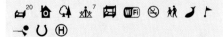

**Awards/Recognition:** Relais & Châteaux; 3 AA Rosettes 2007-2008; 1 Star Michelin 2007

**Location:** B5284, 200yds; A591, 6 miles; M6 jct 36, 12 miles; Windermere, 2 miles

**Attractions:** Windermere; Beatrix Potter Museum; Holker & Levens Halls; Blackwell Arts and Crafts House

An elegant hotel just 2 miles from Lake Windermere, the Cunliffe family along with their long-standing staff excel at making sure you relax under their friendly & professional care. Fresh flowers, crisp linen and log fires in winter are all part of their hospitality. Not only that, some of the guest bedrooms have patio doors, split levels and spa baths, while the suites have private gardens and cedarwood hot tubs. Delicious food is well deserving of their awards and the restaurant popular locally. Of course, this is Wordsworth and Beatrix Potter country, so you can watch wildlife in the beautiful gardens and surrounding grounds or sit and savour the glorious Lakeland scenery.

# LINTHWAITE HOUSE HOTEL

CROOK ROAD, BOWNESS-ON-WINDERMERE, CUMBRIA LA23 3JA
**Tel:** 0845 365 2031 **International:** +44 (0)15394 88600 **Fax:** 015394 88601
**Web:** www.johansens.com/linthwaitehouse **E-mail:** stay@linthwaite.com

***Our inspector loved:*** *The unstuffy ambiance of this hotel with spectacular views of Lake Windermere.*

**Price Guide:**
single £120-£150
double £145-£300
suite £265-£320

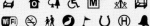

**Awards/Recognition:** Condé Nast Johansens Most Excellent Country House 2007; 3 AA Rosettes 2007-2008; Condé Nast Traveller Gold List 2006

**Location:** B5284, 0.25 miles; Windermere, 2 miles; A591, 2 miles; M6 Jct 36, 14 miles

**Attractions:** Windermere; Beatrix Potter Museums & Dove Cottage; Lake District National Park;

At the heart of the Lake District situated in 14 acres of garden and woodland is Linthwaite House overlooking Lake Windermere and Belle Isle. The hotel combines stylish originality with the best of traditional hospitality. Most bedrooms have lake or garden views whilst the restaurant offers excellent cuisine with the best of fresh, local produce accompanied by a fine selection of wines. There is a 9 hole putting green within the grounds and a par 3 practice hole. You can if you wish, fish for brown trout in the hotel tarn. Fell walks begin at the front door, and you can follow in the footsteps of Wordsworth and Beatrix Potter to explore the spectacular scenery.

# LAKESIDE HOTEL ON LAKE WINDERMERE

LAKESIDE, NEWBY BRIDGE, CUMBRIA LA12 8AT
**Tel:** 0845 365 1978 **International:** +44 (0)15395 30001 **Fax:** 015395 31699
**Web:** www.johansens.com/lakeside **E-mail:** sales@lakesidehotel.co.uk

***Our inspector loved:*** *Morning coffee in the Lakeside Conservatory watching the ducks being fed at 11am!*

**Price Guide:**
single from £150
double/twin £185–£325
suite from £325

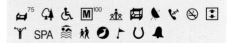

Offering a unique location on the edge of Lake Windermere this classic, traditional Lakeland hotel will have cast its spell on you by the time your visit is over. Many bedrooms have breathtaking lake vistas, and menus in both the award-winning Lakeview Restaurant or Ruskin's Brasserie include Cumbrian favourites. To get a real lakes experience there are cruisers berthed adjacent to the hotel ready for further exploration and adventure. For inclement weather the Pool and Spa, exclusively for hotel residents, has a 17m indoor pool, gym, sauna, steam room and health and beauty suites. The hotel's fully equipped conference centre and syndicate suites offer scope and flexibility for business, so whatever your requirements this old coaching inn's facilities and friendly service will deliver!

**Awards/Recognition:** 2 AA Rosettes 2007-2008

**Location:** A590, 1 mile; M6 jct 36, 15 miles; Newby Bridge, 1 mile

**Attractions:** Windermere Lake Cruisers; Aquarium of the Lakes; Lakeside and Haverthwaite Steam Railway; Holker Hall and Gardens

# CALLOW HALL

MAPPLETON ROAD, ASHBOURNE, DERBYSHIRE DE6 2AA
**Tel:** 0845 365 3221 **International:** +44 (0)1335 300900 **Fax:** 01335 300512
**Web:** www.johansens.com/callowhall **E-mail:** stay@callowhall.co.uk

*Our inspector loved: The evolution of Callow Hall with its newly decorated bedrooms, a timeless pleasure.*

**Price Guide:**
single from £105
double/twin from £150
suite from £210

**Awards/Recognition:** 2 AA Rosettes 2007-2008

**Location:** A515, 2 miles; A52, 3 miles; A50, 10 miles; East Midlands Airport, 24 miles

**Attractions:** Chatsworth House; Kedleston Hall; Peak District National Park; Uttoxeter Racecourse

Overlooking Bentley Brook and the River Dove, you are welcomed to this fine Victorian hall by its former owners son and daughter Anthony and Emma Spencer. Fine antiques and fireplaces combine with ornate ceilings to give a sense of grandeur to this country house, while the bedrooms offer comfortable fabrics and striking vistas across the landscape. The Spencers take great pride in home baking, smoking and curing; skills that have been passed down through the family since 1724. The menu includes local produce and game and Anthony's passion for wines is evident in the extensive list of over 100 labels. Private parties can be accommodated in the formal dining room and groups of 20 in a further function room. Country pursuits including trout fishing can be arranged.

# THE IZAAK WALTON HOTEL

DOVEDALE, NEAR ASHBOURNE, DERBYSHIRE DE6 2AY
**Tel:** 0845 365 2561 **International:** +44 (0)1335 350555 **Fax:** 01335 350539
**Web:** www.johansens.com/izaakwalton **E-mail:** reception@izaakwaltonhotel.com

*Our inspector loved: The wonderful views and location.*

**Price Guide:**
single £110
double/twin from £137

**Location:** A515, 3 miles; A52, 6 miles; Derby, 16 miles; Stoke on Trent, 19 miles

**Attractions:** Chatsworth House; Dovedale and the Peak District; Haddon Hall; Alton Towers

Taking its name from the author of "The Compleat Angler," this lovely 17th Century country house hotel is a fisherman's retreat through and through - from the River Dove that meanders in the valley below, to the interesting fishing memorabilia adorning the walls of the Dovedale Bar in the oldest part of the building. With 35 comfortable bedrooms, containing plenty of period features, the hotel is ideally situated for both leisure and business with its spectacular location and views. The award winning Haddon Restaurant serves creative interpretations of traditional dishes. The hotel can offer excellent fishing on one of the finest Derbyshire trout streams, and private tuition is available by arrangement. Chatsworth House and Haddon Hall are close by and the Staffordshire Potteries are within easy reach.

# EAST LODGE COUNTRY HOUSE HOTEL

ROWSLEY, NR MATLOCK, DERBYSHIRE DE4 2EF
**Tel:** 0845 365 3278 **International:** +44 (0)1629 734474 **Fax:** 01629 733949
**Web:** www.johansens.com/eastlodgecountryhouse **E-mail:** info@eastlodge.com

*Our inspector loved: The gardens which are a total delight, serene by day and magical by evening.*

**Price Guide:**
single from £100
double/twin from £150

**Awards/Recognition:** Condé Nast Johansens Most Excellent Service 2005; 2 AA Rosettes 2007-2008

**Location:** Just off the A6; Chesterfield, 8 miles; M1 jct 29, 18 miles; Derby, 21 miles

**Attractions:** Chatsworth House; Haddon Hall; Cromford Mill World Heritage Site; Peak District

A glorious tree-lined driveway guides you from the Peak District National Park to this elegant country house hotel. As you enter the reception you're enveloped by the warm, hospitable atmosphere that has been effortlessly created by the Hardman Family and their excellent team, who ensure every visit is memorable. The traditional and modern fuse together, with Broadband availability, luxurious bathrooms, a romantic garden room and terrace all merely adding to the charm of this award-winning property. Outside, David Hardman has created splendid gardens. The use of floodlight in the evening is enchanting and the 10 acres of grounds provide tranquil wanders. Beyond, fishing on the River Derwent, within the Chatsworth Estate, can be arranged. This is the nearest hotel to historic Chatsworth House.

# Northcote Manor Country House Hotel

BURRINGTON, UMBERLEIGH, DEVON EX37 9LZ
**Tel:** 0845 365 2087 **International:** +44 (0)1769 560501 **Fax:** 01769 560770
**Web:** www.johansens.com/northcotemanor **E-mail:** rest@northcotemanor.co.uk

*Our inspector loved:* The total peace and first-class service.

**Price Guide:**
single from £100
double from £155
suite from £255

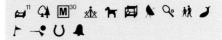

**Awards/Recognition:** 2 AA Rosettes 2006-2007; Condé Nast Johansens Reader Award 2006

**Location:** A377, 0.6 miles; Barnstaple, 14 miles; Exeter, 30 miles

**Attractions:** RHS Rosemoor; Dartington Crystal; Dartmoor and Exmoor; Various National Trust Properties

It is easy to understand why this luxurious 18th-century manor has won numerous accolades over the years. Following a recent refurbishment including a redesign of the spacious sitting rooms, hall, restaurant and bedrooms, Northcote has retained its charmingly unpretentious atmosphere of timeless tranquillity. Savour seasonal gourmet meals in the elegant restaurant while admiring the view of the pretty gardens, and take afternoon tea on the terrace garden that overlooks the Japanese water garden. Sitting high above the Taw River Valley you might feel like doing nothing more than playing a game of croquet, reading a book under a large shady tree or enjoying a relaxing treatment, such as Indian head massage, manicure or pedicure, in the comfort of your own room. Alternatively, there is a challenging golf course next door, outstanding fishing at the end of the drive, tennis and the area hosts some of the best shoots in the county.

# GIDLEIGH PARK

CHAGFORD, DEVON TQ13 8HH
**Tel:** 0845 365 1759 **International:** +44 (0)1647 432367 **Fax:** +44 (0)1647 432574
**Web:** www.johansens.com/gidleighpark **E-mail:** gidleighpark@gidleigh.co.uk

*Our inspector loved: The location and beautiful presentation, a must to visit.*

**Price Guide:** (including dinner)
single £340–£480
double/twin £440–£1200

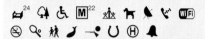

**Awards/Recognition:** 2 Star Michelin 2007; Relais & Châteaux

**Location:** A382, 2.5 miles; A30, 4.79 miles; M5 jct 31, 20 miles; Exeter St. Davids Railway Station, 21 miles

**Attractions:** Dartmoor; Castle Drogo; Exeter Cathedral; The Eden Project

You will appreciate Gidleigh Park for its outstanding international reputation for comfort and gastronomy. A clutch of top culinary awards including 2 Michelin stars for its imaginative cuisine and the wine list, make it one of the best in Britain. Service throughout the hotel is faultless. The bedrooms – 2 of them in a converted chapel – are furnished with original antiques. The public rooms are well appointed and during the cooler months, a fire burns in the lounge's impressive fireplace. Privacy is complete, amidst 54 secluded acres in the Teign Valley. A croquet lawn and a splendid water garden can be found in the grounds. A 360 yard long, par 52 putting course designed by Peter Alliss was opened in 1995.

# LEWTRENCHARD MANOR

LEWDOWN, NEAR OKEHAMPTON, DEVON EX20 4PN
**Tel:** 0845 365 2018 **International:** +44 (0)1566 783222 **Fax:** 01566 783332
**Web:** www.johansens.com/lewtrenchard **E-mail:** info@lewtrenchard.co.uk

*Our inspector loved: Location - ambience - welcoming crackling log fires.*

**Price Guide:**
single £145-£240
double/twin £180-£225
suite £245-£270

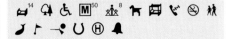

**Awards/Recognition:** 3 AA Rosettes 2007-2008

**Location:** A386, 6.6 miles; A30, 7 miles; M5 jct 31, 33.5 miles

**Attractions:** Exeter Cathedral; Dartmoor; Eden Project; Various Historic Houses, Castle & Gardens

You can tell that this beautiful Jacobean manor has been well-loved, built by the Monk family in 1600 and embellished later by the Victorian hymn writer Rev Sabine Baring Gould, as it has an unmistakeable warmth, and family antiques bump up against ornate ceilings, leaded windows and elegant carved oak staircases. Bedrooms look out over the valley, and another pretty impressive backdrop, the oak-panelled dining room, prepares you for excellent cooking. The estate offers clay pigeon shooting, rough shooting and fishing, making this ideal for your weekend parties, as well as an idyllic setting for weddings and private functions. Exeter is on the doorstep with its cathedral and sophisticated shops, whilst Devon's numerous tourist attractions are all within easy reach.

# THE ARUNDELL ARMS

LIFTON, DEVON PL16 0AA
**Tel:** 0845 365 2394 **International:** +44 (0)1566 784666 **Fax:** 01566 784494
**Web:** www.johansens.com/arundellarms **E-mail:** reservations@arundellarms.com

*Our inspector loved: The wholesome hospitality and comfort after a day in the country.*

**Price Guide:**
single from £99
double/twin from £160
superior from £190

**Awards/Recognition:** 2 AA Rosettes 2007-2008

**Location:** A30, 2 miles; Plymouth, 27.5 miles; M5 jct 31, 40 miles; Exeter, 40 miles

**Attractions:** Eden Project; Various Historic Houses and Gardens; Tintagel

One of England's best-known sporting hotels for more than half a century, The Arundell Arms, a former coaching inn, dates back to Saxon times. Recommended by Condé Nast Johansens for 25 years. The hotel boasts 20 miles of exclusive salmon and trout fishing on the Tamar and 5 of its tributaries, and a famous school of fly fishing. You can experience other country activities such as hill walking, shooting, riding and golf, or check out the surf on wonderful nearby beaches. Alternatively just take some well earned time off and collapse into a comfortable armchair and enjoy the Old World charm of flagstone floors, fires, paintings, antiques and thoroughly delicious gourmet cooking.

# SOAR MILL COVE HOTEL

SOAR MILL COVE, SALCOMBE, SOUTH DEVON TQ7 3DS
**Tel:** 0845 365 2349 **International:** +44 (0)1548 561566 **Fax:** 01548 561223
**Web:** www.johansens.com/soarmillcove **E-mail:** info@soarmillcove.co.uk

***Our inspector loved:*** *Superb location and tastefully created new exclusive intimate cocktail and champagne bar.*

**Price Guide:**
single £89–£180
double/twin £150–£240
suite £260

**Awards/Recognition:** 4 AA Rosettes 2006-2007

**Location:** A381, 1.5 miles; Salcombe, 4 miles; Plymouth, 24 miles

**Attractions:** Salcombe; Dartmoor; South West Coastal Park; Historic Barbican of Plymouth with famous Pilgrim steps

Strolling along golden sandy beaches, fishing in rock pools and exploring local caves – it all seems very 'Famous Five'. This family run hotel offers the right balance of attentive yet unobtrusive service. Nothing is too much trouble at Soar Mill Cove and there is plenty to keep you busy - take the hotels tandem for a spin, find a quiet corner by one of the two pools, enjoy a relaxing massage in "The Ocean Spa", or feast yourself on lobster and crab. Set within 2,000 acres of National Trust countryside between Dartmouth's historic port and The Pilgrim Steps of Plymouth, this is arguably the most dramatic seaside setting, with breathtaking views and coastal paths to die for. Dogs welcome too.

# THE TIDES REACH HOTEL

SOUTH SANDS, SALCOMBE, DEVON TQ8 8LJ
**Tel:** 0845 365 2713  **International:** +44 (0)1548 843466  **Fax:** 01548 843954
**Web:** www.johansens.com/tidesreach  **E-mail:** enquire@tidesreach.com

*Our inspector loved: The stunning location and the unwinding calming atmosphere*

**Price Guide:** (including dinner)
single £78–£170
double/twin £146–£350

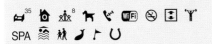

**Awards/Recognition:** 1 AA Rosette 2007-2008

**Location:** A381, 2 miles; M5, 43 miles; Salcombe, 1.7 miles

**Attractions:** Gardens of Overbecks; Plymouth Maritime Museum; South Devon Coastal Path; Dartmoor

A charming south-facing hotel sitting in a sandy cove just inside the mouth of the Salcombe Estuary. Over their 39 years of ownership the Edwards family have gained a reputation for warmth, hospitality and no-nonsense service. Chef Finn Ibsen creates menus with seasonal produce and makes the most of the morning catch from the local fishermen. Most of the immaculate bedrooms come with lovely sea views and offer plenty of flexibility for families. There's an indoor pool, sauna, spa, snooker table and for the very energetic a squash court. For sailing fans why not hire a Hobie Cat, sail into Salcombe for an ice-cream or spot of shopping and then happily retreat from the hordes to the comfort of Tides Reach.

# BUCKLAND-TOUT-SAINTS

GOVETON, KINGSBRIDGE, DEVON TQ7 2DS
**Tel:** 0845 365 3211 **International:** +44 (0)1548 853055 **Fax:** 01548 856261
**Web:** www.johansens.com/bucklandtoutsaints **E-mail:** buckland@tout-saints.co.uk

*Our inspector loved:* This tucked away secret gem within a haven of natural beauty.

**Price Guide:**
single from £80
double/twin £120-£165
suite from £295

Come and enjoy the hospitality of this elegant 300-year-old country house nestled amidst 4 acres of landscaped gardens in idyllic Devon. If you're a nature lover you'll be in paradise, or you may just want to relax in tranquil surroundings. The 16 individually decorated bedrooms have wonderful views of the countryside, while a daily newspaper, mineral water and fluffy bathrobes are all complimentary. The restaurant has won accolades over the years and offers both local and exotic menus complemented by fine wines - take afternoon tea in front of a roaring wood fire or explore the local area with its castles and picturesque villages. You're very close here to the popular sailing and fishing towns of Salcombe and, Dartmouth.

**Awards/Recognition:** 2 AA Rosettes 2007-2008

**Location:** A381, 2 miles; Totnes, 12 miles; Plymouth, 22 miles; M5 jct 29, 40 miles

**Attractions:** Various Historic Houses Castles & Gardens; National Marine Aquarium; Eden Project; Beautiful Coastal Walks and Beaches

# HOTEL RIVIERA

THE ESPLANADE, SIDMOUTH, DEVON EX10 8AY

**Tel:** 0845 365 1904  **International:** +44 (0)1395 515201  **Fax:** 01395 577775
**Web:** www.johansens.com/riviera  **E-mail:** enquiries@hotelriviera.co.uk

*Our inspector loved: Welcome, location and total detail to comfort.*

**Price Guide:** (including 6 course dinner):
single £109–£163
double/twin £218–£304
suite £330–£350

**Awards/Recognition:** 2 AA Rosettes 2007-2008

**Location:** A3052, 2.5 miles; M5 jct 30, 13 miles; Exeter Airport, 10 miles; Honiton Railway Station, 8 miles

**Attractions:** Killerton House and Gardens; Exeter Cathedral; Powderham Castle; Dartmoor

A warm welcome awaits you at this prestigious award-winning hotel. Peter Wharton's Hotel Riviera is arguably one of the most comfortable and most hospitable in the region. The exterior, with its fine Regency façade and bow fronted windows complements the elegance of the interior comprising handsome public rooms and beautifully appointed bedrooms, many with sea views. Perfectly located at the centre of Sidmouth's historic Georgian esplanade, and awarded 4 Stars by both the AA and Visit Britain, the Riviera is committed to providing the very highest standards of excellence, ensuring you a most enjoyable experience. Choose to dine in the attractive salon, with panoramic views across Lyme Bay, and indulge in the superb cuisine, prepared by English and French trained chefs. The exceptional cellar will please any wine connoisseur. Short breaks are available.

# THE HORN OF PLENTY COUNTRY HOUSE HOTEL & RESTAURANT

GULWORTHY, TAVISTOCK, DEVON PL19 8JD
**Tel:** 0845 365 2534 **International:** +44 (0)1822 832528
**Web:** www.johansens.com/hornofplenty **E-mail:** enquiries@thehornofplenty.co.uk

*Our inspector loved:* All the beautiful refurbishments and the location.

**Price Guide:**
single £150–£240
double/twin £160–£250

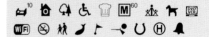

**Awards/Recognition:** 3 AA Rosettes 2007-2008

**Location:** Just off A390; A386, 3.5 miles; A30, 15 miles; Plymouth, 17 miles

**Attractions:** Devon Coastline; The Eden Project; Dartmoor National Park; Buckland Abbey

The warmth and charm of owners Paul Roston and Master Chef Peter Gorton is infectious, as is the friendly, informal atmosphere of this enchanting country house created by their young, efficient staff. Set in 5 acres of spectacular gardens and wild orchards the house oozes character. Some bedrooms have balconies with breathtaking views over the Tamar Valley and luxuries include fluffy towels, robes and the scent of fresh flowers competing with woodsmoke from log fires in winter. The heart of The Horn of Plenty is its kitchen where you're invited to sample a superb selection of food and wine. Fresh produce is sourced locally and menus feature dishes such as John Dory with smoked salmon mousse and tortellini, hot ginger sponge pudding with rhubarb compote!

# ORESTONE MANOR & THE RESTAURANT AT ORESTONE MANOR

ROCKHOUSE LANE, MAIDENCOMBE, TORQUAY, DEVON TQ1 4SX
**Tel:** 0845 365 2095 **International:** +44 (0)1803 328098 **Fax:** 01803 328336
**Web:** www.johansens.com/orestonemanor **E-mail:** enquiries@orestonemanor.com

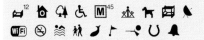
***Our inspector loved:*** *The Idyllic location - welcome and stylish presentation.*

**Price Guide:**
single £99–£149
double/twin £135–£225

**Awards/Recognition:** 2 AA Rosettes 2007-2008

**Location:** On the A379; Torquay, 3 miles; Teignmouth, 4 miles; M5 jct 30, 19 miles

**Attractions:** Dartmoor; Cathedral City of Exeter; National Trust Houses & Gardens; Exmoor

With stunning views across the Torbay coastline and Lyme Bay this was formerly the home of painter John Calcott Horsley RA, renowned for painting the very first Christmas card, and whose celebrated portrait of his brother-in-law, Isambard Kingdom Brunel, hangs in the National Gallery. A colonial theme runs through the house and as expected an excellent afternoon tea is served on the terrace or in the conservatory. The lunch and dinner menu takes inspiration from local seasonal ingredients, with many of the herbs and vegetables coming from its own garden. There is plenty to do nearby, from National Trust properties to Dartmoor, Exmoor and stunning coastal walks.

# Langdon Court Hotel & Restaurant

DOWN THOMAS, PLYMOUTH, DEVON PL9 0DY
**Tel:** 0845 365 1985 **International:** +44 (0)1752 862358 **Fax:** 01752 863428
**Web:** www.johansens.com/langdon **E-mail:** enquiries@langdoncourt.co.uk

**Our inspector loved:** *Inviting friends to a house party in this magical place.*

**Price Guide:**
single from £85
double from £120
exclusive use £5,000

**Location:** Plymouth, 6 miles; A38, 9 miles; M5 jct 31, 40 miles

**Attractions:** Coastal paths of Devon; Plymouth; Various National Trust Properties; Dartmoor

Originally built for Katherine Parr, the sixth wife of Henry VIII, we think she'd be impressed with this Grade II listed Tudor manor's modern incarnation. Beyond its Jacobean walled gardens, well-kept lawns and impressive grey façade lie tiled floors, warmly painted stone walls and classic, uncluttered furnishings. Some of the 12 bedrooms are simply stunning, many with views of the countryside or the gardens. Whether you're a wedding reception, shooting or house party, 3 function suites are available, and the impressive menu served in the modern brasserie, bar or on the terrace specialises in fish and seafood. The hotel has a direct path to the beach at Wembury, access to the coastal paths and is ideally placed for exploring the South Hams countryside.

# WOOLACOMBE BAY HOTEL

SOUTH STREET, WOOLACOMBE, DEVON EX34 7BN
**Tel:** 0845 365 2819 **International:** +44 (0)1271 870388 **Fax:** 01271 870613
**Web:** www.johansens.com/woolacombebay **E-mail:** woolacombe.bayhotel@btinternet.com

**Our inspector loved:** *Everything they have to offer, especially for families.*

**Price Guide:** (including dinner)
single £92–£152
double/twin £184–£304

**Location:** A361, 5 miles; Ilfracombe, 6 miles; Barnstaple, 11 miles; M5 jct 27, 46 miles

**Attractions:** Exmoor; National Trust Coastal Walks; Lynton; RHS Garden Rosemoor

Always impressive at building fine hotels the Victorian's also knew where to position them. Woolacombe Bay Hotel is no exception standing in 6 acres of grounds leading to 3 miles of golden Blue-flag sand. The hotel is packed with activity both indoors and out, from unlimited use of tennis, squash, two pools, billiards, bowls and a health suite there is also power-boating, fishing, shooting and riding that can be arranged. Special rates are also offered at nearby golf clubs. Being energetic is not a requirement however, and you can join others in relaxing in the grounds, which extend to the rolling surf of this magnificent bay. A great hotel to take the family though it can also be a well deserved treat for those with less luggage.

# WATERSMEET HOTEL

MORTEHOE, WOOLACOMBE, DEVON EX34 7EB

**Tel:** 0845 365 2793  **International:** +44 (0)1271 870333  **US toll free:** Reservations: 0800 731 7493  **Fax:** 01271 870890
**Web:** www.johansens.com/watersmeet  **E-mail:** info@watersmeethotel.co.uk

*Our inspector loved: Location, the relaxing, informal atmosphere and the fine menus.*

**Price Guide:** (including dinner)
single £98–£150
double/twin £150–£296
suite £196–£296

**Awards/Recognition:** 1 AA Rosette 2006-2007

**Location:** B3343, 2 miles; A361, 4 miles; M5 jct 27, 50 miles; Barnstaple, 15 miles

**Attractions:** Arlington Court; Saunton Sands Golf Course; National Trust Coastal Walks; Watermouth Castle

A dramatic and beautiful setting greets those arriving at Watersmeet just above Combesgate Beach. Steps lead down to the sandy shore and large picture windows in the reception rooms mean you never have to miss out on the ever-changing coastline. The hotels strength lies in the dedication and care of owners Michael and Amanda James. Bedrooms are in a classical style and all have the most wonderful views, some even have balconies. Quality local ingredients are used in the creative and thoughtfully balanced dishes in the Pavilion restaurant. Here you can marvel over sunsets by candlelight though on warm nights sitting on the terrace listening to the waves is also a tempting option.

# SUMMER LODGE COUNTRY HOUSE HOTEL, RESTAURANT & SPA

9 FORE STREET, EVERSHOT, DORSET DT2 0JR
**Tel:** 0845 365 2381 **International:** +44 (0)1935 482000 **Fax:** +44 (0)1935 482040
**Web:** www.johansens.com/summerlodge **E-mail:** enquiries@summerlodgehotel.com

***Our inspector loved:*** *The sumptuous provision and extravagant interiors.*

**Price Guide:**
single from £195
double/twin £225–£360
suite/master bedroom £425–£495

**Awards/Recognition:** Relais & Châteaux; 3 AA Rosettes 2006-2007

**Location:** A37, 1.5 miles; M5 jct 25, 33.5 miles; Dorchester, 13 miles; Bournemouth, 46 miles

**Attractions:** Thomas Hardy Country; Cerne Abbas; Abbotsbury and Heritage Coast; Sherborne and Shaftesbury

Summer Lodge dates back to 1789. Built for the 2nd Earl of Ilchester, Thomas Hardy was commissioned to draw plans for a second floor by the 6th Earl in 1893. Impeccably restored with 24 gorgeous bedrooms, suites and cottages - many with fireplaces - it combines the finest English furnishings and classical art with the latest technology, including complimentary Wi-Fi. The award-winning restaurant, under Head Chef Steven Titman and Sommelier Eric Zwiebel is a delight and the Lodge's own vegetable garden and extensive wine cellar complement the culinary experience. Lighter meals are available in the well-stocked bar and sumptuous Dorset cream teas are served each afternoon. The spa treatment rooms offer Matis products. Civil weddings, small business meetings and private dining are meticulously catered for.

# STOCK HILL COUNTRY HOUSE HOTEL & RESTAURANT

STOCK HILL, GILLINGHAM, DORSET SP8 5NR

**Tel:** 0845 365 2371 **International:** +44 (0)1747 823626 **Fax:** 01747 825628
**Web:** www.johansens.com/stockhillhouse **E-mail:** reception@stockhillhouse.co.uk

***Our inspector loved:*** *Exceptional hospitality in a beautiful Dorset garden.*

**Price Guide:** (including dinner)
single £145–£165
double £265–£295

**Awards/Recognition:** 3 AA Rosettes 2007-2008

**Location:** On the B3081; A303, 3 miles; Shaftesbury, 6 miles; Bristol, 47 miles

**Attractions:** Stonehenge; Stourhead House & Garden; Salisbury; Longleat

Set within 11 acres of attractive woodlands and beautiful gardens on the borders of 3 counties, this remarkable, 3 Red Star, late Victorian mansion exudes a relaxed charm. Impressive oak doors open to reveal a beautiful period interior. Each bedroom reflects the history and style of the house and offers every comfort you would expect. The restaurant, which is also open for non-residents, displays interesting antiques and curios and has excellent views over the gardens. Romantic candle-lit tables are perfectly positioned to provide privacy, complemented by attentive and friendly service. The highly-acclaimed, award winning cuisine is most imaginative with a range of European flavours. Ingredients are sourced locally and include fresh fish, shellfish and organic vegetables, many harvested from the walled kitchen garden. Sumptuous desserts are a perfect finish to a memorable evening. Completely non-smoking throught the hotel.

# PLUMBER MANOR

STURMINSTER NEWTON, DORSET DT10 2AF

**Tel:** 0845 365 2134  **International:** +44 (0)1258 472507  **Fax:** 01258 473370
**Web:** www.johansens.com/plumbermanor  **E-mail:** book@plumbermanor.com

***Our inspector loved:*** *The feeling of total relaxation and well-being which embraces the visitor immediately.*

**Price Guide:**
single from £95
double/twin £115–£175

**Location:** A357, 1.5 miles; M27 jct 1, 43 miles; Sturminster Newton, 2 miles; Bournemouth, 30 miles

**Attractions:** Cerne Abbas Giant; Kingston Lacy (NT); Stourhead (NT); Sherborne

This imposing Jacobean building of local stone, occupies extensive gardens in the heart of Thomas Hardy's Dorset and has been the home of the Prideaux-Brune family since the early 17th century. There are 6 very comfortable bedrooms in the house and a further 10 spacious rooms in a converted stone barn and courtyard building within the grounds. 3 interconnecting dining rooms comprise the restaurant, where Chef Brian Prideaux-Brune's creative culinary skills have been recognised by all the major food guides. Open for dinner every evening and Sunday lunch. Explore the many churches and villages and the neaby Dorset coastline. Riding can be arranged locally. Closed during February.

# THE PRIORY HOTEL

CHURCH GREEN, WAREHAM, DORSET BH20 4ND

**Tel:** 0845 365 2651 **International:** +44 (0)1929 551666 **Fax:** 01929 554519
**Web:** www.johansens.com/priorywareham **E-mail:** reservations@theprioryhotel.co.uk

***Our inspector loved:*** *The thought, care and tireless effort that goes into this exquisite hotel.*

**Price Guide:**
single from £172
double £215-£315
boathouse suite from £345

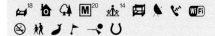

Since the 16th century, the one time Lady St Mary Priory has offered sanctuary to travellers. In Hardy's Dorset, "Far From the Madding Crowd", it placidly stands in immaculate gardens on the bank of the River Frome. The Priory underwent a sympathetic conversion, the result is an unpretentiously charming hotel. The bedrooms are distinctively styled and feature family antiques, many rooms have views of the Purbeck Hills. A 16th-century clay barn has been transformed into the Boathouse, creating 4 spacious luxury suites at the river's edge. The drawing room, residents' lounge and intimate bar create a convivial atmosphere. The Garden Room restaurant is open for breakfast and lunch, while splendid dinners are served in the vaulted stone cellars. There are moorings for guests arriving by boat.

**Location:** A352, 1 miles; M27 jct 1, 32 miles; Poole, 9 miles; Southampton, 42 miles

**Attractions:** Corfe Castle; Lulworth Cove; Athelhampton House and Garden; Jurassic Coast

# MOONFLEET MANOR

FLEET, WEYMOUTH, DORSET DT3 4ED
**Tel:** 0845 365 2074 **International:** +44 (0)1305 786948 **Fax:** 01305 774395
**Web:** www.johansens.com/moonfleetmanor **E-mail:** info@moonfleetmanorhotel.co.uk

***Our inspector loved:*** *This excellent child friendly hotel dedicated to the satisfaction of the discerning family.*

**Price Guide:**
double/twin £170–£270
suite from £310

**Location:** A354, 3 miles; M27 jct 1, 50 miles; Weymouth, 3 miles; Bournemouth, 42 miles

**Attractions:** Chesil Beach and Jurassic Coast; Abbotsbury; Monkey World; Corfe Castle

Overlooking Chesil Beach, a unique feature of the Dorset coast, Moonfleet Manor is both a luxury hotel and a family resort. The use of a variety of unusual antiques and objets d'art from around the world lends a refreshing and individual style to this comfortable and attractive hotel. Bedrooms are beautifully decorated and furnished and a range of amenities ensures that guests enjoy high standards of comfort. Attentive staff work hard to ensure that guests feel at home whatever their age. Moonfleet's dining room, offers an excellent and varied menu based on fresh local produce but bringing culinary styles from around the world. Facilities at the hotel include an indoor swimming pool and squash and tennis courts.

# HEADLAM HALL

HEADLAM, NEAR GAINFORD, DARLINGTON, COUNTY DURHAM DL2 3HA
**Tel:** 0845 365 1827 **International:** +44 (0)1325 730238 **Fax:** 01325 730790
**Web:** www.johansens.com/headlamhall **E-mail:** admin@headlamhall.co.uk

*Our inspector loved: Relaxing in the outdoor spa pool, followed by a swim and sauna.*

**Price Guide:**
single £90–£120
double/twin £110–£140
suite from £150

**Awards/Recognition:** 1 AA Rosette 2007-2008

**Location:** A67, 2 miles; Darlington, 8 miles; A1M jct 58, 8 miles

**Attractions:** Raby Castle; Bowes Museum; Barnard Castle; Historic City of Durham

This 17th-century Jacobean country house stands in beautiful walled gardens evoking an air of splendour and tranquillity and is enveloped by its own golf course and rolling farmland. The bedrooms are individually designed, some with period furniture and others with a more contemporary feel. The main hall has a superb 300-year-old carved oak fireplace with big comfortable sofas and a relaxed ambience. For dinner you can choose between 3 rooms within the restaurant, all offering their own character and fine furnishings, where dishes prepared with fresh, local ingredients can be enjoyed. There is also a stylish brasserie serving more informal food with great views of the surroundings. The new spa provides health and beauty treatments and has a swimming pool, outdoor hydrotherapy spa pool, sauna, steam room and fully-equipped gym. Play tennis on the hotel's court or golf at the excellent 9-hole course with pro shop and driving range.

# THE SWAN HOTEL AT BIBURY

BIBURY, GLOUCESTERSHIRE GL7 5NW
**Tel:** 0845 365 2709 **International:** +44 (0)1285 740695 **Fax:** 01285 740473
**Web:** www.johansens.com/swanhotelatbibury **E-mail:** info@swanhotel.co.uk

***Our inspector loved:*** *The picturesque location in a pretty village set right on the river.*

**Price Guide:**
single £99–£155
double/twin £145–£265

**Location:** Just off B4425; A40, 8.7 miles; M40, 34.4 miles; M4 jct 16, 63.4 miles

**Attractions:** Bibury Trout Farm; Arlington Row; Cirencester; Chipping Campden

Recommended by Condé Nast Johansens since 1983, this 17th century coaching inn is the perfect Cotswolds base for country lovers, fishermen and walkers, and acknowledges the needs of the sophisticated modern-day traveller. The hotel has its own fishing rights for keen anglers and a moated ornamental garden to enjoy on a summer's evening. Bibury village is delightful with masses of honey-coloured stonework, picturesque ponds, the trout-filled River Coln and a complete sense of lazy serenity. Oak panelling, plush carpets and sumptuous fabrics create an eclectic background for the fine paintings and antiques that decorate the Swan's interiors, and eccentric bedrooms are superbly appointed with luxury bathrooms. Dine in the Café Swan or unique Gallery Restaurant.

# THE DIAL HOUSE

THE CHESTNUTS, HIGH STREET, BOURTON-ON-THE-WATER, GLOUCESTERSHIRE GL54 2AN

**Tel:** 0845 365 2463 **International:** +44 (0)1451 822244 **Fax:** 01451 810126
**Web:** www.johansens.com/dialhouse **E-mail:** info@dialhousehotel.com

*Our inspector loved:* The stylish decoration combined with the comfortable and relaxed feel.

**Price Guide:**
single £55–£89
double £120–£160
suite £180

Feel that you're stepping into a period drama at this beautiful family-run hotel, built in 1698 of Cotswold stone in an unspoiled village where the little River Windrush flows down the main street under "toy town" bridges. Exuding sophisticated English country style, The Dial House is filled with large inglenook fireplaces, exposed timber beams, monks' chairs, poor boxes, secret cupboards, water wells and stone arches. There is so much you'll find memorable, and every bedroom has gorgeous details from hand-painted wallpaper to lavish big beds, deep baths and exquisite fabrics. Mouth-watering cuisine is served in intimate dining rooms where like the rest of the hotel innovative style and high standards reign.

**Location:** A429, 0.65 miles; A40, 5 miles; Cheltenham, 19.5 miles

**Attractions:** Stow-on-the-Wold; Warwick Castle; Shakespeare country; Blenheim Palace

# HOTEL ON THE PARK

EVESHAM ROAD, CHELTENHAM, GLOUCESTERSHIRE GL52 2AH
**Tel:** 0845 365 1903  **International:** +44 (0)1242 518898  **Fax:** 01242 511526
**Web:** www.johansens.com/hotelonthepark  **E-mail:** stay@hotelonthepark.co.uk

***Our inspector loved:*** *The fabulous aromatherapy baths and massaging beds - heaven!*

**Price Guide:**
single from £106.50
double/twin from £129.50–£139.50

**Awards/Recognition:** 2 AA Rosettes 2006-2007

**Location:** Just off A435; Cheltenham, 5-min walk; M5 jct 10, 3.3 miles

**Attractions:** Sudeley Castle; The Cotswolds; Stratford-upon-Avon; Cheltenham Racecourse

As you would expect in a spa city this attractive wisteria-clad townhouse has amazing bathrooms! They range from an infinity spa bathroom, through to those with state-of-the-art whirlpool baths and several with aromatherapy and chromatherapy to energise or relax you. The infinity bath's gently cascading water is enhanced by a spectrum cycle of colours, controlled according to your mood. Bedrooms are traditional with a contemporary twist and well furnished with antiques. The overall atmosphere here is welcoming and relaxed. Parkers the brasserie features imaginative, vibrant menus and good wine lists. The well-stocked library is ideal if you want to be alone with a book. Cheltenham's shops, theatres and historic attractions are within walking distance, and the National Hunt Racecourse is nearby.

# COWLEY MANOR

COWLEY, NR CHELTENHAM, GLOUCESTERSHIRE GL53 9NL
**Tel:** 0845 365 3452 **International:** +44 (0)1242 870900 **Fax:** 01242 870901
**Web:** www.johansens.com/cowleymanor **E-mail:** stay@cowleymanor.com

*Our inspector loved:* The contemporary style and beautiful grounds.

**Price Guide:**
double £245-£470

**Location:** A435, 1.8 miles; Cheltenham, 6 miles; M5 Jct 11A, 9 1.8 miles; Oxford, 40 1.8 miles

**Attractions:** The beautiful Cotswolds; Cirencester; Oxford

The imposing classical exterior belies a truly impressive chic and contemporary interior, all set in 55 acres of Grade I listed gardens. You sense that the fine details, friendly and efficient service are born from a true understanding of today's modern traveller. The interiors are works of art in themselves; in one room, flamboyant lime-green walls and red laminate tables are offset by the high 1850's ceilings. The billiard room is lined with leather walls. Bedrooms have a feeling of space and light and the bathrooms are positively palatial. The panelled dining room combines classical architecture with modern elegance; locally sourced produce inspires delicious menus. Sleek lines of the award winning spa, C-Side, blend into the natural surroundings around the indoor and outdoor pools. All this just 1.5 hours from London in the stunning Cotswolds.

# THE GREENWAY

SHURDINGTON, CHELTENHAM, GLOUCESTERSHIRE GL51 4UG
**Tel:** 0845 365 2514 **International:** +44 (0)1242 862352 **Fax:** 01242 862780
**Web:** www.johansens.com/greenway **E-mail:** info@thegreenway.co.uk

*Our inspector loved:* The warm welcome, friendly and professional staff and beautiful surroundings.

**Price Guide:**
single from £99
double/twin £150–£240

**Awards/Recognition:** 2 AA Rosettes 2007-2008

**Location:** A46, 0.5 miles; M5 jct 11a, 2.5 miles; Bristol Airport, 41.5 miles; Cheltenham, 10-min drive

**Attractions:** Cheltenham Racecourse; The Cotswolds; Shakespeare Country; Gloucester

Set in gentle parkland with the rolling Cotswold hills beyond, The Greenway manages to capture a unique style of its own. This is the perfect place to unwind, where there is a sense of seductively warm hospitality. Elegant public rooms soothe your tired mind with their antique furniture, fresh flowers and roaring log fires in winter, and access to the formal gardens in summer. 11 bedrooms in the main house, a further 10 in the converted Georgian coach house next door, are individually decorated with co-ordinating bathrooms. Peruse the menu for a superb choice of dishes and carefully selected wines in the award-winning conservatory dining room. Plan your day trips to the spa town of Cheltenham, the Cotswold villages and Shakespeare country.

# Charingworth Manor

NR CHIPPING CAMPDEN, GLOUCESTERSHIRE GL55 6NS
**Tel:** 0845 365 3298 **International:** +44 (0)1386 593555 **Fax:** 01386 593353
**Web:** www.johansens.com/charingworthmanor **E-mail:** info.charingworthmanor@classiclodges.co.uk

*Our inspector loved:* The wonderful setting overlooking the beautiful Cotswold countryside.

**Price Guide:**
single £125-£155
double £180-£210
suite £245-£295

**Awards/Recognition:** 2 AA Rosettes 2006-2007

**Location:** B4035, 1 miles; A429, 2.5 miles; Moreton-in-Marsh, 4.5 miles

**Attractions:** Chipping Campden; Cotswolds; Stratford-upon-Avon; Warwick Castle

A captivating 14th century manor house set in a 54 acre estate, with immaculate formal gardens and far-reaching views of the unmatchable Cotswold countryside. During the 1930s, the manor hosted several illustrious guests, including T.S.Eliot who wrote an ode to Charingworth. Individually designed guest rooms are furnished with antiques and fine fabrics, recreating the manor's original charm; two feature impressive four-poster beds and some offer private terraces from which to enjoy the beautiful grounds. The restaurant has a creative menu and offers a good selection of seasonally inspired dishes. On a mild evening you can enjoy strolling through the extensive gardens or during the winter months log fires warm the series of intimate, tapestry-hung public rooms which are inviting retreats from inclement weather.

# COTSWOLD HOUSE HOTEL

HIGH STREET, CHIPPING CAMPDEN, GLOUCESTERSHIRE GL55 6AN
**Tel:** 0845 365 3250 **International:** +44 (0)1386 840330 **Fax:** 01386 840310
**Web:** www.johansens.com/cotswoldhouse **E-mail:** reception@cotswoldhouse.com

*Our inspector loved:* This ultra-stylish treat with fantastic bedrooms.

**Price Guide:**
single from £150
double/twin from £295
suite from £525

**Awards/Recognition:** Condé Nast Johansens Most Excellent Country Hotel 2005; 3 AA Rosettes 2006-2007

**Location:** B4081, 0.25 miles; A44, 2 miles; M5 jct 8, 25 miles

**Attractions:** Shopping in Chipping Campden; Stratford-upon-Avon; Oxford; The Cotswolds

Unashamedly nostalgic, Chipping Campden says no thank you very much to the rigours of modern-day life, but Cotswold House indulges in a witty mix of contemporary style alongside its Regency architecture to create a true feast for the senses. A signature spiral staircase leads to peaceful bedrooms with warm tones, state-of-the-art technology and delightfully original bathrooms, while original artworks adorn the walls, and modern glass sculptures and award-winning lighting, intrigue. The hotel is rightly proud of its kitchen, which has many winning accolades to its credit. You will undoubtedly adore Juliana's Restaurant, serving locally sourced dishes and the informal meals served in Hicks' Brasserie. A Michelin Rising Star for 2007.

# The Noel Arms Hotel

HIGH STREET, CHIPPING CAMPDEN, GLOUCESTERSHIRE GL55 6AT
**Tel:** 0845 365 2608 **International:** +44 (0)1386 840317 **Fax:** 01386 841136
**Web:** www.johansens.com/noelarms **E-mail:** reception@noelarmshotel.com

**Our inspector loved:** *The friendly welcome and comfortable atmosphere.*

**Price Guide:**
single £95
double £130–£220

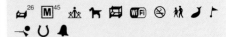

**Location:** On the B4081; A44, 2 miles; A429, 4.5 miles; Moreton-in-Marsh, 8 miles

**Attractions:** Oxford; Cheltenham Spa; Cotswolds; Hidcote Manor Gardens

A long tradition of hospitality awaits you at The Noel Arms. In 1651 the future Charles II rested here after his Scottish army was defeated by Cromwell at the Battle of Worcester, and guests continue to be royally entertained here. Today, a contemporary style has been adopted throughout yet the hotel's long-standing traditional comfort has been maintained. Reminders of the past such as antique furniture and swords are displayed around the hotel, whilst some bedrooms, located in the main house or in the tastefully constructed new wing, have four-poster beds. Each guest room offers the standards you expect from a country hotel. Be tempted by the varied menu that features both British and Continental dishes, or enjoy the gastropub food. Much of the menu consists of Cotswold produce and is served in the conservatory and Dover's Bar. Browse Chipping Campden's delightful shops or the surrounding honey-coloured enchanting Cotswold villages.

# LOWER SLAUGHTER MANOR

LOWER SLAUGHTER, GLOUCESTERSHIRE GL54 2HP
**Tel:** 0845 365 2047 **International:** +44 (0)1451 820456 **Fax:** 01451 822150
**Web:** www.johansens.com/lowerslaughtermanor **E-mail:** info@lowerslaughter.co.uk

*Our inspector loved:* The newly designed and decorated bedrooms, all individual and ultra-chic.

**Price Guide:**
single £170–£465
double £250–£450
garden room £550–£825

**Awards/Recognition:** 2 AA Rosettes 2007-2008

**Location:** A429, 0.5 miles; Stow-on-the-Wold, 4 miles; M5 jct 10, 20 miles; Cheltenham, 21 miles

**Attractions:** Stratford-upon-Avon; Warwick Castle; Sudeley Castle; The Cotswolds

Nothing less than regal, this beautifully restored Grade II listed country manor house positively oozes style. Its "designer" rooms are chic and Continental in flavour, and a contemporary feel teases the exceptional house's historic character. Enjoy the exquisite cuisine alongside a well balanced list of specially selected wines from the Old and New Worlds. The wonderful grounds feature a croquet lawn and, within the delightful walled garden, a unique 2-storey dovecote that dates back to the 15th century. This is a wonderful setting for private parties, business meetings, weddings and civil partnership ceremonies.

# WASHBOURNE

LOWER SLAUGHTER, GLOUCESTERSHIRE GL54 2HS
**Tel:** 0845 365 2791 **International:** +44 (0)1451 822143 **Fax:** 01451 821045
**Web:** www.johansens.com/washbournecourt **E-mail:** info@washbournecourt.co.uk

**Our inspector loved:** *The comtemporary style of the bar combined with the original features of the building.*

**Price Guide:** (including dinner)
single from £115
double/twin from £170

**Awards/Recognition:** 2 AA Rosettes 2006-2007

**Location:** A429, 0.5 miles; Bourton-on-the-Water, 2 miles

**Attractions:** ; Stow-on-the-Wold; Cheltenham; Oxford

Lower Slaughter has been described as one of the prettiest villages in England. The perfect partner to this 17th-century hotel, next to the River Eye and surrounded by 4 acres of private gardens and grounds. Beamed ceilings, stone mullioned windows and original open fireplaces will fulfil all your hopes of a cosy country bolthole, whilst comfortable bedrooms make good use of modern fabrics and tasteful colours. Some in the main building date back over 400 years, new rooms are located in the Coach House. Pray for fine weather, as then you can enjoy breakfast, afternoon tea and light meals on the terrace, but save your appetite for more formal British menus of local produce in the elegant restaurant - not to be missed!

# BURLEIGH COURT

BURLEIGH, MINCHINHAMPTON, NEAR STROUD, GLOUCESTERSHIRE GL5 2PF
**Tel:** 0845 365 3217 **International:** +44 (0)1453 883804 **Fax:** 01453 886870
**Web:** www.johansens.com/burleighgloucestershire **E-mail:** info@burleighcourthotel.co.uk

***Our inspector loved:*** *The spacious bedrooms and wonderful views of the Golden Valley*

**Price Guide:**
single £85-£105
double £125-£145
suite £170

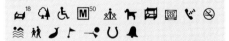

**Awards/Recognition:** 1 AA Rosette 2006-2007

**Location:** A419, 0.5 miles; M4 jct, 28.5 miles; Cirencester, 11.5 miles; Cheltenham, 16 miles

**Attractions:** Cotswolds; Bath; Slimbridge Wildfowl Trust; Westonbirt Arboretum

Journey through honey-stoned Cotswold villages to reach this 18th-century former gentleman's manor. Nestling on a steep hillside overlooking the Golden Valley its relaxed atmosphere and acres of beautifully tended gardens featuring terraces, ponds, pools, hidden pathways and Cotswold stone walls create an idyllic setting. Many bedrooms in the main house have garden views though for families we recommend the coach house rooms, located by a Victorian plunge pool as well as those within the courtyard gardens which offer flexible accommodation. The restaurant has a reputation for classical dishes and a wine cellar to satisfy the most demanding drinker. From here you can easily explore the market towns of Minchinhampton, Tetbury, Cirencester, Painswick and Bibury.

# STONEHOUSE COURT HOTEL

BRISTOL ROAD, STONEHOUSE, GLOUCESTERSHIRE GL10 3RA
**Tel:** 0845 365 2378  **International:** +44 (0)1453 794950  **Fax:** 0871 871 3241
**Web:** www.johansens.com/stonehousecourt  **E-mail:** info@stonehousecourt.co.uk

*Our inspector loved: The newly decorated Henry's Restaurant.*

**Price Guide:**
single from £75
double/twin £90–£140
four poster £180

Overlooking the Cotswold landscape and built in 1601, this outstanding Grade II listed manor house is set in 6 acres of private grounds and offers the largest conference and meeting venue in the area. Comprehensive facilities are available for up to 150 guests, intimate civil wedding ceremonies can be held in the picturesque outdoor pagoda and marquees on the lawn. Relaxation and comfort extend into the individually decorated bedrooms, some located in the original Tudor manor house have fireplaces and mullioned windows with views of the mature gardens. Dinner is served in the lounge or on the terrace, and Henry's restaurant creates delicious dishes using fine local ingredients. Menus include fillet of line caught sea bass, duet of spring lamb, carrot infused pannacotta and apple and lavender mousse.

**Location:** Off the A419; M5 jct 13, 1.7 miles; Stroud, 3.2 miles; Bristol, 29 miles

**Attractions:** Slimbridge Wildfowl Trust; Gloucester Cathedral; Westonbirt Arboretum; Cheltenham Racecorse

# THE GRAPEVINE HOTEL

SHEEP STREET, STOW-ON-THE-WOLD, GLOUCESTERSHIRE GL54 1AU
**Tel:** 0845 365 2508 **International:** +44 (0)1451 830344 **Fax:** 01451 832278
**Web:** www.johansens.com/grapevine **E-mail:** enquiries@vines.co.uk

*Our inspector loved: The friendly welcome
and the lovely vine canopied restaurant.*

**Price Guide:**
single from £85
double/twin from £140

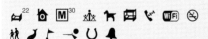

**Awards/Recognition:** 2 AA Rosette 2007-2008

**Location:** On the A436; A429, 0.5 miles

**Attractions:** Oxford; Cheltenham Racecourse;
Stratford-upon-Avon; Cotswolds

The Grapevine Hotel and Stow-on-the-Wold suit one another perfectly, which may
explain the warm welcome that puts you immediately at ease. Outstanding service
provided by loyal staff is certainly the secret of the hotel's success. There are 22 well
furnished bedrooms, including 6 garden rooms across the courtyard. Imaginative
cuisine is served in the relaxed atmosphere of the Conservatory Restaurant, which
has recently been awarded 2 AA rosettes for fine dining. Alternatively you have the
option of eating in the hotel's popular brasserie, La Vigna, offering a wide range of
Mediterranean influenced dishes, or in the hotel's bar, which serves more traditional
English fare. Al fresco dining is available at the hoel's bar and brasserie, during the
summer months. Whether travelling on business or for pleasure, you will return here.
The local landscape offers wide scope for exploration to the numerous picturesque
villages in the Cotswolds. Open over Christmas.

# LORDS OF THE MANOR HOTEL

UPPER SLAUGHTER, NR BOURTON-ON-THE-WATER, GLOUCESTERSHIRE GL54 2JD
**Tel:** 0845 365 2041 **International:** +44 (0)1451 820243 **Fax:** 01451 820696
**Web:** www.johansens.com/lordsofthemanor **E-mail:** enquiries@lordsofthemanor.com

**Our inspector loved:** *This idyllic place to get away from it all; a beautiful setting.*

**Price Guide:**
single from £110
double/twin/suite £170–£320

**Awards/Recognition:** 3 AA Rosettes 2007-2008

**Location:** A429, 2 miles; Stow-on-the-Wold, 4 miles; Oxford, 25miles; London, 70 miles

**Attractions:** Cheltenham; Warwick Castle; Blenheim Palace; Shakespeare Country

You'll be forgiven for imagining yourself as Lord of the Manor at this 17th century honeyed stone house with views over the surrounding meadows in the heart of the Cotswolds. Once home to generations of the Witts family, historically rectors of the parish, the bedrooms pay homage to the women who married into the family by bearing their maiden names; it is difficult not to wonder whether the namesakes were as individual as the rooms are today. Reception rooms burst forth with masses of fresh flowers and blazing fires in winter, but the heart of the house is the dining room where truly delicious dishes are created from locally grown ingredients.

# CALCOT MANOR HOTEL & SPA

NEAR TETBURY, GLOUCESTERSHIRE GL8 8YJ
**Tel:** 0845 365 3220  **International:** +44 (0)1666 890391  **Fax:** 01666 890394
**Web:** www.johansens.com/calcotmanor  **E-mail:** reception@calcotmanor.co.uk

**Our inspector loved:** *The facilities for all ages: crèche, play facility, spa and restaurant.*

**Price Guide:**
double/twin £205–£245
family room £245
family suite £280

**Awards/Recognition:** 2 AA Rosettes 2007-2008; Condé Nast Johansens Most Excellent Meeting Venue 2007

**Location:** On the A4135; Tetbury, 3.5 miles; M5 jct 13, 11 miles; M4 jct 18, 12.5 miles

**Attractions:** Westonbirt Arboretum; Bath; Cotswolds; Cirencester

For excellent family facilities look no further! The delightful family suites feature bunk beds and baby listening devices, while a play area to keep older children entertained has Playstations, Xboxes and a small cinema. The Ofsted registered crèche means you can enjoy quality time away from your little ones in the spa with its 16m pool, steam room, gym, outdoor hot tub and beauty treatments. A farmhouse until 1983, the Manor's stone barns and stables include one of the oldest tithe barns in England. The Barn features the Thomas Suite with digital state-of-the-art audio-visual equipment for conferences. Dinner in the elegant conservatory restaurant is memorable while the ever popular Gumstool Bistro and Bar offers simpler food and local ales.

# THE HARE AND HOUNDS HOTEL

WESTONBIRT, NEAR TETBURY, GLOUCESTERSHIRE GL8 8QL
**Tel:** 0845 365 2518 **International:** +44 (0)1666 880233 **Fax:** 01666 880241
**Web:** www.johansens.com/hareandhounds **E-mail:** enquiries@hareandhoundshotel.com

*Our inspector loved: The spacious new bedrooms in Silkwood Court, all decorated to a high standard*

**Price Guide:**
single from £93
double/twin from £120
superior from £150
suite from £175

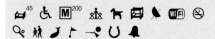

**Location:** On the A433; M4 Jct 17/18, 10/11 miles; Bristol Airport, 33.5 miles

**Attractions:** Westonbirt Arboretum; Tetbury; Bath; Slimbridge Wildfowl & Wetlands Trust

This country hotel stands in well tended grounds alongside Westonbirt Arboretum, home to approximately 18,000 specimens of trees and 17 miles of meandering paths. An idyllic place for quiet escapes; spring and autumn are the most spectacular months for visiting the Arboretum. A combination of blazing log fires, polished parquet floors and club-like public rooms create a convivial atmosphere. There is a choice of carefully appointed suites, as well as interconnecting, ground floor and large family bedrooms. The Westonbirt Restaurant offers well-planned menus featuring traditional favourites influenced by a Continental flavour. The Ballroom, adorned with historic tapestries, is a beautiful setting for any reception or dinner dance. Other well-designed and stylish meeting rooms and suites can cater for up to 200 delegates.

# CORSE LAWN HOUSE HOTEL

CORSE LAWN, NR TEWKESBURY, GLOUCESTERSHIRE GL19 4LZ
**Tel:** 0845 365 3249 **International:** +44 (0)1452 780479/771 **Fax:** 01452 780840
**Web:** www.johansens.com/corselawn **E-mail:** enquiries@corselawn.com

***Our inspector loved:*** *The wonderful welcome from Baba and the team and the great food.*

**Price Guide:**
single £90
double/twin £145
four-poster/suite £165-£175

**Awards/Recognition:** 2 AA Rosettes 2006-2007

**Location:** On the B4211; A438, 3 miles; A417, 6 miles; Cheltenham, 12 miles

**Attractions:** Cotswolds; Malverns; Forest of Dean

Just 6 miles from the M5 and M50, Corse Lawn occupies 12 acres of an unspoilt, typically English hamlet in a peaceful Gloucestershire backwater. The hotel, an elegant Queen Anne listed building set back from the village green offers you charm, history and very good food. As well as the renowned restaurant, there are 3 comfortable drawing rooms, a large lounge bar, and two private dining-cum-conference rooms which can accommodate up to 45 and a smaller room for up to 20. A tennis court, heated indoor swimming pool and croquet lawn adjoin the hotel and most sports and leisure activities can be arranged by prior request. You'll find it ideal for exploring the Cotswolds, Malverns and Forest of Dean. Short breaks are available on request.

# THORNBURY CASTLE

THORNBURY, SOUTH GLOUCESTERSHIRE BS35 1HH

**Tel:** 0845 365 2749 **International:** +44 (0)1454 281182 **Fax:** 01454 416188
**Web:** www.johansens.com/thornburycastle **E-mail:** info@thornburycastle.co.uk

*Our inspector loved:* The romance of such an historic place.

**Price Guide:**
single from £110
double/twin from £140
suite from £295

**Awards/Recognition:** 2 AA Rosettes 2006-2007

**Location:** B4061, 0.5 miles; A38, 2 miles; M5 jct 14, 5 miles; M5 jct 16, 6 miles

**Attractions:** Bath; Cardiff; The Cotswolds; Bristol

Built in 1511 by Edward Stafford, third Duke of Buckingham. Thornbury Castle was once owned by Henry VIII, who stayed there in 1535 with Anne Boleyn. You can live out all your romantic fantasies amidst the colourful history, rich furnishings, ornate oriel windows, suits of armour, panelled walls and large open fireplaces, and the 25 carefully restored bedchambers that retain many period details. The castle is acclaimed for its food, which features dishes such as Gloucestershire Old Spot pork, fresh south coast fish, local seasonal vegetables and cheeses and organic free-range eggs. You'll often see the chef picking herbs from the garden. Personally guided tours will introduce you to little-known areas of this magnificent building as well as the famous places nearby.

# ESSEBORNE MANOR

HURSTBOURNE TARRANT, ANDOVER, HAMPSHIRE SP11 0ER
**Tel:** 0845 365 3284 **International:** +44 (0)1264 736444 **Fax:** 01264 736725
**Web:** www.johansens.com/essebornemanor **E-mail:** info@esseborne-manor.co.uk

***Our inspector loved:*** *The welcoming atmosphere in the restaurant which brings visitors back time after time.*

**Price Guide:**
single £98–£130
double/twin £125–£180
suite £250

**Awards/Recognition:** 2 AA Rosettes 2006-2007

**Location:** Just Off A343; M4 jct 13, 13 miles; Andover, 7 miles; Heathrow Airport 55 miles

**Attractions:** Salisbury and Winchester Cathedrals; Stonehenge; Highclere Castle; Newbury Racecourse

Esseborne Manor is small, unpretentious yet stylish. The present house was built at the end of the 19th century and carries the name used to record details of the local village in the Domesday Book. It is set in a pleasing garden amid the rich farmland and natural beauty of the North Wessex Downs. Owners Ian and Lucilla Hamilton, have established the restful atmosphere of a private country home. The bedrooms include a luxurious suite with a giant sunken Jacuzzi bath; some bedrooms are reached via a courtyard.and others are delightful cottage rooms with their own patios overlooking the garden. Head Chef Steve Ratic's fine 2 AA Rosette-awarded cooking can be fully appreciated in the new dining room. Meetings and private parties can also be accommodated.

# AUDLEYS WOOD

ALTON ROAD, BASINGSTOKE, HAMPSHIRE RG25 2JT
**Tel:** 0845 365 2899 **International:** +44 (0)1256 817555 **Fax:** 01256 817500
**Web:** www.johansens.com/audleyswood **E-mail:** info@audleyswood.com

***Our inspector loved:*** *7 acres of wooded grounds – a wonderful setting for this newly restored Victorian gem.*

**Price Guide:**
double from £129
weekends from £85

**Location:** Just off A339; M3 jct6, 2 miles; Basingstoke, 3 miles; Heathrow Airport, 36 miles

**Attractions:** Jane Austen House; Watercress Line Steam Railway; Newbury Racecourse; Winchester Cathedral

This Hampshire retreat, once a Victorian manor house, has been painstakingly transformed into an intimate, chic country hotel. Stained-glass windows are lit by candles, log fires evoke a cosy ambience and the magnificent Stucco ceiling in the Great Hall adds a sense of grandeur. Comfortable bedrooms have special touches such as nightcaps by the bed and desirable toiletries. Build up an appetite with a brisk walk through the surrounding woodland before returning for drinks in the oak-panelled cocktail bar. Enjoy unashamedly British menus, which draw heavily on the produce of the area, accompanied by vintage wines from around the world in the stylish Gallery restaurant that features an unusual minstrels' gallery.

# TYLNEY HALL

ROTHERWICK, HOOK, HAMPSHIRE RG27 9AZ
**Tel:** 0845 365 2782 **International:** +44 (0)1256 764881 **Fax:** 01256 768141
**Web:** www.johansens.com/tylneyhall **E-mail:** reservations@tylneyhall.com

**Our inspector loved:** *The grandeur of the house in its wonderful garden setting.*

**Price Guide:**
single from £150
double/twin from £195
suite from £330

**Location:** A30, 1 mile; M3 jct5, 3 miles; Basingstoke, 6.5 miles; Heathrow, 32 miles

**Attractions:** Watercress Line steam railway; Antiques at Hartley Wintney; West Green House and Gardens; Milestones Museum

Arriving there in the evening, with floodlights and the forecourt fountain, it is easy to imagine partying in a private stately home. Set in 66 acres of ornamental gardens and parkland, Tylney Hall typifies the great houses of another era. Apéritifs are taken in the panelled library bar; haute cuisine is served in the glass-domed award winning Oak Room restaurant. The health and leisure facilities include 2 heated pools and whirlpool, solarium, fitness studio, beauty and hairdressing, sauna, tennis, croquet and snooker. Surrounding the hotel are wooded trails ideal for jogging. Functions for up to 100 people are catered for in the Tylney Suite or Chestnut Suite; there are a further 10 private banqueting rooms. Tylney Hall is licensed to hold wedding ceremonies on-site.

# THE MONTAGU ARMS HOTEL

PALACE LANE, BEAULIEU, NEW FOREST, HAMPSHIRE SO42 7ZL
**Tel:** 0845 365 2601 **International:** +44 (0)1590 612324 **Fax:** 01590 612188
**Web:** www.johansens.com/montaguarms **E-mail:** reservations@montaguarmshotel.co.uk

*Our inspector loved: The delicious offerings in the Terrace Restaurant masterminded by Chef Shaun Hill.*

**Price Guide:**
single from £145
double/twin £190–£200
suites £221–£294

In the heart of the New Forest, this small oasis of luxury has 23 beautifully decorated bedrooms and suites and attentive levels of service. The Montagu Arms is suitable for exclusive use, weddings and conferences for 10 to 100 guests. The Terrace Restaurant, Voted Best Hampshire Restaurant, by Which? Good Food Guide 2007 overlooks the secluded gardens, and head chef Scott Foy is happy to cater for specific occasions and tastes. Under the guidance of Shaun Hill, Director of Cooking, the Oakwood and Paris Rooms provide a more intimate setting for family celebrations and private dining. The New Forest has easy access to sailing on the Solent and good riding in the forest, both activites can be arranged. The hotel has its own fully-crewed luxury 84ft yacht that can accommodate up to 12 guests for a day's sailing.

**Awards/Recognition:** 2 AA Rosettes 2006-2007

**Location:** On the B3054; A326, 3.3 miles; M27 jct 2, 14 miles; Southampton, 20.5 miles

**Attractions:** Beaulieu Estate; Exbury Gardens; Buckler's Hard; Walking in the New Forest

# New Park Manor & Bath House Spa

LYNDHURST ROAD, BROCKENHURST, NEW FOREST, HAMPSHIRE SO42 7QH
**Tel:** 0845 365 2084 **International:** +44 (0)1590 623467 **Fax:** 01590 622268
**Web:** www.johansens.com/newparkmanor **E-mail:** info@newparkmanorhotel.co.uk

***Our inspector loved:*** *The splendid blend of the traditional and modern.*

**Price Guide:**
double/twin £155–£275
four poster £245–£315

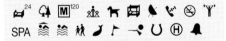

**Awards/Recognition:** 2 AA Rosettes 2006-2007

**Location:** A337, 0.5 mile; M27 jct 1, 6.5 miles; Brockenhurst, 1 mile; Southampton, 18 miles

**Attractions:** On site Equestrian Centre; Beaulieu; Lymington Harbour; Isle of Wight

Escape to this Grade II listed former Charles II hunting lodge for a taste of history mixed with contemporary style and technology. Bedrooms have fine views of the surrounding parklands and forest, and some have LCD TV screens in the bathrooms! The Equestrian Centre has a BHS trained stable crew or you can check out the nearby coast and sailing on the Solent. The Bath House Spa offers treatments that are inspired by the rural setting: hay and moss wraps, holistic natural therapies, thermal spa treatments and techno-gym. Later, you can chat about the day's ride or sailing in the lively Polo Bar, enjoy a romantic dinner in the restaurant or impress your friends with a party in the lovely New Forest Room with its picture windows.

# Passford House Hotel

MOUNT PLEASANT LANE, LYMINGTON, HAMPSHIRE SO41 8LS
**Tel:** 0845 365 2097 **International:** +44 (0)1590 682398 **Fax:** 01590 683494
**Web:** www.johansens.com/passfordhouse **E-mail:** sales@passfordhousehotel.co.uk

***Our inspector loved:*** *The extensive grounds - all set in a very quiet and relaxing spot.*

**Price Guide:**
single from £95
double/twin from £120
principle from £240

The former home of Lord Arthur Cecil this English Country House is all about taking things leisurely. Depending on the weather there is an indoor and outdoor pool, a multi-gym, sauna, pool table, croquet lawn, pétanque and tennis court. Bedrooms are traditional and in the stable yard a 2-bedroom suite with kitchenette is ideal for families. The restaurant prides itself on the creativity of its dishes. Beyond the hotel's 9 acres of gardens and parkland are charming New Forest villages such as Sway, lovely Georgian Lymington, numerous golf courses, riding and trekking centres, cycling paths, beautiful walks, and of course sailing on the Solent.

**Location:** A337, 1 mile; M27 jct1, 12.5 miles; Lymington, 1.5 miles; Southampton Airport, 24 miles

**Attractions:** New Forest; Beaulieu Motor Museum; Lymington Quay and Isle of Wight; Bucklers Hard

# WESTOVER HALL

PARK LANE, MILFORD-ON-SEA, HAMPSHIRE SO41 0PT
**Tel:** 0845 365 3425  **International:** +44 (0)1590 643044  **Fax:** 01590 644490
**Web:** www.johansens.com/westoverhall  **E-mail:** info@westoverhallhotel.com

**Our inspector loved:** *This superb 19th century house, the exquisite bedrooms and the wonderful views.*

**Price Guide:**
double from £200
superior from £260

**Awards/Recognition:** 2 AA Rosettes 2007-2008

**Location:** A337, 3 miles; M27 jct 1, 17 miles; Lymington, 3 miles; Bournemouth, 13 miles

**Attractions:** New Forest; Lymington; Beaulieu and Exbury; Hurst Castle

Westover Hall effortlessly combines stately grandeur with a home-from-home atmosphere. Use the hotel as a base for local excursions, or stroll down to the private beach hut on the pebble sea front and watch the yachts on the Solent. The main hall is encircled with oak panelling and illuminated through pre-Raphaelite stained glass windows. Guestrooms boast high ceilings and period features, offset by elegant furnishings and individual touches, most enjoy views of the Solent and the Isle of Wight. The oak-panelled dining room, showcasing a collection of art and photography, is at once impressive and intimate. The daily menu comprises Modern European dishes, all artistically presented and using local produce. Wile away the rest of the evening in the contemporary bar, or in a well-padded, fireside armchair in the lounge.

# CHEWTON GLEN

NEW MILTON, NEW FOREST, HAMPSHIRE BH25 6QS
**Tel:** 0845 365 3233 **International:** +44 (0)1425 275341 **US toll free:** US toll free 1 800 344 5087 **Fax:** 01425 272310
**Web:** www.johansens.com/chewtonglen **E-mail:** reservations@chewtonglen.com

*Our inspector loved: The newly presented lounges - sumptuous and scrumptious. Hot crumpets on a cold day and cool champagne when its hot.*

**Price Guide:**
double £295–£461
suites £467–£1250

**Awards/Recognition:** Relais & Châteaux; 3 AA Rosettes 2007-2008; Condé Nast Traveller Gold List 2006

**Location:** A35, 2 miles; M27 jct 1, 14 miles; Highcliffe, 1 mile; Heathrow, 85 miles

**Attractions:** New Forest; Bournemouth; Lymington; Isle of Wight

Arrive with high expectations and you certainly won't be disappointed. Chewton Glen is set in 130 acres of gardens and parkland on the edge of the New Forest, not far from the sea. Bedrooms are the ultimate in luxury, with marble bathrooms, cosy bathrobes and views over the grounds . Head chef Luke Matthews creates suprising and innovative dishes using fresh local produce, and the wine list is impressive. You'll be tempted to spend much of your time in the stunning spa, with its magnificent 17 metre swimming pool, steam, sauna, treatment rooms, gym and hydrotherapy pool. Outside there's another pool, sun terrace, croquet lawn, tennis and a 9-hole par 3 course. What more could you really want?

# Chilworth Manor

CHILWORTH, SOUTHAMPTON, HAMPSHIRE SO16 7PT
**Tel:** 0845 365 3234 **International:** +44 (0)23 8076 7333 **Fax:** 023 8076 6392
**Web:** www.johansens.com/chilworth **E-mail:** sales@chilworth-manor.co.uk

*Our inspector loved:* The new indoor pool and leisure facilities.

**Price Guide:**
single £55-£150
double £110-£165
suite £185-£195

**Location:** Off the A27; M3 jct 14, 1 mile; Southampton, 4 miles; Southampton International Airport, 4 miles.

**Attractions:** New Forest; National Motor Museum Beaulieu; Cathedral City of Winchester; Marwell Zoo.

A long tree-lined drive sweeps you towards this imposing Edwardian manor house, set in 12 landscaped acres of glorious Hampshire countryside. Its mellow, cream coloured stone exterior is highlighted by tall, sparkling sash windows and heavy, dark oak front doors open onto a magnificent galleried hall. All bedrooms are well furnished with every comfort, including 24-hour room service. You can dine leisurely on imaginative cuisine while enjoying views over manicured lawns, or if you're feeling more energetic there's a jogging route and hard tennis court within the grounds.and a new indoor pool and leisure facility. Southampton's shopping and nightlife are in easy reach, as is cathedral city of Winchester. Extensive purpose-built conference and meeting facilities are available.

# HOTEL TERRAVINA

174 WOODLANDS ROAD, WOODLANDS, NEW FOREST, SOUTHAMPTON, HAMPSHIRE SO40 7GL
**Tel:** 0845 365 2871 **International:** +44 (0)23 8029 3784 **Fax:** 023 8029 3627
**Web:** www.johansens.com/hotelterravina **E-mail:** info@hotelterravina.co.uk

*Our inspector loved:* The ambience of this exciting new venture - prepare to enjoy!

**Price Guide:** (room only)
double £110-£180

**Location:** A336, 1 mile; M27 jct 2, 4 miles; Southampton, 7 miles Southampton Airport 9 miles

**Attractions:** Walking and Riding in the New Forest; Beaulieu; Lyndhurst; Lymington

The New Forest was planted over 1,000 years ago and covers 90,000 acres. A favourite with walkers, cyclists and drivers, this is an ideal base for enjoying rural Hampshire life. Located just west of Southampton, this new hotel is a handsome "turn-of-the-century" building that has been transformed from an ordinary, everyday stopover, into a welcoming, non-smoking hotel of excellence that aims to satisfy your every requirement. Spacious and uncluttered whose star features are comfortable bedrooms that make good use of modern fabrics and tasteful colours. The Californian-themed dining room with on-view, open-plan kitchen is focused on delivering imaginative, seasonal food with a wine cellar that offers plenty of complementing temptations.

# CASTLE HOUSE

CASTLE STREET, HEREFORD, HEREFORDSHIRE HR1 2NW
**Tel:** 0845 365 3225 **International:** +44 (0)1432 356321 **Fax:** 01432 365909
**Web:** www.johansens.com/castlehse **E-mail:** info@castlehse.co.uk

*Our inspector loved:* The elegant decor and super postion overlooking the old moat

**Price Guide:**
single £120
double £175
suite £185–£220

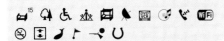

**Awards/Recognition:** 3 AA Rosettes 2007-2008

**Location:** Off the A438; A49, 0.8 miles; M4 jct 20, 43 miles

**Attractions:** Mappa Mundi & Chained Library at Hereford Cathedral; Ludlow; Hay on Wye; Cheltenham

Hard to believe this peaceful hotel is in the heart of a city and just 100m from Hereford cathedral. As soon as you step though the door of its immaculate Georgian façade you find yourself in a bright lobby area dominated by the grand staircase. You'll be warmly greeted and taken up to comfortable bedrooms which offer personal touches of fresh flowers, bowls of fruit and a decanter filled with a complimentary tipple. The Castle House Restaurant serves carefully presented English dishes with a European twist, such as fillet of Hereford beef with sweet potato dauphinoise, caramelised shallots and wild mushroom compote. A beautifully landscaped garden runs down to the old castle moat and is a wonderful place to enjoy afternoon tea after a day exploring this historic area.

# SHENDISH MANOR HOTEL & GOLF CLUB

LONDON ROAD, APSLEY, HEMEL HEMPSTEAD, HERTFORDSHIRE HP3 OAA
**Tel:** 0845 365 3427 **International:** +44 (0)1442232220 **Fax:** 01442 230683
**Web:** www.johansens.com/shendishmanor **E-mail:** sales@shendish-manor.com

***Our inspector loved:*** *The lovely "Folly" in the garden- licensed for Civil Weddings.*

**Price Guide:**
single £149.95
double £164.90
premier £179.95-£194.90

A stunning Jacobean manor house set in 160 acres of parkland and formal gardens, Shendish Manor has recently been lovingly refurbished, restoring its former glory. Light, modern wallcoverings and furnishings and contemporary yet classic touches beautifully offset the high ceilings and proportions of the former stately home. 18 premier rooms are located in the original manor house, a further 52 rooms are found in the new wing; all are individually decorated with pretty furnishings and are immediately inviting. The beautiful orangery houses the restaurant and would make a gorgeous wedding or reception venue and the traditional garden folly is licensed for civil weddings. Henry Cotton originally designed the par 70 golf course and which has more recently been extended by Donald Steel.

**Location:** Off the A4251; M25 jct 20, 2.5 miles; Luton Airport, 14 miles

**Attractions:** The Roman City of St.Albans; Woburn Abbey and Safari Park; Whipsnade Zoo; Hatfield House

# WEST LODGE PARK COUNTRY HOUSE HOTEL

COCKFOSTERS ROAD, HADLEY WOOD, BARNET, HERTFORDSHIRE EN4 0PY
**Tel:** 0845 365 2794 **International:** +44 (0)20 8216 3900 **Fax:** 020 8216 3937
**Web:** www.johansens.com/westlodgepark **E-mail:** westlodgepark@bealeshotels.co.uk

*Our inspector loved: The beauty of the grounds - a joy whatever the season.*

**Price Guide:**
single £85–£155
double/twin from £120–£175

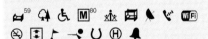

**Awards/Recognition:** 2 AA Rosettes 2006-2007

**Location:** Just off A111; M25 jct 24, 1.6 miles; London, 14.5 miles; Stansted Airport, 32 miles

**Attractions:** St Albans Abbey; Hatfield House; Kenwood; Alexandra Palace

West Lodge Park is a country house hotel which stands in 34 acres of parklands and gardens featuring a lake and arboretum. Run by the Beale family for over 60 years, the house was originally a gentleman's country seat, rebuilt in 1838 on the site of an earlier keeper's lodge. In the public rooms, antiques, original paintings and period furnishings create a restful atmosphere. The individually furnished bedrooms, many of which enjoy country views, have a full range of modern amenities. Well presented cuisine is available in the restaurant. Beauty rooms feature Elemis products. Guests can enjoy free membership and a complimentary taxi to the nearby leisure centre.

# St Michael's Manor

ST MICHAEL'S VILLAGE, FISHPOOL STREET, ST ALBANS, HERTFORDSHIRE AL3 4RY
**Tel:** 0845 365 2359 **International:** +44 (0)1727 864444 **Fax:** 01727 848909
**Web:** www.johansens.com/stmichaelsmanor **E-mail:** reservations@stmichaelsmanor.com

***Our inspector loved:*** *A peaceful oasis created by the lake and gardens.*

**Price Guide:**
single £145–£230
double/twin £180–£320
suite £250–£310

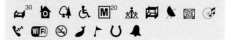

**Awards/Recognition:** AA 2 Rosettes 2007-2008

**Location:** A5183, 1.5 miles; A405, 2 miles; M25, 4 miles; Luton Airport, 11.7 miles

**Attractions:** St Albans Roman Remains; St Albans Abbey; Hatfield House; London

Everyone loves a rare gem and this is certainly one of them! The hospitable Newling Ward family have owned and run St Michael's Manor for the past 40 years, and in that time have created a peaceful, elegant charm. Many of the bedrooms - some with four-poster beds, some sitting-room suites - overlook the picturesque grounds with wide sweeping lawns and beautiful lake. If you tip-toe quietly you'll see all manner of wildlife, or you can enjoy garden views from the conservatory dining room. Dinners are tantalisingly tasty, and if you're a vegetarian you'll be very happy with the excellent selection of dishes. The Roman remains of Verulamium and Verulam golf course - Home of the Ryder Cup - are within easy reach.

# EASTWELL MANOR

BOUGHTON LEES, NEAR ASHFORD, KENT TN25 4HR
**Tel:** 0845 365 3279  **International:** +44 (0)1233 213000  **Fax:** 01233 635530
**Web:** www.johansens.com/eastwellmanor  **E-mail:** enquiries@eastwellmanor.co.uk

***Our inspector loved:*** *This fine old building with its panelling and atmosphere of centuries of hospitality.*

**Price Guide:**
single From £110
double/twin £140–£295
suites £230–£445

**Awards/Recognition:** 2 AA Rosettes 2006-2007

**Location:** A251, 0.5 miles; M20 jct 9, 2.5 miles; Ashford International Station, 4.5 miles; Gatwick Airport, 55 miles

**Attractions:** Canterbury Cathedral; Leeds Castle; Rye - Ancient Town

Come to the "Garden of England", and stay at historical Eastwell Manor, dating back to the 16th century when Richard Plantagenet, son of Richard III, lived on the estate. The impressive grounds are perfectly matched by rather splendid interiors, featuring exquisite plasterwork, carved oak panelling and antiques adorning public rooms. Some bedrooms and suites, have fine views across the gardens and meet all your creature comforts and there are 19 courtyard apartments giving 39 more bedrooms. Outside, is a formal Italian garden, scented rose gardens and attractive lawns and parkland, as well as the smart new health and fitness spa with indoor and outdoor pools, hydrotherapy pool, sauna, steam room, technogym and 15 treatment rooms. A 9 hole golf course will be available to guests very soon.

# THE SPA HOTEL

MOUNT EPHRAIM, ROYAL TUNBRIDGE WELLS, KENT TN4 8XJ
**Tel:** 0845 365 2693  **International:** +44 (0)1892 520331  **Fax:** 01892 510575
**Web:** www.johansens.com/spahotel  **E-mail:** reservations@spahotel.co.uk

*Our inspector loved: The recently and stylishly refurbished bedrooms.*

**Price Guide:** (room only)
single £105–£120
double/twin £150–£210

**Awards/Recognition:** 1 AA Rosette 2007-2008

**Location:** On the A264; M25 jct 5, 14.5 miles; Gatwick Airport, 22.5 miles

**Attractions:** Hever Castle; Chartwell; Groombridge Place; The Pantiles

Originally built in 1766 as a country mansion The Spa has been a hotel for over a century and it has retained standards of service reminiscent of life in Georgian and Regency England. The bedrooms are individually furnished and many offer spectacular views. The Spa prides itself on the excellence of its cuisine. The grand, award-winning Restaurant features the freshest produce from Kentish farms and London markets complemented by a carefully selected wine list. Within the hotel is Spa Health equipped to the highest standards including an indoor swimming pool, fully equipped state-of-the-art resistance gymnasium, cardio-vascular gymnasium, steam room, floodlit hard tennis court and jogging track.

# EAVES HALL

EAVES HALL LANE, WADDINGTON, CLITHEROE, LANCASHIRE BB7 3JG
**Tel:** 0845 365 3280 **International:** +44 (0)1200 425 271 **Fax:** 01200 425 131
**Web:** www.johansens.com/eaveshall **E-mail:** reservations@eaveshall.co.uk

**Our inspector loved:** *The manicured gardens and grounds of this Georgian Lancashire manor house.*

**Price Guide:**
single £78–£125
double/twin £120–£250

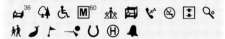

**Location:** A59, 1 mile; M6 jct 31, 12 miles; Clitheroe, 0.5 miles; Manchester Airport, 45 miles

**Attractions:** Clitheroe Castle; Skipton Castle; Lake District; Trough of Bowland

At the heart of the Ribble Valley you will find this splendid Georgian-style manor house surrounded by 7 acres of landscaped gardens. The bedrooms and suites are of a high standard and many offer superb views across the gardens. Further accommodation can be found in 2 self-catering cottages within the grounds, Peels Cottage and The Lodge, which sleep 4 to 5 people and feature fully-equipped kitchens. Menus are based on the finest and freshest ingredients and can be enjoyed in the warm and inviting atmosphere of the restaurant, which affords splendid views across the surrounding countryside. Eaves Hall is the perfect location for weddings and small meetings, with a ballroom and a further meeting room accommodating up to 60 people.

# THE FARINGTON LODGE HOTEL

STANFIELD ROAD, FARRINGTON, LEYLAND, PRESTON, LANCASHIRE PR25 4QR
**Tel:** 0845 365 3429 **International:** +44 (0)1772 421321 **Fax:** 01772 455388
**Web:** www.johansens.com/faringtonlodge **E-mail:** enquires@faringtonlodge.co.uk

**Our inspector loved:** *The new bedrooms in this converted Georgian hotel.*

**Price Guide:**
single £95-£115
double £115-£150

**Location:** B5254, 150yds; M6 jct 28/29, 1.25 miles; Preston, 7 miles; Manchester Airport, 32 miles

**Attractions:** Camalot Theme Park; Leyland Vehicle Museum; Blackpool; Trough of Bowland

Ideally situated for exploring Lancashire with its intriguing past, impressive coastline and beautiful countryside, this Grade II listed Georgian building is set in 3 acres of private gardens and has been sympathetically and stylishly enhanced. The interiors effortlessly combine modern luxury with lavish traditional touches such as hand-painted silk wallpaper and original period features, all softly lit under shimmering chandeliers. The elegantly furnished guest rooms are named after military vehicles built at the infamous Leyland factory and most enjoy views of the pretty gardens; an additional 17 stylish new rooms will soon be available. The Garden Restaurant is renowned throughout the area for its creative menus and we are assured that only the freshest, locally sourced ingredients are used in dishes that combine classical influences with fresh contemporary flourishes.

# THE GIBBON BRIDGE HOTEL

NEAR CHIPPING, FOREST OF BOWLAND, LANCASHIRE PR3 2TQ
**Tel:** 0845 365 2501  **International:** +44 (0)1995 61456  **Fax:** 01995 61277
**Web:** www.johansens.com/gibbonbridge  **E-mail:** reception@gibbon–bridge.co.uk

***Our inspector loved:*** *Dining alfresco in one of the thatched Pegolas in the beautiful countryside.*

**Price Guide:**
single £80–£120
double/twin £120
suite £150–£250

**Location:** Chipping, 1 miles; B6243, 5 miles; M6 jct 31a, 7.5 mile; Preston, 12 miles

**Attractions:** Historic Market Towns and Villages; Clitheroe Castle; Pendle Witches Trail; Forest of Bowland - AONB

Now officially recognised as the Centre of the Kingdom, this area, in the heart of Lancashire, is a favourite of the Queen, and where proprietor Janet Simpson and her late mother Margaret have created a welcoming, peaceful retreat. The buildings combine traditional architecture and interesting Gothic masonry, a theme that has been carried into the well-appointed bedrooms with their four-posters, half-testers and Gothic brass beds. Overlooking the garden, the restaurant is renowned for its imaginative dishes using home-grown vegetables and herbs, and alfresco dining can be enjoyed in one of the 3 Julian & Christian designed thatched pergolas perfect for an informal, unique experience. If you're seeking a venue for business meetings and conferences, the hotel can offer that "something a bit different", and the garden bandstand is perfect for musical repertoires or civil wedding ceremonies.

133

# STAPLEFORD PARK COUNTRY HOUSE HOTEL & SPORTING ESTATE

STAPLEFORD, NEAR MELTON MOWBRAY, LEICESTERSHIRE LE14 2EF
**Tel:** 0845 365 2367 **International:** +44 (0)1572 787 000 **Fax:** 01572 787 001
**Web:** www.johansens.com/staplefordpark **E-mail:** reservations@stapleford.co.uk

*Our inspector loved:* The 3-level Sanderson Suite with its mullioned windows.

**Price Guide:**
double/twin £250–£465
suites from £575

**Awards/Recognition:** 2 AA Rosettes 2007-2008

**Location:** B676, 1 mile; M1 jct 21a, 40-min drive; Melton Mowbray, 12-min drive; East Midlands Airport, 40-min drive

**Attractions:** Belvoir Castle; Rutland Water; Burghley House; Stamford

Casual luxury is the byword at this 16th-century stately home and sporting estate. Once coveted by Edward, Prince of Wales, his mother Queen Victoria forbade him to buy it for fear that his morals would be corrupted by the Leicestershire hunting society! You can only live in hope, because today its "lifestyle experience" is more to do with superb comfort than potential corruption. Voted Top UK Hotel for Leisure Facilities by Condé Nast Traveller and with innumerable awards for style and hospitality, its bedrooms and 2 self-contained cottages have been created by famous names such as Mulberry, Wedgwood, Zoffany and Crabtree & Evelyn. The restaurant offers British with European influenced menus carefully prepared to the highest standards and matched by an excellent wine list.

# THE GEORGE OF STAMFORD

ST MARTINS, STAMFORD, LINCOLNSHIRE PE9 2LB
**Tel:** 0845 365 3295  **International:** +44 (0)1780 750750  **Fax:** 01780 750701
**Web:** www.johansens.com/georgeofstamford  **E-mail:** reservations@georgehotelofstamford.com

***Our inspector loved:*** *The warm and welcoming feel of this charming old English coaching inn.*

**Price Guide:**
single from £85
double from £125
suite from £165

**Awards/Recognition:** 1 AA Rosette 2006-2007

**Location:** A1, 1 mile; Peterborough, 10 miles; London 60 min train

**Attractions:** Burghley House; Rutland Water;

Historic Stamford was described by Walter Scott as the finest view between London and Edinburgh and as a well travelled man he was probably right. He was a frequent visitor to this engaging coaching Inn whose own history as a hostelry goes back some 900 years. Plenty of deep wood panelling and high wood beamed ceilings tell of an intriguing and fascinating past. Guest rooms retain traditional charms and are decorated with pretty floral fabrics and individual touches. The Restaurant serves a formidable menu using the best of local produce (complemented by an excellent wine cellar) whilst on warm nights you can enjoy the informal Garden Lounge. Afternoon tea is a delight and a very good idea after taking a long stroll around Burghley House just a short walk away.

# 41

41 BUCKINGHAM PALACE ROAD, LONDON SW1W 0PS
**Tel:** 0845 365 3601 **International:** +44 (0)20 7300 0041 **Fax:** +44 (0)20 7300 0141
**Web:** www.johansens.com/41buckinghampalaceroad **E-mail:** book41@rchmail.com

**Our inspector loved:** *The two new hospitality suites. Perfect for small meetings with overnight stays.*

**Price Guide:**
king bedded from £295
junior suite from £495
master suite from £695

**Awards/Recognition:** 5 AA Rosettes 2006-2007

**Location:** Victoria station, 5-min walk; Eurostar, 2.5 miles; Heathrow airport, 15 miles; Stansted Airport, 37 miles

**Attractions:** Buckingham Palace; London Eye; Houses of Parliament; Hyde Park

Adjacent to St James's Park, overlooking the Royal Mews and Buckingham Palace, 41 offers guests a discreet and secluded entrance, magnificent architectural features, beautiful furniture and club-like qualities. Natural light floods the Executive Lounge where continental and English breakfast and a variety of tasty snacks are served. 28 bedrooms and suites, some split level are furnished with traditional mahogany and black leather décor. Here you can relax on the world's most comfortable, handmade English mattresses and step on pure wool carpets. The marble bathrooms have bespoke baths. Every bedroom features an iPod docking station, movies, music and Internet access with complimentary Wi-Fi broadband available. A state-of-the-art boardroom offers ISDN teleconferencing and private dining. 41 offers secretarial support, chauffeur driven cars, butler and chef services.

# THE MAYFLOWER HOTEL

26-28 TREBOVIR ROAD, LONDON SW5 9NJ
**Tel:** 0845 365 2591 **International:** +44 (0)20 7370 0991 **Fax:** 020 7370 0994
**Web:** www.johansens.com/mayflower **E-mail:** info@mayflower-group.co.uk

**Our inspector loved:** *The new extended Garden, great for breakfast and evening drinks.*

**Price Guide:**
double £120-£155
suite £130-£195

**Awards/Recognition:** 4 AA Rosettes 2007-2008

**Location:** Earls Court Underground Station, 2-min walk; M4 jct1, 8 miles; Heathrow Airport, 14 miles; Waterloo International, 5 miles

**Attractions:** Buckingham Palace; Harrods; Victoria and Albert Museum; Hyde Park

A sleek fusion of Eastern influences in the centre of London, The Mayflower is perfect if you're travelling alone or on business. Stylish compact guest rooms are rich in pale stone, vibrant fabrics and Indian and Oriental antiques. Stylish bathrooms sparkle with slate and chrome and have walk-in showers. A Continental buffet breakfast is served in the downstairs dining room or, when the weather is fine, in the new extended Patio garden. You can grab a caffeine or vitamin C fix in the coffee and juice bar before heading out to Knightsbridge or Chelsea, or visit the V&A and Natural History and Science Museums. The hotel is close to the famous Earl's Court Exhibition Centre.

# TWENTY NEVERN SQUARE

20 NEVERN SQUARE, LONDON SW5 9PD
**Tel:** 0845 365 2769 **International:** +44 (0)20 7565 9555 **Fax:** 020 7565 9444
**Web:** www.johansens.com/twentynevernsquare **E-mail:** hotel@twentynevernsquare.co.uk

*Our inspector loved:* The georgous Pasha Suite!

**Price Guide:**
double/twin £130–£165
suite £275

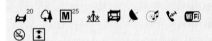

**Awards/Recognition:** 4 AA Rosettes 2007-2008

**Location:** Earls Court Underground, 2-min walk; M4, 8 miles; Heathrow Airport, 14 miles; Gatwick Airport, 35 miles

**Attractions:** Victoria and Albert Museum; Natural History Museum; Harrods; Hyde Park

To say that a unique hospitality experience awaits you at this elegant 4-star townhouse hotel wouldn't be overselling it, as it's sumptuously restored, compact bedrooms emphasise natural materials, hand-carved beds and white marble. Choose the delicate silks of the Chinese Room or a touch of opulence in the Rococo Room, and if you want to spoil someone the grandeur of the Pasha Suite's four-poster and balcony is a perfect treat! Breakfast is served in the light, bright Conservatory opening onto a decked balcony area, and gym facilities are available by arrangement. You're close to Earl's Court and Olympia Exhibition Centres, and a mere 10 minutes from some of London's finest shops, restaurants, theatres and attractions such as the V&A and Science Museums.

# HENDON HALL HOTEL

ASHLEY LANE, HENDON, LONDON NW4 1HF
**Tel:** 0845 365 1839 **International:** +44 (0)20 8203 3341 **Fax:** 020 8457 2502
**Web:** www.johansens.com/hendonhall **E-mail:** info@hendonhall.com

*Our inspector loved:* Georgian splendour in North London, the refurbishment is a triumph!

**Price Guide:**
double from £125
deluxe from £140
suite from £210

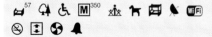

**Awards/Recognition:** 2 AA Rosettes 2007-2008

**Location:** Hendon Underground, 1 mile; M1, 2 miles; Thameslink, 1.5 miles; Luton Airport, 26 miles

**Attractions:** Wembley Stadium; RAF Museum; Alexandra Palace; Hampstead Heath

Historic actor David Garrick once owned this beautiful manor house and still today it loves to play host to a fun, well-travelled and sophisticated crowd. It has been beautifully restored with an eye to detail, incorporating modern luxuries into the traditional framework of the building. Bedrooms are charming with crisp white linen and a welcoming seasonal tipple. Fringe Restaurant has a creative modern twist and the kitchens will put together a picnic hamper for you to enjoy in the garden or take up to Hampstead Heath, Kenwood House or Primrose Hill. There is always plenty going on in this great neighbourhood and staff are great at pointing you in the right direction. Floor to ceiling windows flood the private rooms with daylight and at night they make stunning settings for receptions and dinner parties.

# KENSINGTON HOUSE HOTEL

15-16 PRINCE OF WALES TERRACE, KENSINGTON, LONDON W8 5PQ
**Tel:** 0845 365 1936 **International:** +44 (0)20 7937 2345 **Fax:** 020 7368 6700
**Web:** www.johansens.com/kensingtonhouse **E-mail:** reservations@kenhouse.com

*Our inspector loved: Location, location! Just perfect for exploring Kensington and Chelsea*

**Price Guide:**
single £150
double/twin £175-£195
junior suites £215

**Location:** High Street Kensington Underground, 0.3 miles; M4, 8 miles; Heathrow, 14 miles; Gatwick, 37 miles

**Attractions:** Kensington Palace; Harrods; Hyde Park; London Eye

This charming townhouse located just off Kensington High Street, looks out over delightful mews houses, leafy streets and City rooftops. The atmosphere is relaxed, service informal yet professional, and bright, airy bedrooms with tall, ornate windows and modern furnishings add freshness to classic design. You can slip between crisp linen sheets and snuggle up in cosy bathrobes, and for those travelling en famille, 2 junior suites convert into a family room. The Tiger Bar is a perfect venue for coffee and pre dinner drinks, where menus of traditional and modern dishes have a range of influences. The serenity of Kensington Gardens is just a gentle stroll away, while some of the capital's most fashionable shops, restaurants and cultural attractions are within walking distance.

# THE MILESTONE HOTEL & APARTMENTS

1 KENSINGTON COURT, LONDON W8 5DL

**Tel:** 0845 365 2594  **International:** +44 (0)20 7917 1000  **US toll free:** 1 877 955 1515  **Fax:**+44 (0)20 7917 1010
**Web:** www.johansens.com/milestone  **E-mail:** bookms@rchmail.com

***Our inspector loved:*** *The regal Prince Albert Suite, with it's open fireplace, elaborate ceilings and four poster bed, fit for a king!*

**Price Guide:** (Room only, excluding VAT)
double £310-£490
suite £570-£910

**Awards/Recognition:** 2 AA Rosettes 2007-2008

**Location:** Kensington High Street, 5-min walk; Paddington Heathrow Express, 2.18 miles; Heathrow Airport, 13.6 miles; Gatwick Airport, 37 miles

**Attractions:** Kensington Palace and Gardens; Portabello Road; Harrods; Buckingham Palace

A beautifully appointed Condé Nast Johansens award-winning property located opposite Kensington Palace and Gardens and Hyde Park. The Milestone will give you an education in Victorian splendor as well as the utmost in comfort and service. Its apartments, bedrooms and suites, all with complimentary WiFi, are individually designed with antiques - some with private balconies. You can relax in the panelled Park Lounge or dine in Cheneston's restaurant, which bears the original spelling of Kensington. The Stables bar is perfect for evening drinks and the fitness centre, with it's resistance pool and spa treatments, is a great place to unwind. The Milestone is a short walk from Kensington and Knightsbridge, and a brief taxi ride to the London's West End. The Royal Albert Hall and all the museums in Exhibition Road are also just a stroll away.

# BEAUFORT HOUSE

45 BEAUFORT GARDENS, KNIGHTSBRIDGE, LONDON SW3 1PN
**Tel:** 0845 365 3029  **International:** +44 (0)20 7584 2600  **US toll free: US toll free:** 1 800 23 5463  **Fax:** 020 7584 6532
**Web:** www.johansens.com/beauforthouseapartments  **E-mail:** info@beauforthouse.co.uk

*Our inspector loved:* Great apartments in a suberb location. I am looking forward to the refurbishment in 2008.

**Price Guide:** (room only excluding VAT)
£230–£650

**Location:** Knightsbridge Underground, 3-min walk; Victoria Station, 2 miles; Heathrow, 14 miles; Gatwick, 28 miles

**Attractions:** Harrods; Hyde Park; Buckingham Palace; Victoria and Albert Museum

On a quiet and exclusive, tree-lined Regency cul-de-sac, are 21 self-contained luxury apartments, ranging in size from intimate 1-bedroomed to spacious 4-bedroomed accommodation. Enjoy the privacy and comfortable atmosphere of your own home together with the benefits of a first-class hotel. All apartments have direct dial telephones with voice mail, personal safes, satellite television, DVD players, iPod connectors, and high speed broadband access. Some benefit from balconies or patios. A daily maid is included at no additional charge, and full laundry/dry cleaning services are available. The 24 hour Guests Services team are happy to organise your theatre tickets, restaurant bookings, or chauffeur. You won't need a car to shop however, as you are in the heart of Knightsbridge, just 250 yards from Harrods.

# THE CAPITAL HOTEL & RESTAURANT

22 BASIL STREET, KNIGHTSBRIDGE, LONDON SW3 1AT
**Tel:** 0845 365 2413  **International:** +44 (0)20 7589 5171  **Fax:** 020 7225 0011
**Web:** www.johansens.com/capital  **E-mail:** reservations@capitalhotel.co.uk

***Our inspector loved:*** *The most perfect venue for an exceptional dining exerience, especially the stunning private rooms for larger gatherings.*

**Price Guide:**
single £175–£210
double/twin £215–£365
suite £390–£850

**Awards/Recognition:** 2 Star Michelin 2007; Conde Nast Traveller Gold List Best Hotel for Food in UK 2006

**Location:** Knightsbridge Underground, 2-min walk; Victoria Station, 2 miles; Heathrow, 14 miles; Gatwick, 28 miles

**Attractions:** Harrods; Hyde Park; Buckingham Palace; Victoria and Albert Museum

Established 35 years ago at its exclusive Knightsbridge address, The Capital remains the only hotel restaurant in London to hold 2 coveted Michelin Stars. Head Chef Eric Chavot's French inspired cuisine is acclaimed as 'faultlessly assured' by even the most discriminating critics. The London bakery owned by the Capital Group, supplies all the bread and pastries for the restaurant and a mouth-watering afternoon tea in the Sitting Room. The excellent wine list features wine from the Hotel's own vineyard in the Loire Valley in France. The 49 individually designed bedrooms are the height of luxury and comfort with their super king-sized beds, handmade mattresses, Egyptian cotton sheets and marble bathrooms. Three stunning event spaces, The Cadogan Suite, The Eaton Suite and The Sitting Room, are available for private dining.

# THE EGERTON HOUSE HOTEL

17-19 EGERTON TERRACE, KNIGHTSBRIDGE, LONDON SW3 2BX
**Tel:** 0845 365 2483 **International:** +44 (0)20 7589 2412 **Fax:** +44 (0)20 7584 6540
**Web:** www.johansens.com/egertonhouse **E-mail:** bookeg@rchmail.com

*Our inspector loved:* The specially programmed Video iPods in each room.

**Price Guide:**
double £235–£255
suite £295–£395

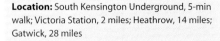

**Location:** South Kensington Underground, 5-min walk; Victoria Station, 2 miles; Heathrow, 14 miles; Gatwick, 28 miles

**Attractions:** Harrods; Victoria and Albert Museum; Hyde Park; Buckingham Palace

This quiet townhouse hotel's owners have restyled it to suit the 21st century without abandoning its Victorian roots. Rooms and suites are individually designed with an eclectic mix of Italian Rococo and contemporary furnishings. All offer 24 hour service. Original artworks and antiques complete the look, while sleek accessories include flat-screen TVs, WiFi and specially programmed Video iPods. Breakfast is served in the lower ground floor dining room, a stunning space full of glass and light with ivory leather banquette, and in the cosy, muted drawing room and bar you might feel like you've joined a discreet private club. Set on a residential Knightsbridge street, you can walk a leafy 3-minutes to Harrods and venture further to all of central London's attractions.

# JUMEIRAH CARLTON TOWER

ON CADOGAN PLACE, LONDON SW1X 9PY
**Tel:** 0845 365 1932  **International:** +44 (0)20 7235 1234  **Fax:** +44 (0)20 7235 9129
**Web:** www.johansens.com/carltontower  **E-mail:** JCTinfo@jumeirah.com

**Our inspector loved:** *The exquisite GILT Champagne Lounge, with its gorgeous glass bubbles!*

**Price Guide:** (excluding VAT)
double from £239
suite from £339

**Awards/Recognition:** Condé Nast Johansens Most Excellent London Hotel 2006

**Location:** Knightsbridge Underground, 5-min walk; Waterloo Eurostar terminal, 15-min drive; Heathrow, 15 miles; Gatwick, 30 miles

**Attractions:** Harrods; Harvey Nichols; Hyde Park; Buckingham Palace

Overlooking the private, leafy gardens of Cadogan Place, the ultra-modern is combined with traditional hospitality at this 5-star luxury hotel. Perfect whether you're in London for business or pleasure, Harrods and fabulous shopping are within walking distance and the West End and City can easily be reached by tube or taxi. A quiet and stylish elegance infuses the hotel, where spacious bedrooms and suites offer memorable views. Arguably London's finest, the Presidential Suite boasts private sauna, enhanced security and exceptional personalized service. If you enjoy a good steak, head to The Rib Room, or check out the eclectic mix of restaurants and bars including the exclusive GILT Champagne Lounge. The luxurious rooftop health club reveals a fitness facility, an indoor 20m swimming pool, a state-of-the-art golf simulator featuring 42 world renowned courses and luxurious spa treatments.

# JUMEIRAH LOWNDES HOTEL

21 LOWNDES STREET, KNIGHTSBRIDGE, LONDON SW1X 9ES
**Tel:** 0845 365 1934 **International:** +44 (0)20 7823 1234 **Fax:** 020 7235 1154
**Web:** www.johansens.com/lowndes **E-mail:** JLHinfo@jumeirah.com

***Our inspector loved:*** *Sipping a delicious latte in the busy vibrant Mimosa Bar & Restaurant.*

**Price Guide:** (room only, excluding VAT)
double from £199
suite from £299

**Location:** Knightsbridge Underground, 5-min walk; Waterloo Eurostar Terminal, 15-min drive; Heathrow, 15 miles; Gatwick, 30 miles

**Attractions:** Harrods; Harvey Nichols; Hyde Park; Buckingham Palace

Following an extensive refurbishment, the Jumeirah Lowndes Hotel fully lives up to its chic boutique retreat credentials, offering you a luxurious urban sanctuary minutes from Hyde Park, Sloane Street and Duke of York Square. The new sixth floor with its suites, all themed in blue, silver and grey shades, is – literally – the icing on top of the renovation! The other stylish rooms and suites maximise light and space. Elsewhere, the lobby has been remodelled to create flowing areas with an art deco influence and the Mimosa Bar & Restaurant serves Mediterranean cuisine on the terrace overlooking Lowndes Square. Head to the heart of the hotel, the bar, where a relaxed vibe is created by cool Balearic beats. Other special touches include the luxurious Temple Spa amenities. Guests have access to all facilities, including The Peak Health Club & Spa, at adjacent sister hotel the Jumeirah Carlton Tower.

# THE SUMNER

54 UPPER BERKELEY STREET, MARBLE ARCH, LONDON W1H 7QR
**Tel:** 0845 365 2703 **International:** +44 (0)20 7723 2244 **Fax:** 0870 705 8767
**Web:** www.johansens.com/thesumner **E-mail:** hotel@thesumner.com

*Our inspector loved: The great location of this charming hotel. Oxford Street on the door step and Hyde Park a stroll away.*

**Price Guide:** (including breakfast)
double/twin £130–£150
deluxe £160

**Location:** Marble Arch Underground station, 2-min walk; Oxford Street, 2-min walk; Hyde Park, 5-min walk; Paddington station, 0.8 miles

**Attractions:** Wallace Collection; Buckingham Palace; Piccadilly Circus; Madame Tussauds

The Sumner is perfect if you're a fashionista whose surroundings are as important as your wardrobe. An intimate Georgian townhouse, a stone's throw from shopping on Bond Street and South Molton Street, it's been refurbished to create contemporary and elegant bedrooms, furnished with designer fabrics and chic lighting. All also feature 26'' flat-screen TVs and Wi-Fi. The modern breakfast room in the basement serves an extensive buffet to set you up for pounding the pavements, and after a long day you can rest aching feet in the cosy sitting room. Hyde Park, the Wallace Collection and Soho are all within walking distance of Upper Berkeley Street, and Marylebone's bustling restaurant scene is tempting if you still feel the need to flex your credit card!

# THE MANDEVILLE HOTEL

MANDEVILLE PLACE, LONDON W1U 2BE
**Tel:** 0845 365 2589 **International:** +44 (0)20 7935 5599 **Fax:** 020 7935 9588
**Web:** www.johansens.com/mandeville **E-mail:** info@mandeville.co.uk

***Our inspector loved:*** *Afternoon Tea in the DeVille Restaurant followed by a cocktail in the outrageous De Vigne Bar.*

**Price Guide:** (Room only, excluding VAT)
single £275
double/twin £325
suite £500

**Location:** Bond Street Underground, 5-min walk; Paddington Heathrow Express, 1.88 miles; Heathrow Airport, 17 miles; Gatwick Airport, 30 miles

**Attractions:** Oxford Street; Hyde Park; Madame Tussards; Buckingham Palace

In fashionable Marylebone Village and nominated for Most Excellent London Hotel 2007 by Condé Nast Johansens, the Mandeville's ethos is one of style, modern opulence and personalised service. Its sleek sophistication doesn't mean you can't relax and feel at home, however. The bedroom's elegant design emphasises comfort and space, with decadent fabrics and comfy chairs. The attic penthouse suite has it's own private terrace and separate entrance, while the stunning De Vigne Bar features an eye-catching silver and glass bar and dark brown suede banquettes. A theatrical theme dreamed up by world famous Interior Designer, Stephen Ryan, sets the stage for you to enjoy delicious modern British food in the De Ville restaurant. Wander just a few minutes from Marylebone to find Oxford Street, Bond Street and Mayfair.

# SOFITEL ST JAMES

6 WATERLOO PLACE, LONDON SW1Y 4AN

**Tel:** 0845 365 2351  **International:** +44 (0)20 7747 2200  **Fax:** +44 (0) 20 7747 2210
**Web:** www.johansens.com/stjames  **E-mail:** H3144@accor.com

***Our inspector loved:*** *The sexy St James Bar and the new bar menu - I was tempted to try a Black Pearl....*

**Price Guide:** (room only, excluding VAT)
single from £275
double from £320
suite £430-£1,200

**Location:** Piccadilly underground, 5-min walk; Waterloo Eurostar, 2 miles; Heathrow, 16 miles; Gatwick, 28 miles

**Attractions:** Trafalgar Square; Buckingham Palace; London Eye; National Gallery

Grand and imposing, this Grade II listed building on the corner of Waterloo Place and Pall Mall is the former home of the Cox's and King's bank, whose original artwork is still proudly displayed and cleverly balances out the hotel's contemporary design. The sophisticated bedrooms and suites have ultra modern technology and bathrooms, in which black and white marble complements granite tops and chrome fittings. French flair and refined food are hallmarks of the buzzing Brasserie Roux, and a large selection of Champagnes and cocktails can be found in the St James Bar. For afternoon tea you'll adore the eclectic Rose Lounge. You can also enjoy a pampering session in the hotel's fitness and massage centre.

# THE RICHMOND GATE HOTEL AND RESTAURANT

RICHMOND HILL, RICHMOND-UPON-THAMES, SURREY TW10 6RP
**Tel:** 0845 365 2674 **International:** +44 (0)20 8940 0061 **Fax:** 020 8332 0354
**Web:** www.johansens.com/richmondgate **E-mail:** richmondgate@foliohotels.com

***Our inspector loved:*** *This beautiful Georgian building is so welcoming - I've seen it in both rain and sunshine, and it never fails to cheer me up!*

**Price Guide:**
double/twin from £135
four poster from £195

**Awards/Recognition:** 2 AA Rosettes 2007-2008

**Location:** On the B353; Richmond Underground Station, 1 mile; Central London, 7 miles; Heathrow Airport, 7 miles

**Attractions:** Hampton Court Palace; Kew Gardens; Richmond Hill

Even though you're on the edge of London you could almost be in the country as this Georgian house with its Victorian walled garden stands on the crest of Richmond Hill with commanding views of the river Thames. As for the bedrooms, you can enjoy every comfort of the present with the elegance of the past including luxury four-poster bedrooms and suites. Space for weddings, meetings, parties and private dining is very flexible, and the award winning 2 AA Rosette restaurant Gates on the Park offers imaginative menus complemented by an exciting range of over 60 wines from around the world. Cedars Leisure club has a beautiful 20m indoor pool, which can be a welcome retreat after a day spent shopping in Richmond or walking through the park.

# 51 BUCKINGHAM GATE LUXURY SUITES AND APARTMENTS

51 BUCKINGHAM GATE, WESTMINSTER, LONDON SW1E 6AF
**Tel:** 0845 365 2653 **International:** +44 (0)20 7769 7766 **Fax:** 020 7828 5909
**Web:** www.johansens.com/buckinghamgate **E-mail:** info@51-buckinghamgate.co.uk

**Our inspector loved:** *The Spa at Fifty-One, great Sodashi treatments!*

**Price Guide:**
suites £405–£975
prime ministers suite p.o.a

**Awards/Recognition:** 5 AA Rosettes 2006-2007

**Location:** Victoria station, 10-min walk; Waterloo, Eurostar, 2 miles; Heathrow Airport, 16 miles; Gatwick Airport, 28 miles

**Attractions:** Houses of Parliment; Buckingham Palace; St James Park; London Eye

You'll want for nothing at 51 Buckingham Gate, an attractive Victorian town house that offers contemporary style and luxury on a grand scale. Privacy, relaxation and superb service is delivered by multilingual staff. Designated suites have 16-hour personal butler service, limousine pick-up and a mouthwatering range of special amenities. Other suites and apartments range from junior to the 5-bedroom Prime Minister's Suite, all of which are packed with sophisticated technology. Fully-equipped kitchens, as well as 24-hour room service, are available, or you can call on a team of talented chefs to prepare a private dinner. Enjoy the exclusive Spa and Sodashi treatments and don't let jet-lag slow you down with the jet-lag recovery service.

# CANNIZARO HOUSE

WEST SIDE, WIMBLEDON COMMON, LONDON SW19 4UE
**Tel:** 0845 365 3222 **International:** +44 (0)208 879 1464 **Fax:** 020 8970 2753
**Web:** www.johansens.com/cannizarohouse **E-mail:** info@cannizarohouse.com

***Our inspector loved:*** *The new look Cannizario, fabulous bar and restaurant.*

**Price Guide:**
double/twin from £155
feature room from £185

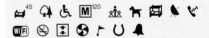

**Awards/Recognition:** 2 AA Rosettes 2006-2007

**Location:** Wimbledon Station, 1 mile; M25, 12 miles; Heathrow Airport, 17 miles; Gatwick Airport, 20 miles

**Attractions:** All England Lawn and Tennis Club and Museum; Kew Gardens; Hampton Court; London attractions

This captivating Georgian mansion sits on the edge of Wimbledon Common, and while its sweeping lawns, ornamental lake and formal gardens create an atmosphere of country living, you're still well located for trips to London's city centre and West End. The house has played host to distinguished individuals including King George III, Oscar Wilde, William Pitt and Henry James, and you will feel rather special amongst the sumptuous interiors with fine antiques, gilded mirrors and ornate fireplaces, along with a contemporary new light bar. Bedrooms are luxurious; some have four-posters, and views over Cannizaro Park. Award-winning modern British and European food is served in the Common restaurant or you can enjoy tea on the terrace and cocktails in the chic Cannizaro Bar.`

# CONGHAM HALL

GRIMSTON, KING'S LYNN, NORFOLK PE32 1AH
**Tel:** 0845 365 3244 **International:** +44 (0)1485 600250 **Fax:** 01485 601191
**Web:** www.johansens.com/conghamhall **E-mail:** info@conghamhallhotel.co.uk

***Our inspector loved:*** *The lovely setting for this stately home and the warm and friendly welcome.*

**Price Guide:**
single from £105
double/twin from £180
suite from £315

**Location:** A148, 2 miles; M11, 55 miles; King's Lynn, 6 miles; Norwich, 38 miles

**Attractions:** Sandringham; North Norfolk Coast; Houghton Hall; Holkham Hall

This pretty house, situated in acres of parkland, slips seamlessly into the role of a comfortable country hotel, where all that is good about the pleasures of country living comes to the fore. Classic interiors, fresh flowers, homemade pot pourri and roaring log fires blend into a welcoming, relaxed atmosphere. The hotel's renowned herb garden grows over 700 varieties of herb, many used by the chef to create modern English dishes accenting fresh local produce and fish from the local Norfolk markets, or try the home-made preserves at your breakfast table. A programme of events ranging from gardening, antiques and wine master classes are available. This is the ideal base for a tour of the spectacular north Norfolk coastline with its sandy beaches, teeming wildlife and welcoming hostelries.

# FAWSLEY HALL

FAWSLEY, NEAR DAVENTRY, NORTHAMPTONSHIRE NN11 3BA
**Tel:** 0845 365 3291 **International:** +44 (0)1327 892000 **Fax:** 01327 892001
**Web:** www.johansens.com/fawsleyhall **E-mail:** reservations@fawsleyhall.com

*Our inspector loved: The exciting split-level bedrooms in the new Knightley Court.*

**Price Guide:**
single from £159
double/twin from £199
suite from £389

In grounds landscaped by Capability Brown, Fawsley Hall holds many clues to its illustrious past, from the vaulted hall to the Queen Elizabeth I chamber. Go on a magical history tour in bedrooms offering Tudor, Georgian, Victorian and "classic modern" styles. The Knightley Restaurant has established a reputation as the county's finest, while the Old Laundry Bar provides light meals at lunchtime. The recently opened Knightley Court provides an additional 8 Georgian bedrooms, a cinema, syndicate rooms and a magnificent function room holding 150 guests for private dinners, weddings or conferences. Escape to the Georgian cellar where you will find the spa, beauty salon, fitness studio, sauna and spa bath.

**Awards/Recognition:** 3 AA Rosettes 2007-2008

**Location:** A361, 1 mile; M1 jct 16, 10 miles; Daventry, 8 miles; Birmingham International Airport, 35 miles

**Attractions:** Sulgrave Manor; Althorp; Blenheim Palace; Warwick Castle

# RUSHTON HALL

RUSHTON, NEAR KETTERING, NORTHAMPTONSHIRE NN14 1RR
**Tel:** 0845 365 2316 **International:** +44 (0)1536 713001 **Fax:** 01536 713010
**Web:** www.johansens.com/rushtonhall **E-mail:** enquiries@rushtonhall.com

***Our inspector loved:*** *The truly Great Hall with its panelling, portraits and fireplace.*

**Price Guide:**
superior from £140
state room from £160
four poster from £250

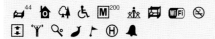

**Awards/Recognition:** 2 AA Rosettes 2006-2007

**Location:** A6003, 3 miles; M1 jct 19, 20 miles; Kettering, 5 miles; Birmingham International, 48 miles

**Attractions:** The Triangular Lodge; Rockingham Castle; Althorp; Rockingham Motor Racing Circuit

It is an exciting feeling to pass through the imposing iron gates, up the sweeping drive and catch sight of this stunning, 4 Star, Grade I listed hall. An elegant hotel with high levels of service. Beautiful linen fold panelling and original 16th-century floors are adorned by stylish, comfortable furnishings and rich drapes. There is the spectacular great hall with vaulted ceiling, an intimate library and a most charming drawing room. Bedrooms include four-posters and spacious state rooms which delight with a mix of sumptuous furnishings, antiques and eccentricities. Led by Adrian Coulthard the Brasserie and Restaurant serve imaginative seasonal menus. The tempting smells from the kitchen include the daily baking of breads, cakes and pastries. A swimmimg pool and spa will open early in 2008.

# WHITTLEBURY HALL

WHITTLEBURY, NEAR TOWCESTER, NORTHAMPTONSHIRE NN12 8QH
**Tel:** 0845 365 2804 **International:** +44 (0)1327 857857 **Fax:** 01327 858987
**Web:** www.johansens.com/whittleburyhall **E-mail:** sales@whittleburyhall.co.uk

*Our inspector loved:* The fine dining in Murrays Restaurant.

**Price Guide:**
single £150
double/twin £175
suite £290

**Awards/Recognition:** 2 AA Rosettes 2006-2007

**Location:** A143, 1 miles; A5, 2 miles; M1 jct 15, 11 miles; Towcester, 4 miles

**Attractions:** Silverstone Motor Racing Circuit; Towcester Racecourse; Oxford; Althorp

Whittlebury Hall is built in the Georgian style with interiors of contemporary furnishings and fabrics. The spacious bedrooms feature modern touches and thoughtful extras; 3 superbly appointed, individually-styled suites have a whirlpool spa bath and shower. You can enjoy an apèritif in the aptly named Silverstone Bar decorated with motor racing memorabilia, before tasting Italian dishes at Bentleys. Alternatively, try Astons Restaurant with menus that blend classic and contemporary cuisine or the award winning Murrays Restaurant, for the latest in food trends. The management training centre can accommodate up to 450 delegates and for relaxation The Spa and The Leisure Club include a range of heat and ice experiences, a gym, swimming pool and treatment suite where over 60 treatments are available for body, mind and soul.

# MATFEN HALL

MATFEN, NEWCASTLE-UPON-TYNE, NORTHUMBERLAND NE20 0RH
**Tel:** 0845 365 2057 **International:** +44 (0)1661 886500 **Fax:** 01661 886055
**Web:** www.johansens.com/matfenhall **E-mail:** info@matfenhall.com

**Our inspector loved:** *Playing a round of golf and then being pampered in the spa.*

**Price Guide:**
single from £115–£190
double from £175–£270

**Awards/Recognition:** 2 AA Rosettes 2007-2008; Condé Nast Johansens Most Excellent Venue 2006

**Location:** B6318, 1.5 miles; A69, 6 miles; Newcastle, 17 miles; Newcastle International. Airport, 11 miles

**Attractions:** Hadrians Wall; Alnwick Gardens; Belsay and Wallington Halls; Beamish Museum

Built in 1830, Matfen Hall has been carefully restored by Sir Hugh and Lady Blackett so that today, this magnificent family seat provides the perfect escape. The impressively pillared Great Hall features stained-glass windows whilst the bedrooms are individually decorated combining traditional and contemporary style. The Library and Print Room Restaurant serves highly accredited modern English cuisine. The championship golf course is rated as one of the finest in the North East and offers players 27 holes plus a 9 hole par 3 course and golf academy. The spa offers superb treatments and amenities including a 16m pool, 5 treatment suites including a duet treatment room, crystal steam room, salt grotto, herbal sauna, tropical feature shower, ice fountain and and the latest techno-gym equipment.

# LACE MARKET HOTEL

29-31, HIGH PAVEMENT, THE LACE MARKET, NOTTINGHAM, NOTTINGHAMSHIRE NG1 1HE
**Tel:** 0845 365 1973 **International:** +44 (0)115 852 3232 **Fax:** 0115 852 3223
**Web:** www.johansens.com/lacemarkethotel **E-mail:** stay@lacemarkethotel.co.uk

*Our inspector loved: The lively and cosy in-house Cock & Hoop pub and its imaginative cuisine.*

**Price Guide:** (room only)
small single £95
double/twin £119–£139
superior/studios £189-£239

**Awards/Recognition:** Condé Nast Johansens Most Excellent City Hotel 2007

**Location:** City Centre; M1 jct 26, 5 miles; Nottingham East Midlands Airport, 15 miles

**Attractions:** Nottingham Castle; Theatre Royal; National Ice Centre

Just yards from Nottingham's most fashionable shops and the National Arena, this privately-owned boutique hotel has a loyal following from music industry and A-list celebrities, and you'll see why. Join them in their appreciation of its luxurious accommodation, gastro pub, upmarket brasserie and chic cocktail bar -all under one roof! Bedrooms are individually designed with unique artwork, and superior rooms and studios have eye catching views from bed and bath. Recently licensed for weddings, the hotel is perfect for an intimate ceremony with loved ones and there are four venue rooms to choose from. Newlyweds can also use the beautiful grounds of St. Mary's Church next door for photographs. You can obtain complimentary access to the nearby Virgin Active Health Club, complete with indoor pool, full gym facilities and fitness classes.

# LANGAR HALL

LANGAR, NOTTINGHAMSHIRE NG13 9HG
**Tel:** 0845 365 1983  **International:** +44 (0)1949 860559  **Fax:** 01949 861045
**Web:** www.johansens.com/langarhall  **E-mail:** imogen@langarhall.com

**Our inspector loved:** *The old world charm, the tranquillity, and the imaginative food.*

**Price Guide:**
single from £75
double/twin from £150
suite £210

**Location:** A52, 4 miles; A46, 5 miles; Nottingham, 19 miles; East Midlands Airport, 26 miles

**Attractions:** Belvoir Castle; Trent Bridge cricket; Nottingham Castle; Stilton cheese making

Combining the charm of a traditional private home and good country living Langar Hall stands quietly secluded, overlooking parkland where sheep graze among ancient trees. The family home of Imogen Skirving, its site is historic, and the house itself dates back to 1837. Today, bedrooms are delightful with lovely views of the gardens and moat, the restaurant - very popular locally - serves English dishes of local meat, poultry, game, fish, and garden vegetables in season. Beyond the croquet lawn you can get lost in a romantic network of medieval fishponds teeming with carp, and further afield, the hotel is perfect for cricket at Trent Bridge, trips to Belvoir Castle and visits to the academics at Nottingham University. Dogs can also enjoy the Hall's comforts by prior arrangement.

# YE OLDE BELL

BARNBY MOOR, RETFORD, NOTTINGHAMSHIRE DN22 8QS
**Tel:** 0845 365 3457 **International:** +44 (0)1777 705121 **Fax:** 01777 860424
**Web:** www.johansens.com/yeoldebell **E-mail:** enquiries@yeoldebell.net

*Our inspector loved: The combination of the beautifully appointed refurbished bedrooms and the old world charm of the public rooms.*

**Price Guide:**
single from £80
double from £125
suite from £225

**Awards/Recognition:** 1 AA Rosette 2006-2007

**Location:** On A638; M1 jct 30, 18 miles; Retford, 3 miles

**Attractions:** Sherwood Forest; Historic City of Lincoln; Nottingham Castle

This cosy family-run hotel, formally a 16th century farm and one of England's oldest coaching inns, is brimming with quality, character and a history of hospitality. The distinguished visitors book with names including Charlie Chaplin, Oliver Reed and, more recently, Louis Theroux, illustrates the many people who have been charmed by this hotel's warm and welcoming atmosphere. There is an on going programme of sympathetic re-design and recently a series of bedrooms was completed in a fresh classic style, introducing neutral and warm colours. Inside, a homely feeling is created in the lounge with open fires. The 'St Leger Bar' is great for a light snack whilst the pretty wood paneled "Restaurant 1650" is ideal for intimate meals or can be taken over for receptions and civil ceremonies. Lovely gardens can be used for weddings and events.

# PHYLLIS COURT CLUB

MARLOW ROAD, HENLEY-ON-THAMES, OXFORDSHIRE RG9 2HT
**Tel:** 0845 365 2107  **International:** +44 (0)1491 570500  **Fax:** 01491 570528
**Web:** www.johansens.com/phylliscourt  **E-mail:** enquiries@phylliscourt.co.uk

**Our inspector loved:** *The gracious and traditional surroundings, and riverside setting.*

**Price Guide:**
single £98-£136
double/twin £140-£169

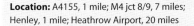

**Location:** A4155, 1 mile; M4 jct 8/9, 7 miles; Henley, 1 mile; Heathrow Airport, 20 miles

**Attractions:** Henley; Riverside Walks; Marlow; Ascot

As a resident guest you become a temporary member of a club whose past visitors have included Prince Albert, King George V and Edward, Prince of Wales. Enjoying an unparalleled position on the Thames overlooking the Henley Royal Regatta course since 1906, the Club was founded by a group of friends and London businessmen, but in its distant past played host to Oliver Cromwell and William II's first Royal Court. Today, following an extensive luxury refurbishment of the reception, lounge and bar, Phyllis Court retains great character and tradition alongside high standards of hospitality. Offering comfortable bedrooms, a fine dining restaurant, delicious afternoon tea and the contemporary-styled Orangery, with its innovative menu and view of the garden and river, you are guaranteed a memorable stay. Corporate events, weddings and parties can be arranged by request. Private hospitality boxes are available on the finishing line.

# LE MANOIR AUX QUAT' SAISONS

GREAT MILTON, OXFORDSHIRE OX44 7PD
**Tel:** 0845 365 2014  **International:** +44 (0)1844 278881  **Fax:** 01844 278847
**Web:** www.johansens.com/lemanoirauxquatsaisons  **E-mail:** lemanoir@blanc.co.uk

*Our inspector loved: The very special magical feeling of Le Manoir and its exceptional staff.*

**Price Guide:** (including French breakfast)
double/twin £380–£540
suites £575–£1340

**Awards/Recognition:** 2 Star Michelin 2007; 5 AA Rosettes 2007-2008; Relais & Châteaux

**Location:** A329, 0.20 miles; M40 J7/8a, 2 miles; Oxford, 8 miles; Heathrow Airport, 40 miles

**Attractions:** Oxford; Blenheim Palace; Cotswolds; Henley

This beautiful 15th century, golden stone house is the culmination of Chef Patron, Raymond Blanc's vision to create a hotel and restaurant where guests find perfection in food, comfort and service, and it's the only country house to have retained 2 Michelin stars for 22 years. Set in 7 acres of stunning grounds with its own organic herb and vegetable gardens, there are 32 beautifully designed suites and bedrooms. If you're really passionate about food, you can enjoy a course at 'The Raymond Blanc Cookery School' and in summer they run a series of Junior Chef days to inspire young talent. There are chocolate tastings, organic wine tastings and a music festival amongst the events organized to add a certain 'je ne sais quoi' to your visit.

# THE SPRINGS HOTEL & GOLF CLUB

NORTH STOKE, WALLINGFORD, OXFORDSHIRE OX10 6BE
**Tel:** 0845 365 2697 **International:** +44 (0)1491 836687 **Fax:** 01491 836877
**Web:** www.johansens.com/springshotel **E-mail:** info@thespringshotel.com

*Our inspector loved:* The lakeside views from the restaurant and the refurbished golf club.

**Price Guide:**
single from £95
double/twin from £110
suite from £155

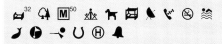

**Awards/Recognition:** 1 AA Rosette 2006-2007

**Location:** A4074, 0.1 miles; M40, 15 miles; Wallingford, 2 miles; Heathrow, 40 miles

**Attractions:** Oxford; Blenheim Palace; Henley; Basildon Park (NT)

Dating from 1874 this very early fine English Mock Tudor style house is set in 6 acres in the heart of the beautiful Thames Valley. Large south-facing windows overlook a spring-fed lake, from which the hotel takes its name. Many of the comfortable bedrooms and suites share this lake view, whilst others overlook the quiet woodland that surrounds the hotel. Private balconies provide patios for summer relaxation. The award-winning Lakeside Restaurant's menu offers fresh local produce and a well-stocked cellar of fine international wines. Leisure facilities include an 18-hole par 72 golf course, clubhouse and putting green, an outdoor swimming pool, sauna and touring bicycles. You can enjoy these facilities for business or pleasure or even participate in a themed weekend.

# HAMBLETON HALL

HAMBLETON, OAKHAM, RUTLAND LE15 8TH
**Tel:** 0845 365 1809 **International:** +44 (0)1572 756991 **Fax:** 01572 724721
**Web:** www.johansens.com/hambletonhall **E-mail:** hotel@hambletonhall.com

*Our inspector loved:* The warm colours and welcoming fire in the bar.

**Price Guide:**
single from £170
double/twin £200–£365
suite £500–£600

Originally a Victorian mansion, Hambleton Hall celebrated its 25th year as a hotel in 2005, and continues to attract acclaim for achieving near perfection. Artful blends of flowers from local hedgerows and London flower markets add splashes of colour to the bedrooms. The Croquet Pavillion a 2 bedroom suite with living and breakfast rooms is a luxurious additional option. In the Michelin-starred restaurant, chef Aaron Patterson and his team offer strongly seasonal menus - Grouse, Scottish ceps, chanterelles, partridge and woodcock all appear when they're supposed to, accompanied by vegetables, herbs and salads from the Hall's garden. If you're feeling energetic you can embark on walks around the lake and there are opportunities for tennis, swimming, golf and sailing, otherwise you can browse for hidden treasures in Oakham's antique shops.

**Awards/Recognition:** 1 Star Michelin 2007; Relais & Châteaux; 4 AA Rosettes 2007-2008

**Location:** A606, 2 miles; Oakham, 2 miles; A1(M), 10 miles; East Midlands International Airport, 40 miles

**Attractions:** Rutland Water;  Burghley House; Rockingham Castle; Barnsdale Gardens

# Hotel Inspector, pages 56-57

# beasts? Go wild on a safari to Ken

# travelmail

## AN INSPECTOR CALLS

**His mission: To test hotel hospitality to the limit**

SITTING on a peninsula overlooking Rutland Water, Hambleton Hall is the former Victorian hunting lodge where Noel Coward famously wrote Hay Fever.

Since 1979, it has been owned and managed by Tim and Stefa Hart, parents of two highly celebrated London restaurateurs, Sam and Eddie Hart, whose outlets include Quo Vadis.

Hambleton Hall promises its guests a 'luxurious and relaxing escape' — hardly original, but as we drove along the three-mile peninsula, observing the lush, verdent and seemingly endless countryside on the other side of the water, escape seemed the operative word. I felt like Jack climbing his beanstalk, not knowing what was at the top. The village, with a population of just over a 100 and boasting a delightful 12th-century church at its heart, could not have been further from the calamity of the M25 we had left behind two hours earlier.

But it was a surprise to see the hotel car park full of Aston Martins (well, there were only two), and Maseratis (one, actually).

Once we had swallowed our prejudices and manoeuvred our bags past a fleet of suspiciously clean wellies in the entrance hall, we almost fell on to three sets of couples taking coffee on the sofa by a large log fire.

Their discussions seemed to have a common theme. 'Yes, well, my redundancy has worked out really rather well, so, George, you shouldn't worry too much,' said a red-faced man in a pin-stripe suit. We were warmly greeted by the immaculate general manager, Chris Hurst, and then shown to our room by a cheerful receptionist.

'One thing I should tell you about the room, which I don't think was mentioned when you booked...' she said, with a frightening pause. 'The shower is attached to the bath, so you can't stand up in it. I stayed in this room after being snowed in. Aside from that, I was extremely comfortable.'

Although not enormous, the room was just as she had said, 'extremely comfortable', though for an extra £70 we could have had a lake-facing vista rather than a view towards the kitchens.

This is the sort of place where the 'smart attire' rule for dinner is taken seriously — but it had a variety of interpretations, ranging from psychedelic orange ties to well-cut dinner jackets.

Don't ask me why, but I asked for a Bullshot before dinner. It's like a Bloody Mary, only made with beef bouillon instead of tomato juice. Although it wasn't on the cocktail list, the young Bulgarian waiter had no problem rustling one up.

Working in the kitchen is Aaron Patterson, who has maintained the restaurant's Michelin-star status since 1986. We decided to put him through his paces by ordering the £60 tasting menu. The highlights were the scallops and the exquisitely presented assiette of puddings.

A stay at Hambleton Hall isn't cheap, but it's a rare treat — and hard to define. It's old fashioned without being stuffy and if you combine it with a visit to nearby Burghley, the grandest house of the Elizabethan age and once home of Sir William Cecil, I can't think of many better ways to spend a weekend.

*Hambleton Hall,*
*Hambleton,*
*Oakham,*
*Rutland LE15 8TH*
*tel: 01572 756 991, hambletonhall.co...*
*Doubles from £230 b&b*
★★★★★

Picture: LIONEL HEAP

## WEB WISDOM

Read what the Inspector has to say about other hotels in the UK at travelmail.co.uk

# DINHAM HALL

LUDLOW, SHROPSHIRE SY8 1EJ

**Tel:** 0845 365 3266 **International:** +44 (0)1584 876464 **Fax:** 01584 876019
**Web:** www.johansens.com/dinhamhall **E-mail:** info@dinhamhall.co.uk

***Our inspector loved:*** *The location, exploring Ludlow at your leisure then delicious dining at Dinham Hall - lunch or dinner.*

**Price Guide:**
single from £95
double/twin from £140
suite from £240

**Awards/Recognition:** 2 AA Rosettes 2006-2007

**Location:** A49, 1 mile; Hereford, 20 miles; Shrewsbury, 35 miles; Birmingham, 50 miles

**Attractions:** Ludlow Castle; Ironbridge; Welsh Marches; Powis Castle

James Garnett, General Manager of Dinham Hall, is keen that you enjoy your visit to Ludlow, described by architectural critics as the most beautiful country town in England, and the delights start here at this Georgian townhouse. Built in 1792 as a town residence for a wealthy landowner it once housed schoolboys from Ludlow College who cheekily inscribed their names on window ledges in some of the superb rooms and suites that overlook the gardens or castle. Public spaces beckon with comfortable sofas, leather armchairs, open fires and fresh flowers, and excellent lunch and dinner menus use local ingredients, most sourced within a 30-mile radius. The Merchant Suite, with its 14th-century timbers, the Green Room and Orangery are available for private dining.

# STON EASTON PARK

STON EASTON, BATH, SOMERSET BA3 4DF
**Tel:** 0845 365 2376 **International:** +44 (0)1761 241631 **Fax:** 01761 241377
**Web:** www.johansens.com/stoneastonpark **E-mail:** info@stoneaston.co.uk

***Our inspector loved:*** *Feeling of bygone era, offering every comfort for 21st century*

**Price Guide:**
single from £145
double/twin £175–£420
four-poster £240–£420

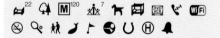

**Awards/Recognition:** 2 AA Rosettes 2007-2008

**Location:** just off A37 miles; Bath, 14 miles; Brsitol Airport 19 miles

**Attractions:** Thermae Bath Spa; Wells Cathedral; Glastonbury Tor and Abbey; Cheddar Gorge and caves

Jean Monro - an acknowledged expert on 18th-century decoration supervised the design and furnishings of this noble Grade I Palladian mansion and in so doing created the perfect partner for the romantic grounds and parkland landscaped by Humphrey Repton in 1792. The exceptional architecture and decoration features will impress even an untrained eye though it is the warm and unobtrusive service that really makes you feel at home. Herbs and vegetables are grown in the Victorian kitchen garden & help influence the creation of English and French dishes. If you are really after peaceful solitude then book the private suite in the 17th-century Gardener's Cottage, on the wooded banks of the River Norr.

# AVON GORGE HOTEL

SION HILL, CLIFTON, BRISTOL, SOMERSET BS8 4LD
**Tel:** 0845 365 3451  **International:** +44 (0)117 973 8955  **Fax:** 0117 923 8125
**Web:** www.johansens.com/avongorge  **E-mail:** info@avongorge-hotel-bristol.com

*Our inspector loved: The wonderful terrace overlooking the Clifton Suspension Bridge, a fantastic location.*

**Price Guide:**
single £120
double £130-£140
suite £160-£255

**Location:** B3129, 0.2 miles; City Centre, 2 miles; Bristol Temple Meads Station, 3 miles; Bristol Airport, 20 miles

**Attractions:** Clifton Suspension Bridge; Bristol Zoo; SS Great Britain; Cheddar Gorge

Staying in the city could hardly be better than at this fashionable boutique hotel, situated in Bristol's trendy Clifton village and with terraces and views overlooking the spectacular Avon Gorge and the Clifton suspension bridge. As a top Bristol restaurant, The Bridge Café delivers inspired dishes using locally sourced produce and its 'all-most' all weather dining deck for alfresco entertaining has breathtaking views. The White Lion Bar and Terrace is a renowned haunt with gastro style dishes and excellent wines, beers and ales. A variety of private rooms including a terrace for summer barbeques and drinks, makes this a great venue all year round for companies or friends getting together.

# COMBE HOUSE HOTEL

HOLFORD, NEAR BRIDGWATER, SOMERSET TA5 1RZ
**Tel:** 0845 365 3240 **International:** +44 (0)1278 741382
**Web:** www.johansens.com/combehouseholford **E-mail:** enquiries@combehouse.co.uk

*Our inspector loved:* Breathtaking location - fine dining and wanting to return.

**Price Guide:**
single £72.50-£95
double £125-£150
suite £140-£165

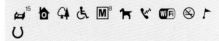

**Awards/Recognition:** 1 AA Rosette 2006-2007

**Location:** A39, 0.5 miles; M5 jct 23/24, 20 miles; Bristol Airport, 25 miles

**Attractions:** Somerset light Railway; Quantock Hills; Hestercombe Gardens; Dunster Castle

Surrounded by 4 acres of grounds and the wooded valleys of the Quantock Hills nature lovers will adore Combe House with its fine varieties of shrubs , an ancient yew, a bubbling stream and an organic kitchen garden bursting with vegetables and soft fruit. On summer evenings you might even catch sight of wild deer emerging from the forest to graze. Accommodation ranges from standard to superior rooms with king or super-king-size beds, luxury toiletries, fluffy robes and views over the garden. There is also a four-poster bridal suite. The restaurant offers dishes based on recipes from all over the world combining meat and game from local farms and shoots. Fish from Brixham, shellfish from the Bristol Channel, and of course, Somerset cheeses.

# CHARLTON HOUSE & THE SHARPHAM PARK RESTAURANT

CHARLTON ROAD, SHEPTON MALLET, SOMERSET BA4 4PR
**Tel:** 0845 365 2876 **International:** +44 (0)1749 342008 **Fax:** 01749 346362
**Web:** www.johansens.com/charltonhouse **E-mail:** enquiry@charltonhouse.com

**Our inspector loved:** *Atmosphere - First class dining and the Spa, It really is a must*

**Price Guide:**
single from £140
double £180-£375
suite £465-£565

**Awards/Recognition:** 2 AA Rosettes 2007-2008

**Location:** Off the A361; A303, 28 miles

**Attractions:** Bath; Longleat House; Stourhead; Wells Cathedral

An early 17th century country house that combines the grandeur of a country retreat with inviting homeliness. The owners, Roger and Monty Saul, know a thing or two about creativity having founded Mulberry Design Company. Every where you look there are luxurious fabrics, eclectic touches and a sense of the elegant yet informal. Several bedrooms feature grand bathrooms, striking four-poster beds and working fireplaces; others offer a particularly intimate atmosphere with private gardens. The Sharpham Park Restaurant, under the imaginative eye of Elisha Carter uses organic ingredients from its own farm; organic spelt, White Park Beef and Vension. For a bit of heavenly nurturing Monty's spa makes its own products freshly by hand, with ingredients chosen for their purity and therapeutic values.

# The Castle at Taunton

CASTLE GREEN, TAUNTON, SOMERSET TA1 1NF
**Tel:** 0845 365 2415 **International:** +44 (0)1823 272671 **Fax:** 01823 336066
**Web:** www.johansens.com/castleattaunton **E-mail:** reception@the-castle-hotel.com

*Our inspector loved: The whole experience of visiting this beautiful hotel.*

**Price Guide:**
single from £135
double from £230
suite from £330

**Awards/Recognition:** 1 Star Michelin 2007; 3 AA Rosettes 2006-2007

**Location:** Town Centre; M5 jct 25, 3 miles

**Attractions:** Exmoor; Somerset Levels; Wells Cathedral; Hestercombe Gardens

In the heart of the West Country, The Castle at Taunton has been welcoming travellers to explore the region's plethora of attractions since the 12th century. Run by the Chapman family for over 50 years, this former Norman fortress serves as a convivial gateway to the land of King Arthur and features 44 bedrooms, all of which are individually appointed. Gastronomes will be delighted with the award-winning restaurant whose Head Chef Richard Guest has won a Michelin star. Ambitious dishes include Brixham crab cakes with marinated cauliflower, red mullet minestrone and a celebration of British beef comprising steamed oxtail pudding, roast fillet of South Devon beef and ox tongue sauce. Alternatively, there is the more informal BRAZZ, The Castle's contemporary brasserie, where delicious food created from fresh local produce is served. Conference planners should note that meetings for up to 100 delegates can be accommodated.

# MOUNT SOMERSET COUNTRY HOUSE HOTEL

HENLADE, TAUNTON, SOMERSET TA3 5NB
**Tel:** 0845 365 2076 **International:** +44 (0)1823 442500 **Fax:** 01823 442900
**Web:** www.johansens.com/mountsomerset **E-mail:** info@mountsomersethotel.co.uk

***Our inspector loved:*** *The overall welcome - total comfort - and fine cuisine.*

**Price Guide:**
single £120-£160
double £180-£200
suite £225-£270

**Awards/Recognition:** 2 AA Rosettes 2007-2008; Condé Nast Johansens Most Excellent Country Hotel 2006

**Location:** A358, 1 mile; M5 jct 25, 3 miles; Taunton, 6 miles

**Attractions:** Glastonbury; Wells Cathedral; Exmoor; Various National Trust Properties

This elegant Regency residence sits high on the slopes of the Blackdown Hills, overlooking miles of lovely countryside. The hotel is rich in intricate craftsmanship and displays fine original features. Its owners have committed themselves to creating an atmosphere where you can relax, confident that your needs are taken care of. The bedrooms are very comfortable and many offer views across the Quantock Hills, all have luxurious bathrooms some with spa baths. Light lunches, teas, coffees and home-made cakes draw you into the beautifully furnished drawing room. The restaurant offers excellent menus and fine wines supported by a team of chefs working together to create dishes that will exceed your expectations. Nearby places of interest include Glastonbury Abbey and Wells Cathedral. Enjoy special breaks throughout the year.

# HOAR CROSS HALL SPA RESORT

HOAR CROSS, NEAR YOXALL, STAFFORDSHIRE DE13 8QS
**Tel:** 0845 365 1864 **International:** +44 (0)1283 575671 **Fax:** 01283 575652
**Web:** www.johansens.com/hoarcrosshall **E-mail:** info@hoarcross.co.uk

*Our inspector loved: This excellent fully inclusive spa resort with all its facilities and treatments.*

**Price Guide:** (fully inclusive of spa treatment, breakfast, lunch and dinner)
single £175-£195
double/twin £320-£370
single/double/twin suite £220–£440

**Location:** A515, 2 miles; A50, 8 miles; Lichfield, 8 miles; M6 jct 12 or 15, 22 miles

**Attractions:** In the heart of The National Forest; Historic Lichfield

The only stately home spa resort in England and Winner of England's Leading Resort at the World Travel Awards 2005/6. Surrounded by 100 acres of beautiful landscaped grounds. Oak panelling, tapestries, rich furnishings and paintings adorn the interior. A Jacobean staircase leads up to the bedrooms, all with crown tester or four-poster beds. Penthouses have private saunas and balconies overlooking the treetops. Gilded ceilings and William Morris wallpaper in the ballroom set the scene for the dining room, where a superb à la carte menu is offered. Trained professionals are ready to assist with yoga, meditation, tai chi, pilates, dance classes and aqua-aerobics. The spa features seawater and hydrotherapy swimming pools, baths, flotation therapy, saunas, a 4000 sq ft gymnasium, steam rooms, water grottos, saunariums, aromatherapy room, aerobics and yoga suites. A PGA golf academy is also available.

# BRUDENELL HOTEL

THE PARADE, ALDEBURGH, SUFFOLK IP15 5BU

**Tel:** 0845 365 3209  **International:** +44 (0)1728 452071  **Fax:** 01728 454082
**Web:** www.johansens.com/brudenell  **E-mail:** info@brudenellhotel.co.uk

***Our inspector loved:*** *Entering at the front entrance and seeing the sea beyond.*

**Price Guide:**
single £62-£94
double £100-£182
deluxe £150–£224

**Awards/Recognition:** 2 AA Rosettes 2006-2007

**Location:** A1094, 1 mile; A12, 7 miles; Ipswich, 26 miles; Lavenham, 48 miles

**Attractions:** Snape Maltings; Framlingham Castle; Orford Castle; Thorpeness

Escape the city hustle at this contemporary seaside charmer. Light, airy and relaxed, fresh modern décor and furnishings complement the occasional piece of driftwood, and welcoming staff attend to your every whim. Cleverly arranged interiors mean that most rooms enjoy panoramic sea views, and the AA two Rosette awarded restaurant immediately on the seafront makes you feel as if you are on an ocean liner. Fresh fish and grills are the speciality. Aldeburgh has something for everybody - scenic walks past pastel-coloured houses and fishermen's huts, superb boutique shopping, highly acclaimed restaurants and the annual Aldeburgh Festival. If you love history, there are many historic buildings, castles and an abbey in the area. Bring your wellies as the marshes are a haven for wading birds and heaven for birdwatchers.

# RAVENWOOD HALL COUNTRY HOTEL & RESTAURANT

ROUGHAM, BURY ST. EDMUNDS, SUFFOLK IP30 9JA
**Tel:** 0845 365 2139 **International:** +44 (0)1359 270345 **Fax:** 01359 270788
**Web:** www.johansens.com/ravenwoodhall **E-mail:** enquiries@ravenwoodhall.co.uk

*Our inspector loved: The absolute wow factor of the new Garden Room Bar Restaurant - no, its not another Conservatory!*

**Price Guide:**
mews £97.50–£120
main house £108.50–£165
superior £130–£195

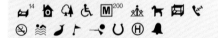

**Awards/Recognition:** 2 AA Rosettes 2007-2008

**Location:** Just off A14 jct 45; Bury St. Edmunds, 4 miles

**Attractions:** Cambridge; Long Melford; Lavenham; Newmarket Racecourse

Nestling within 7 acres of lawns and woodlands in the heart of Suffolk lies Ravenwood Hall. This fine building dates back to 1530 and retains many of its original features. The restaurant is decorated with carved timbers and a huge inglenook fireplace from Tudor times, creating a delightfully intimate atmosphere in which to enjoy imaginative cuisine. The menu is a combination of adventurous and classical dishes, featuring some long forgotten English recipes. The Hall's extensive cellars are stocked with some of the finest vintages, along with a selection of rare ports and brandies. Comfortable bedrooms are furnished with antiques, reflecting the historic tradition of the Hall. the new garden room overlooks the patio, pool and summer house. A wide range of leisure facilities is available for guests, including a croquet lawn and heated swimming pool.

# THE ICKWORTH HOTEL AND APARTMENTS

HORRINGER, BURY ST EDMUNDS, SUFFOLK IP29 5QE
**Tel:** 0845 365 2539 **International:** +44 (0)1284 735350 **Fax:** 01284 736300
**Web:** www.johansens.com/ickworth **E-mail:** info@ickworthhotel.com

***Our inspector loved:*** *The grandeur of driving across the deer park to get to the Hotel.*

**Price Guide:**
single/double/suite £185–£738

**Awards/Recognition:** 2 AA Rosettes 2006-2007

**Location:** A143, 0.5 miles; A14 jct 42, 2.7 miles; Bury St Edmunds, 5-min drive

**Attractions:** Newmarket Racecourse; Ely; Cambridge; Lavenham

At last! The perfect retreat for couples and families, where children are special guests and you can happily pop them into the safe hands of the crèche or Club/Blu - stuffed full of table football, ping pong and computer games - while you head off to ride, swim or indulge in extreme pampering at the Aquae Sulis Retreat. The hotel's airy rooms have been decorated in a delightful mix of classic, traditional and contemporary furnishings, all adding a dash of style and warmth. Bedrooms are diverse in size and design, while the Dower House, a short bicycle ride across the estate, houses stunning apartments for large families or groups of friends. Treat yourselves in Frederick's restaurant, or eat more informally in the Grand Conservatory.

# HINTLESHAM HALL

HINTLESHAM, IPSWICH, SUFFOLK IP8 3NS

**Tel:** 0845 365 1857 **International:** +44 (0)1473 652334 **Fax:** 01473 652463
**Web:** www.johansens.com/hintleshamhall **E-mail:** reservations@hintleshamhall.com

**Our inspector loved:** *The magnificent new Black and Gold Bar.*

**Price Guide:**
single £110–£195
double/twin £140–£280
suite £350–£495

SPA

**Awards/Recognition:** 3 AA Rosettes 2006-2007

**Location:** A1071, 1 mile; Ipswich, 4 miles; Lavenham, 13.5 miles; Bury St Edmunds, 30 miles

**Attractions:** Constable Country; Newmarket Racecourse; Aldeburgh

You'll be constantly surprised by this house and its evolving styles. A splendid Georgian façade hides its 16th-century origins to which the Tudor red-brick at the back of the hall is a clue. The Stuart period is evoked by the magnificent carved oak staircase leading to the hall's north wing. This mix works well, with lofty Georgian reception rooms contrasting with timbered Tudor rooms. The well-balanced menus will appeal to every taste. Whether feeling decadent or health-conscious why not play at an associated championship size golf course or take time out in the Health Club with state-of-the-art gym and beauty/sport treatment rooms.

# THE SWAN HOTEL

HIGH STREET, LAVENHAM, SUDBURY, SUFFOLK CO10 9QA
**Tel:** 0845 365 2708 **International:** +44 (0)1787 247477 **Fax:** 01787 248286
**Web:** www.johansens.com/theswanlavenham **E-mail:** info@theswanatlavenham.co.uk

***Our inspector loved:*** *The "oh so cosy" seating areas created by the historic beams and different ceiling heights.*

**Price Guide:**
single £60- £100
double/twin £120–£200
four poster/suite £145–£270

**Awards/Recognition:** 2 AA Rosettes 2007-2008

**Location:** On the A1141; A131, 7 miles; Stansted Airport, 39 miles

**Attractions:** Gainsboroughs House; Constable Country; Bury St Edmunds; Cambridge

Medieval goes modern at this hotel in the Tudor village of Lavenham, where today's indulgences sit contentedly alongside 15th-century oak beams, flagged floors and inglenook fireplaces. Re-discovered medieval wall paintings have influenced interiors, and in bedrooms decorated with calming colours you can run your hands over natural fabrics which evoke the town's wool trade history. Retreat to comfortable lounge areas and the Old Bar, with its brick floor, or stake a claim on a table in the elegant AA two rosette Gallery Restaurant. Priding itself on its food, the hotel diligently sources fresh Suffolk and Norfolk produce. In summer it's lovely to eat outside in the courtyard. The Swan is a perfect base for enjoying this area's abundant history, culture and unspoilt countryside.

# THE WESTLETON CROWN

THE STREET, WESTLETON, NEAR SOUTHWOLD, SUFFOLK IP17 3AD
**Tel:** 0845 365 2731 **International:** +44 (0)1728 648777 **Fax:** 01728 648239
**Web:** www.johansens.com/westletoncrown **E-mail:** info@westletoncrown.co.uk

***Our inspector loved:*** *The bird illustrations of their room namesakes.*

**Price Guide:**
single £85
double/twin £95–£170

**Awards/Recognition:** 2 AA Rosettes 2007-2008

**Location:** On the B1125; A12, 3.9 miles; Southwold, 7 miles; Aldeburgh, 8 miles

**Attractions:** Dunwich Heath (NT); Snape Maltings and Music Festival; Minsmere RPSB Bird Reserve; Southwold Pier

You'll be very happy to drop your bags at this historic coaching inn that dates back to the 12th century. Bedrooms, some located in converted stables and cottages, are furnished in a fresh country style, and each is named after a species of bird - you'll spot them in the lovely canvas photographs. Hearty breakfasts, light meals in the bar or more elegant dining in the restaurant and conservatory are all created with passion and served by the efficient team that prides itself on making sure you're happy. A range of local ales in the bar is always tempting. You're close to the Suffolk Heritage Coast and its unspoiled heathlands, nature reserves, beaches and wild salt marshes, as well as the quintessential English seaside towns of Aldeburgh and Southwold.

# SECKFORD HALL

WOODBRIDGE, SUFFOLK IP13 6NU
**Tel:** 0845 365 2319 **International:** +44 (0)1394 385678 **Fax:** 01394 380610
**Web:** www.johansens.com/seckfordhall **E-mail:** reception@seckford.co.uk

*Our inspector loved:* The beautiful Tudor Panelling and Carving.

**Price Guide:**
single £85–£145
double/twin £140–£215
suite £180–£215

**Awards/Recognition:** 2 AA Rosettes 2007-2008

**Location:** Off the A12; Woodbridge, 2 miles; Ipswich, 9.5 miles

**Attractions:** Suton Hoo; Constable Country; Aldeburgh; Snape Maltings

Seckford Hall dates from 1530 and it is said that Elizabeth I once held court here. Set in 34 acres of parkland with sweeping lawns and a willow fringed lake the house is furnished as a private residence with many fine period pieces. The panelled rooms, beamed ceilings, carved doors and great stone fireplaces are set against the splendour of English oak. Local delicacies such as the house speciality, lobster, feature on the à la carte menu. The courtyard area was converted from a giant Tudor tithe barn, dairy and coach house and now incorporates 10 charming cottage-style suites and a leisure complex, which includes a heated swimming pool, exercise machines, spa bath and beauty salon. You may also use the fully equipped Business Lounge.

# GRAYSHOTT SPA

HEADLEY ROAD, GRAYSHOTT, NEAR HINDHEAD, SURREY GU26 6JJ
**Tel:** 0845 365 1789 **International:** +44 (0)1428 602020 **Fax:** 01428 609769
**Web:** www.johansens.com/grayshottspa **E-mail:** reservations@grayshottspa.com

***Our inspector loved:*** *The complete sense of tranquility from the moment you arrive.*

**Price Guide:** (including meals and use of facilities. minimum 2 night stay)
single from £199
double from £195 per person double occupancy

**Location:** A3, 2 miles; M25 jct 10, 22 miles; Guildford, 15 miles; Heathrow Airport, 37 miles

**Attractions:** Devil's Punch Bowl (NT); Frensham

Set in 47 acres of gardens, lawns and woodland Grayshott Spa comprises 36 treatment rooms and boasts a highly acclaimed reputation for its natural therapies. Health consultants, dieticians and a professional fitness team are able to create bespoke sessions and one to one tuition classes in Yoga, Pilates and Tai Chi. Alternatively the golf and tennis academies offer personal training. Before taking dinner in the Dining Room or Conservatory Restaurant, guests may enjoy a drink in Bubbles where a variety of organic wines, champagnes, juices and hot drinks are served. The healthy eating menu at the restaurant upholds the healthy living ethos that is apparent throughout Grayshott Spa. All rooms and new Junior Suites, pictured above, have been refurbished with style and comfort in mind.

# LYTHE HILL HOTEL & SPA

PETWORTH ROAD, HASLEMERE, SURREY GU27 3BQ
**Tel:** 0845 365 2052  **International:** +44 (0)1428 651251  **Fax:** 01428 644131
**Web:** www.johansens.com/lythehill  **E-mail:** lythe@lythehill.co.uk

**Our inspector loved:** *The stylish new lounge and bar area - it's bright and uplifting whatever the weather!*

**Price Guide:** (room only)
double £160–£295
suite £260–£350

**Location:** B2131; A3, 5.2 miles; Guildford, 19 miles; London Waterloo, 50-min train/metro

**Attractions:** Petworth House; Lurgashall Winery; Ramster Gardens; Haslemere Museum

Cradled by the Surrey foothills is Lythe Hill Hotel & Spa, comprising of an unusual cluster of ancient buildings – parts of which date from the 14th century. While most of the well appointed accommodation is in the more recently converted part of the hotel, 5 rooms can be found in the Tudor House, including the Henry VIII room with a four-poster bed dated 1614. There are 2 restaurants: the Auberge de France and the 'Dining Room' with a choice of imaginative English dishes. Complemented by over 200 international wines. The Amarna leisure facility has a 16 x 8 metre swimming pool, steam room and sauna, gym, hairdressing, treatment rooms and a nail bar. National Trust hillside adjoining the hotel grounds provides interesting walks and views over the surrounding countryside.

# FOXHILLS

STONEHILL ROAD, OTTERSHAW, SURREY KT16 0EL
**Tel:** 0845 365 1756 **International:** +44 (0)1932 872050 **Fax:** 01932 874762
**Web:** www.johansens.com/foxhills **E-mail:** reservations@foxhills.co.uk

*Our inspector loved:* The new bar and restaurant XIX - the atmosphere is relaxed and welcoming and the black and white photographs are fascinating!

**Price Guide:** (room only)
double/twin from £180
suite from £220

Located in a staggering 400 acres you could be forgiven for imagining yourself lost in the heart of the English countryside. Here you will find an elegant stone manor house which has something for everyone. 3 golf courses, 11 tennis courts and an array of sporting facilities. Bedrooms include courtyard-style garden rooms, and a recently opened wing which can be hired exclusively for family parties, business functions or weddings. You will appreciate the 3 restaurants offering award winning cuisine and may well fall in love with Foxhills' conservatory-style dining room, with its tall, mullioned windows and views . Elsewhere, many parts of the manor are dedicated family-friendly zones, but a stunning adult-only spa is due to open at the end of 2008.

**Location:** A319, 1.5 miles; M25 junction 11, 2.5 miles; Woking Station, 6-min drive; Heathrow Airport, 13 miles

**Attractions:** Windsor Castle; Hampton Court Palace; Thorpe Park; Wisley RHS Garden

# DEANS PLACE HOTEL

SEAFORD ROAD, ALFRISTON, EAST SUSSEX BN26 5TW
**Tel:** 0845 365 3264 **International:** +44 (0)1323 870248 **Fax:** 01323 870918
**Web:** www.johansens.com/deansplacehotel **E-mail:** mail@deansplacehotel.co.uk

***Our inspector loved:*** *The tranquil garden setting with its manicured lawns, wooden sculptures and magnificent views of the South Downs.*

**Price Guide:**
single from £74
double from £95
family from £140

**Awards/Recognition:** 1 AA Rosette 2006-2007

**Location:** A27, 1 mile; M23 (A23), 15 miles; Lewes, 10 miles; Gatwick Airport, 40 miles

**Attractions:** Glyndebourne; Alfriston Clergy House; Eastbourne; South Downs Way

Deans Place Hotel is situated amongst 4 acres of beautifully landscaped gardens with the rolling South Downs as a backdrop. This location creates the perfect retreat where experienced and attentive staff provide an atmosphere of comfortable sophistication. Bedrooms have views over the meadow and hills beyond; many overlook the heated swimming pool. Others look out to the garden, croquet lawn and stream. Fine International cuisine, using fresh local produce when available, is prepared by the hotel's excellent chef, whose creativity provides a memorable dining experience within a spacious, light atmosphere. The adjacent Friston Bar is the ideal place for meeting friends over a quiet drink in front of a roaring log fire. The large terrace, offers you al fresco dining on balmy summer evenings.

# THE POWDERMILLS

POWDERMILL LANE, BATTLE, EAST SUSSEX TN33 0SP
**Tel:** 0845 365 2648 **International:** +44 (0)1424 775511 **Fax:** 01424 774540
**Web:** www.johansens.com/powdermills **E-mail:** powdc@aol.com

***Our inspector loved:*** *The stunning new suite with views over the upper lake.*

**Price Guide:**
single from £105
double/twin from £130
suites from £195

The PowderMills, once the site for the production of the finest gunpowder in Europe is now an 18th-century listed country house skilfully converted into an elegant hotel. The beautiful grounds encompass 150 acres of parks, woodland and a 7-acre specimen fishing lake.Close to the historic town of Battle, the hotel adjoins the famous battlefield of 1066 and has been thoughtfully furnished with locally acquired antiques and paintings. On cooler days welcoming log fires burn in the entrance hall and drawing room. Many of the individually decorated bedrooms and junior suites have four-poster beds. Fine classical cooking by chef James Penn is served in the award winning Orangery Restaurant, whilst light meals and snacks are available in the library and conservatory.

**Awards/Recognition:** 1 AA Rosette 2007-2008

**Location:** A21 (A2100), 3 miles; M25 jct5, 50 miles; Battle, 1 mile; Gatwick Airport, 48 miles

**Attractions:** Battle Abbey; Cinque Port Rye; Bodiam Castle; Hastings Old Town

# LANSDOWNE PLACE, BOUTIQUE HOTEL & SPA

LANSDOWNE PLACE, BRIGHTON, EAST SUSSEX BN3 1HQ
**Tel:** 0845 365 1987  **International:** +44 (0)1273 736266  **Fax:** 01273 729802
**Web:** www.johansens.com/lansdowneplace  **E-mail:** info@lansdowneplace.co.uk

***Our inspector loved:*** *The stylish bedrooms and the ultra restful spa facility.*

**Price Guide:**
single from £90
double £140–£400

**Location:** On the A259; A23, 1.5 miles; Brighton Railway Station, 1.3 miles; Gatwick Airport, 40 miles

**Attractions:** Town Centre; The Royal Pavilion; Brighton Racecourse; Lewes

Describing itself as "touch of a class in Brighton's cosmopolitan hub", Lansdowne Place doesn't disappoint. As soon as you enter its spacious seafront lobby you're enveloped by a stylish blend of classic and contemporary. Rooms pay homage to the grandeur of Regency Brighton, with rich fabrics, elegant wallpaper and period lamps, and after a day exploring the south coast you can chill out in the spa before indulging in an Espa treatment inspired by the sea - salt and oil scrubs, aromatherapy facials and detoxifying algae wraps. The Grill's Restaurant uses locally sourced and organic produce where possible, and afterwards you can head to the lounge bar, glass of champagne firmly in hand, and settle yourself on a leopard print bar stool.

# THE GRAND HOTEL

KING EDWARD'S PARADE, EASTBOURNE, EAST SUSSEX BN21 4EQ
**Tel:** 0845 365 2504  **International:** +44 (0)1323 412345  **Fax:** 01323 412233
**Web:** www.johansens.com/grandeastbourne  **E-mail:** reservations@grandeastbourne.com

***Our inspector loved:*** *Traditional service, impeccably delivered.*

**Price Guide:**
single £150–£480
double/twin £180–£510
suite £360–£510

A grand old dame of the Victorian era, the Grand's majestic façade conceals reception rooms adorned with rich fabrics, and many of the 152 bedrooms have vast proportions,all recently refurbished to include every comfort with attractive bathrooms.There are numerous places in which to relax, and a good choice of restaurants and bars - the Mirabelle in particular achieves exceptional standards of fine dining. New leisure facilities include indoor and outdoor pools, gym, sauna, spa bath, steam room, snooker tables, a hair salon and 8 beauty rooms. If you're seeking a peaceful retreat you'll be more than happy with the tranquil atmosphere The Grand Hotel - pastimes include afternoon tea, a nearby golf club,walks along the Downs, sea fishing and trips to nearby theatres.

**Awards/Recognition:** 2 AA Rosettes 2007-2008

**Location:** On the Seafront; A22, 7.5 miles; M23 jct 11, 23 miles; Gatwick Airport, 48 miles

**Attractions:** Beachy Head; Sovereign Harbour; Drusilla's Zoo; The English Wine Centre

# ASHDOWN PARK HOTEL AND COUNTRY CLUB

WYCH CROSS, FOREST ROW, EAST SUSSEX RH18 5JR
**Tel:** 0845 365 2896  **International:** +44 (0)1342 824988  **Fax:** 01342 826206
**Web:** www.johansens.com/ashdownpark  **E-mail:** reservations@ashdownpark.com

**Our inspector loved:** *The newly presented and updated leisure facilities.*

**Price Guide:**
single £150–£370
double/twin £180–£320
suite £330–£400

**Awards/Recognition:** 2 AA Rosettes 2007-2008;

**Location:** A22, 0.5 miles; M25 jct 6, 15 miles; East Grinstead, 5 miles; Gatwick Airport, 16 miles

**Attractions:** Ashdown Forest; Bluebell Railway; Wakehurst Place Gardens; Lingfield Park Racecourse

A grand, rambling 19th-century mansion overlooking nearly 200 acres of landscaped gardens, Ashdown Park is ideally situated to satisfy the needs of escapees from urban stress. You can amble through the grounds and nearby woodland paths, retire to the indoor pool, steam room and sauna or pamper yourself with a visit to the beauty salon. The more energetic among you can indulge in a game of tennis or croquet, and for golfers who cannot survive a weekend without a round, there is an indoor and outdoor driving range and 18-hole par 3 golf course. The Anderida restaurant's menu and wine list are well constructed, with a service that is discreet and attentive.

# HORSTED PLACE COUNTRY HOUSE HOTEL

LITTLE HORSTED, EAST SUSSEX TN22 5TS

**Tel:** 0845 365 1893 **International:** +44 (0)1825 750581 **Fax:** 01825 750459
**Web:** www.johansens.com/horstedplace **E-mail:** hotel@horstedplace.co.uk

Horsted Place sits amidst the peace of the Sussex Downs. This splendid Victorian Gothic Mansion, built in 1851, features an interior predominantly styled by the celebrated Victorian architect, Augustus Pugin. In former years the Queen and Prince Philip were frequent visitors. Guests today are invited to enjoy the excellent service offered by a committed staff. Chef Allan Garth offers a daily fixed price menu as well as the seasonal à la carte menu. The Terrace Room is an elegant and airy private function room, licensed for weddings for up to 100 guests. The smaller Morning Room and Library are ideal for boardroom-style meetings and intimate dinner parties, and the self-contained management centre offers privacy and exclusivity for business meetings in a contemporary setting.

*Our inspector loved:* This welcoming and elegant country house.

**Price Guide:**
double/twin from £130
suite from £220

**Awards/Recognition:** 2 AA Rosettes 2006-2007

**Location:** On the A26; A22, 0.5 miles; Lewes, 6 miles; Gatwick, 25 miles

**Attractions:** Glyndebourne Opera; Sheffield Park Gardens; Bluebell Railway; Regency Brighton

# NEWICK PARK

NEWICK, NEAR LEWES, EAST SUSSEX BN8 4SB
**Tel:** 0845 365 2085  **International:** +44 (0)1825 723633  **Fax:** 01825 723969
**Web:** www.johansens.com/newickpark  **E-mail:** bookings@newickpark.co.uk

***Our inspector loved:*** *The relaxed informality of a fine house in a classic rolling downland setting.*

**Price Guide:**
single from £125
double/twin from £165

**Awards/Recognition:** 2 AA Rosettes 2007-2008

**Location:** A272, 1 mile; M23 jct 11, 18 miles; Lewes, 8 miles; Gatwick Airport, 28 miles

**Attractions:** Racing at Goodwood; Opera at Glyndebourne; Regency Brighton; Bluebell Railway

This magnificent Grade II listed Georgian country house is set in 200 acres of beautiful parkland and landscaped gardens overlooking the Longford River and South Downs. Whilst situated in a convenient location near to the main road and rail routes and only 30 minutes from Gatwick Airport the hotel maintains an atmosphere of complete tranquility and privacy. Bedrooms are decorated in a classic style featuring elegant antiques and friendly staff ensure that you receive a warm welcome. The exquisite dining room offers culinary delights carefully prepared by Head Chef, Chris Moore. The house and grounds are ideal for weddings, conferences and private parties and The Dell gardens primarily planted in Victorian times include a rare collection of Royal Ferns. Exclusive use can be arranged by appointment.

# RYE LODGE

HILDER'S CLIFF, RYE, EAST SUSSEX TN31 7LD
**Tel:** 0845 365 2317  **International:** +44 (0)1797 223838  **Fax:** 01797 223585
**Web:** www.johansens.com/ryelodge  **E-mail:** info@ryelodge.co.uk

***Our inspector loved:*** *The smiling staff who will really go 'the extra mile' to make your stay memorable.*

**Price Guide:**
single from £85
double £140–£200

Rye Lodge is a traditional hotel in the beautiful town of Rye with stunning views across the Estuary and Romney Marshes. The interior décor of the hotel pays homage to its Edwardian exterior that complements a cosy atmosphere. Several of the spacious bedrooms benefit from decked roof terraces. Dining in the Terrace Restaurant with its high ceiling, large windows and elegant Regency-style furniture create a romantic ambience and the hotel's Venetian Leisure Centre is a great place to unwind. Rye is also well known for its hauntings: a ghostly monk is said to parade the hotel's car park and although the owners of 14 years have never seen this cowled spectre, the lands surrounding Rye Lodge were once chapel gardens and monastic cloisters.

**Location:** A259/A268, 0.5 mile; M20 jct 10, 15 miles; Gatwick Airport, 53 miles

**Attractions:** Ancient Rye; Leeds Castle; Bodiam Castles; Sissinghurst

# DALE HILL

TICEHURST, NEAR TUNBRIDGE WELLS, EAST SUSSEX TN5 7DQ
**Tel:** 0845 365 3259  **International:** +44 (0)1580 200112  **Fax:** 01580 201249
**Web:** www.johansens.com/dalehill  **E-mail:** info@dalehill.co.uk

***Our inspector loved:*** *Spacious and comfortable with terrific golf.*

**Price Guide:**
single £110–£130
double/twin £120–£250

**Awards/Recognition:** 1 AA Rosette 2006-2007

**Location:** A21, 1 mile; M25 jct 5, 26 miles; Tunbridge Wells, 11 miles; Gatwick Airport, 57 miles

**Attractions:** Bewl Water; Tunbridge Wells Pantiles; Lamberhurst Vineyard; Bedgebury Pinetum

This stylish,hotel offers you the best of all worlds. Comfortable rooms, award-winning dishes and a fully-equipped health club are an impressive start. Keen golfers can choose between two 18-hole courses, a gently undulating 6,093 yards par 70 and a new, challenging championship standard course designed by former US Masters champion Ian Woosnam. Just a 20-minute drive away, under the same ownership as the hotel, is the Nick Faldo designed Chart Hills course hailed as "the best new course in England". Packages allow you to play both championship courses. You can enjoy glorious views from a choice of restaurants where delicious dishes are complemented by an excellent wine list. If you like fly-fishing then Bewl Water is nearby.

# AMBERLEY CASTLE

AMBERLEY, NEAR ARUNDEL, WEST SUSSEX BN18 9LT
**Tel:** 0845 365 3612 **International:** +44 (0)1798 831992 **Fax:** 01798 831998
**Web:** www.johansens.com/amberleycastle **E-mail:** info@amberleycastle.co.uk

*Our inspector loved:* The unique ambience of being a guest in a real castle - live the dream!

**Price Guide:** (room only)
accommodation £155–£395
suite £235–£395
breakfast £12–£17

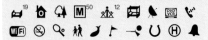

**Awards/Recognition:** 3 AA Rosettes 2006-2007; Relais & Châteaux

**Location:** A29, 3 miles; M23 jct 11, 30 miles; Arundel, 5 miles; Gatwick Airport, 34 miles

**Attractions:** Goodwood Estate; Petworth House; Polo at Cowdray Park

At 900 years Amberley Castle is almost as old as time itself. Set between the rolling South Downs and the calming expanses of the Amberley Wildbrooks. The massive 14th century curtain walls, battlements and mighty portcullis were once built to withstand unwelcome visitors! The opposite is true today, as you will receive a warm and personal welcome and the ultimate in contemporary luxury. 5 distinctive suites have been added in the Bishopric by the main gateway. Each room is individually designed and has its own whirlpool bath. The exquisite 12th-century Queen's Room is the perfect setting for the creative cuisine of the head chef and his team. Amberley Castle is a natural first choice for romantic or cultural weekends, sporting breaks or confidential executive meetings.

# BAILIFFSCOURT HOTEL & SPA

CLIMPING, WEST SUSSEX BN17 5RW
**Tel:** 0845 365 3025  **International:** +44 (0)1903 723511  **Fax:** 01903 723107
**Web:** www.johansens.com/bailiffscourt  **E-mail:** bailiffscourt@hshotels.co.uk

***Our inspector loved:*** *This extraordinary architectural feast - hotel and surrounding buildings will delight.*

**Price Guide:** (including dinner)
single from £165
double from £245
suite from £410

**Awards/Recognition:** 2 AA Rosettes 2006-2007

**Location:** A259, 1 mile; M27 jct 1, 30 miles; Arundel, 6 miles; Gatwick Airport, 44 miles

**Attractions:** Arundel Castle; Goodwood Estate; Chichester Festival Theatre; The Beach

Feel that you've stepped back in time at this perfectly preserved "medieval" manor and out-buildings built in the 1930s using authentic material salvaged from historic old buildings. Gnarled 15th-century beams and gothic mullioned windows recreate the Middle Ages, and many luxurious rooms offer four-poster beds, open log fires and beautiful views across the surrounding countryside. Menus are varied, and in summer you can eat out in the rose-clad courtyard or walled garden. The award-winning health spa features an outdoor Californian hot tub, indoor spa pool, sauna, gym, hammocks and 6 beauty rooms. 2 tennis courts and a croquet lawn complete the on-site leisure facilities, while a private pathway leads 100yds down to Climping beach, ideal for your morning walk.

# MILLSTREAM HOTEL

BOSHAM, NEAR CHICHESTER, WEST SUSSEX PO18 8HL
**Tel:** 0845 365 2067 **International:** +44 (0)1243 573234 **Fax:** 01243 573459
**Web:** www.johansens.com/millstream **E-mail:** info@millstream-hotel.co.uk

**Our inspector loved:** *The delightful setting and guest comfort.*

**Price Guide:**
single £82–£92
double/twin £142–£162
suite £166–£212

Rich in heritage, Bosham village is depicted in the Bayeux Tapestry and King Harold is thought to be buried, alongside King Canute's daughter, in the local Saxon church. This is a yachtsman's idyll on the banks of Chichester Harbour. And close to the harbour is The Millstream a restored 18th-century malthouse and adjoining cottages linked to The Grange, a small English manor house. Across the bridge you will find Waterside a thatched cottage with 2 delightful suites. The bedrooms are decorated in chintz fabrics and pastel tones, while the bar, drawing room and restaurant have been stylishly refurbished. Great emphasis is place on the seasonality and freshness of ingredients used in the restaurant. Locally caught fish like lemon sole, wild sea bass and Selsey crab often feature on the lunch and dinner menus. During winter take a good-value "Hibernation Break".

**Location:** A27, 3 miles; M27 jct 12, 8 miles; Chichester, 4 miles; Gatwick Airport, 45 miles

**Attractions:** Goodwood House and Estate; Chichester Harbour; Chichester Festival Theatre; Fishbourne Roman Palace

# OCKENDEN MANOR

OCKENDEN LANE, CUCKFIELD, WEST SUSSEX RH17 5LD
**Tel:** 0845 365 2093  **International:** +44 (0)1444 416111  **Fax:** 01444 415549
**Web:** www.johansens.com/ockendenmanor  **E-mail:** reservations@ockenden-manor.com

***Our inspector loved:*** *This lovely Elizabethan Manor in its timeless setting.*

**Price Guide:**
single from £110
double from £175
suite from £295

**Awards/Recognition:** 3 AA Rosettes 2007-2008
1 Michelin Star 2007

**Location:** A272, 0.5 mile; M23 jct 10, 4 miles;
Haywards Heath, 2 miles; Gatwick Airport, 18 miles

**Attractions:** Wakehurst and Nymans Gardens;
Glyndebourne Opera; Regency Brighton; Bluebell
Railway

Discover Sussex and Kent, The Garden of England from Ockendon Manor, first recorded in 1520 and now a hotel of great character, charm and hospitality. Rooms are all highly individual, you can climb your private staircase to Thomas or Elizabeth, gaze out across the glorious Sussex countryside from Victoria's bay window or choose Charles, with its handsome four-poster bed. This highly seductive romantic ambience reaches into the wood-panelled restaurant with its beautiful handpainted ceiling, where you can enjoy innovative cooking and an extensive wine list which includes a splendid choice of first-growth clarets. A lovely conservatory, part of the Ockendon Suite, opens onto the lawns where marquees can be set up for summer celebrations. Private dining can be arranged subject to availability.

# The Spread Eagle Hotel & Health Spa

SOUTH STREET, MIDHURST, WEST SUSSEX GU29 9NH
**Tel:** 0845 365 2695 **International:** +44 (0)1730 816911 **Fax:** 01730 815668
**Web:** www.johansens.com/spreadeaglemidhurst **E-mail:** reservations@spreadeagle-midhurst.com.

*Our inspector loved:* The many improvements at this fine old hotel, which in 2007 celebrated 50 years of family ownership.

**Price Guide:**
single £80-£205
double £99-£375
suite £375-£500

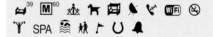

**Awards/Recognition:** 2 AA Rosettes 2007-2008

**Location:** Town Centre; Just off A272/286, 0.2 miles; M25 jct 9, 31 miles; Gatwick Airport, 38 miles

**Attractions:** Petworth; Cowdray Park; Goodwood House and Estate; Chichester Cathedral

Although it's one of England's oldest hotels, dating from 1430 and is rich in charms and period features, The Spread Eagle boasts an outstanding modern Health Spa – with an impressive vaulted glass ceiling and plenty of wet areas. In the restaurant Gary Morton-Jones creates a modern classic menu using seasonal flavours and plenty of local ingredients. The bedrooms are delightful, many with antiques and some with four-posters. The White Room contains a 'secret passage' and is said to have been used by smugglers in their attempt to evade the King's men. This is a great area to explore, after which a cream tea at the Spread Eagle will be well deserved. Childrens high-teas can be arranged and well-behaved dogs are allowed in some bedrooms.

# THE VERMONT HOTEL

CASTLE GARTH, NEWCASTLE-UPON-TYNE, TYNE & WEAR NE1 1RQ
**Tel:** 0845 365 2714  **International:** +44 (0)191 233 1010  **Fax:** 0191 233 1234
**Web:** www.johansens.com/vermont  **E-mail:** info@vermont-hotel.co.uk

**Our inspector loved:** *The excellent service in this City Hotel next to The Castle in the Centre of Newcastle.*

**Price Guide:**
single/double £130
suites from £240

**Awards/Recognition:** 1 AA Rosette 2006-2007

**Location:** A1 M, 2 miles; Newcastle International. Airport, 7 miles

**Attractions:** Newcastle Cathedral; Castle Keep; Durham

The Vermont is Newcastle's only 4-star independent hotel, located next to the Castle, overlooking the Cathedral and the Tyne and Millennium Bridges. This impressive 12 storey, Manhattan-style tower is close to the shops, theatres, galleries, universities and railway station. With direct access to the Quayside and on site free car parking. The 101 bedrooms and suites are a combination of classical and modern design with i-Pod docking stations and 24-hour service.7 meeting rooms are available for special occasions and private dining. The Bridge Restaurant affords spectacular views of the Tyne Bridge, alternatively there is the Redwood Bar, open until late. For those wishing to sample the atmosphere of the famous Quayside, go to Martha's Bar & Courtyard on the ground floor.

# Nailcote Hall

NAILCOTE LANE, BERKSWELL, NEAR SOLIHULL, WARWICKSHIRE CV7 7DE
**Tel:** 0845 365 2078  **International:** +44 (0)2476 466174  **Fax:** 02476 470720
**Web:** www.johansens.com/nailcotehall  **E-mail:** info@nailcotehall.co.uk

*Our inspector loved:* The Elizabethan Mulberry bedroom for its furnishings and views

**Price Guide:**
single £185
double/twin £200
suite £200–£305

Located in the heart of England, Nailcote Hall is a charming Elizabethan country house built in 1640 and used by Oliver Cromwell and his troops during the Civil War. In more peaceful times and fully restored today, it not only tempts you into the intimate Tudor surrounds of the Oak Room restaurant and offers luxury accommodation, it also boasts impressive leisure facilities. Which include a swimming pool, gym, solarium and sauna, outside, all-weather tennis courts, pétanque, croquet, a challenging 9-hole par-3 golf course and putting green - host to the British Championship Professional Short Course Championship. Right in the heart of England, Nailcote Hall is within 15 minutes' drive of the castle towns of Kenilworth and Warwick, Coventry Cathedral, Birmingham International Airport/Station and the NEC.

**Awards/Recognition:** 2 AA Rosettes 2006-2007

**Location:** A452, 2 miles; M42 jct 5, 7 miles; Balsall Common, 3 miles; Birmingham International, 9 miles

**Attractions:** Warwick Castle; Kenilworth Castle; Royal Leamington Spa; Coventry Cathedral

# MALLORY COURT

HARBURY LANE, BISHOPS TACHBROOK, LEAMINGTON SPA, WARWICKSHIRE CV33 9QB
**Tel:** 0845 365 2053 **International:** +44 (0)1926 330214 **Fax:** 01926 451714
**Web:** www.johansens.com/mallorycourt **E-mail:** reception@mallory.co.uk

*Our inspector loved: The sumptuous bedrooms and wonderful menus.*

**Price Guide:**
double (single occupancy) from £125
double from £135
master rooms from £270

**Awards/Recognition:** 1 Star Michelin 2007; 3 AA Rosettes 2006-2007 (Main Restaurant); 1 AA Rosette (Brasserie) 2007-2008; Relais & Châteaux

**Location:** A452, 1 mile; M40 jct 14 (North) & jct 13 (South), 2 miles; Royal Leamington Spa, 2 miles; Birmingham International, 23 miles

**Attractions:** Warwick Castle; Blenheim Palace; Kenilworth Castle; Packwood House

Surrounded by 10 acres of attractive gardens Mallory Court boasts a stunning backdrop across the beautiful Warwickshire countryside, a stone's throw from Stratford-upon-Avon and Warwick Castle. Sip champagne on the terrace before heading off to the Royal Shakespeare Theatre, and for those who don't wish to venture far, cosy up beside log fires. The 30 bedrooms are luxuriously appointed with stunning views across the grounds. The restaurant will happily create tailor-made menus, or simply suspend your diet with roasted Skye scallops, chicken with Avruga caviar, braised shoulder and roasted fillet of Lighthorne lamb and hot passion fruit soufflé ! September 2005 saw the opening of the more informal, yet excellent brasserie for that lighter menu. A truly ravishing venue for weddings and business events.

# BILLESLEY MANOR

BILLESLEY, ALCESTER, NR STRATFORD-UPON-AVON, WARWICKSHIRE B49 6NF
**Tel:** 0845 365 3036  **International:** +44 (0)1789 279955  **Fax:** 01789 764145
**Web:** www.johansens.com/billesley  **E-mail:** bookings@billesleymanor.co.uk

**Our inspector loved:** *The intense dark green of the "sculpted" topiary against the grey local limestone of the main building.*

**Price Guide:**
single £125
double/twin from £180
suite £250

**Awards/Recognition:** 2 AA Rosettes 2006-2007

**Location:** A46, 1 mile; M40 jct 15, 10 miles; Stratford-upon-Avon, 3 miles; Birmingham International Airport, 23 miles

**Attractions:** Shakespeare's Stratford-upon-Avon; Warwick Castle; Ragley Hall; Cotswolds

Right in the heart of England this 16th-century manor house's topiary garden, sun terrace and inevitable Shakespearian connection make it a perfect base for exploring Stratford-upon-Avon, just a few minutes away, but there is plenty to keep you happy within its 11 acres. The Spa incorporates an indoor heated pool, gym, beauty rooms, sauna, solarium and healthy eating bistro. Tennis courts and a croquet lawn are also available. The Cedar Barns offer impressive conference facilities incorporating state-of-the-art equipment, and you can request corporate events such as clay pigeon shooting, archery and quad biking. The house's 72 bedrooms include four-poster rooms and suites, many with garden views, an excellent standard of cuisine is served in the acclaimed Stuart restaurant.

# ETTINGTON PARK

ALDERMINSTER, STRATFORD-UPON-AVON, WARWICKSHIRE CV37 8BU
**Tel:** 0845 365 3286 **International:** +44 (0)1789 450123 **Fax:** 01789 450472
**Web:** www.johansens.com/ettingtonpark **E-mail:** ettingtonpark@handpicked.co.uk

***Our inspector loved:*** *The 21st century bedrooms within a neo-gothic building.*

**Price Guide:**
single from £129
double/twin from £149
suite from £267

**Awards/Recognition:** 2 AA Rosettes 2007-2008

**Location:** A3400, 1 mile; M40 jct 15, 8 miles; Stratford-Upon-Avon, 5 miles; Birmingham International, 31 miles

**Attractions:** Royal Shakespeare Theatre; Warwick Castle; Blenheim Palace; Heritage Motor Centre

Ettington Park resides in 40 acres of Warwickshire parkland with terraced gardens and tended lawns. Its foundations date back at least 1000 years and the building is mentioned in the Domesday Book. Interiors are enhanced by fresh flowers, antiques and fine paintings, amidst such comfortable surroundings all you are required to do is relax, especially in the indoor pool and sauna. The bon viveur will be perfectly at home in the dining room, with its elegant 18th-century Rococo ceiling and excellent French and English dishes accompanied by a fine choice of wines. If you wish to arrange a private party or business meeting there are conference facilities to meet your needs. Both the panelled Long Gallery and the 12th-century Chapel make exceptional venues.

# Ardencote Manor Hotel, Country Club & Spa

LYE GREEN ROAD, CLAVERDON, NR WARWICK, WARWICKSHIRE CV35 8LT
**Tel:** 0845 365 3615 **International:** +44 (0)1926 843111 **Fax:** 01926 842646
**Web:** www.johansens.com/ardencote **E-mail:** hotel@ardencote.com

***Our inspector loved:*** *The food and service in The Lodge Restaurant.*

**Price Guide:**
single from £90
double from £130
suite from £240

**Awards/Recognition:** 2 AA Rosettes 2006-2007

**Location:** A4189, 1 mile; Warwick, 5-min drive; M40 exit 16, 12-min drive; Birmingham International, 20-min drive

**Attractions:** Warwick Castle; Stratford-upon-Avon; Kenilworth; Hatton Locks

Built as a Gentlemen's residence in 1860, and now under private ownership, the house has been sympathetically refurbished and substantially extended to create a luxury hotel retaining its traditional elegance and appealing intimacy. Make the most of the well appointed bedrooms – many with views over the lake and gardens – and extensive sports and leisure facilities, including an indoor pool, spa bath, outdoor whirlpool, sauna and steamrooms. Squash and tennis courts, fully equipped gymnasia and 9-hole golf course are also provided. The spa offers an extensive choice of relaxing, holistic treatments. And dinner at the award-winning lakeside Lodge restaurant is a treat. Visits to Warwick Castle are available (at special rates) through the hotel, and you can brush up on your Shakespeare in Stratford-upon-Avon.

# WROXALL ABBEY ESTATE

BIRMINGHAM ROAD, WROXALL, NEAR WARWICK, WARWICKSHIRE CV35 7NB
**Tel:** 0845 365 2835 **International:** +44 (0)1926 484470 **Fax:** 01926 485206
**Web:** www.johansens.com/wroxallcourt **E-mail:** reservation@wroxall.com

***Our inspector loved:*** *Wren's Chapel and the walled garden.*

**Price Guide:**
single from £89
double from £109
suite from £249

**Location:** On the A4141; M42 jct 5, 12 miles; Warwick, 5 miles; Birmingham International Airport, 16 miles

**Attractions:** Warwick Castle; Stratford-upon-Avon; NEC

This recently restored and impressive listed building, set in 27 acres of landscaped gardens, features comfortable public rooms and a beautiful chapel that define the character of this country estate, once the home of Sir Christopher Wren. A spacious marquee situated in the grounds will accommodate all your entertainment needs, whether a wedding or a special anniversary party. You'll find that this is a romantic place for the perfect escape, where each bedroom is different - many have four-poster beds and original marble fireplaces, whilst bathrooms have separate walk-in showers and whirlpool baths. Whatever the occasion, you'll find a choice of menus to suit your mood, from the a la carte to the informal bistro menu, which are both served in the elegant Sonnets restaurant, next to the classic Broadwood Bar and Garden Lounge.

# LUCKNAM PARK, BATH

COLERNE, CHIPPENHAM, WILTSHIRE SN14 8AZ
**Tel:** 0845 365 2048  **International:** +44 (0)1225 742777  **Fax:** 01225 743536
**Web:** www.johansens.com/lucknampark  **E-mail:** reservations@lucknampark.co.uk

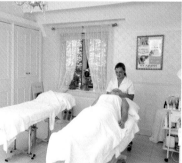

**Our inspector loved:** *The beautiful mile long driveway that sets you up for a wonderfully luxurious experience.*

**Price Guide:** (room only)
single/double/twin from £255
suite from £560

**Awards/Recognition:** 1 Star Michelin 2007; Relais & Châteaux; 3 AA Rosettes 2007-2008

**Location:** A420, 1.5 miles; M4 jct 18, 9 miles; Bristol, 20 miles

**Attractions:** Bath; Lacock; Castle Combe; Westonbirt Arboretum

Built in 1720 at the end of a mile long beech and lime tree lined avenue, this magnificent Palladian mansion, with its 5 AA red stars has always been host to fine society and sophisticated living. The delicate aura of historical context is reflected in fine art and antiques dating from the late Georgian and early Victorian periods. Award winning cuisine can be enjoyed in the elegant Park Restaurant, where tables are laid with exquisite porcelain, silver and glassware, accompanied with excellent wines from an extensive cellar. Set within the gardens of the hotel is the beauty salon offering an impressive range of treatments. A new luxury spa is due to open in the Summer of 2008. The Equestrian Centre welcomes complete beginners, experienced riders and also accepts liveries. Winners in 2007 of the Andrew Harper Grand Hideaway of the year award and the Relais & Châteaux Welcome Trophy.

# WOOLLEY GRANGE

WOOLLEY GREEN, BRADFORD-ON-AVON, WILTSHIRE BA15 1TX
**Tel:** 0845 365 2831 **International:** +44 (0)1225 864705 **Fax:** 01225 864059
**Web:** www.johansens.com/woolleygrange **E-mail:** info@woolleygrangehotel.co.uk

**Our inspector loved:** *A lovely hotel in a pretty location, a perfect retreat for all the family.*

**Price Guide:**
single from £120
double/twin £150–£280
suite from £200–£365

**Awards/Recognition:** 2 AA Rosettes 2006-2007

**Location:** Just off B3105; M4 jct 18, 16 miles; Bath, 8 miles

**Attractions:** Longleat Safari Park; Bath Thermae Spa; Bradford-on-Avon; Stonehenge

Gorgeous views, slightly eclectic, warm and very homey. A 17th-century Jacobean manor manages to be both luxurious and extremely accommodating to its younger guests. In the Victorian coach house there's a huge games room and well-equipped nursery where full-time nannies will look after your children for 2 hours at a time from 10am-4.45pm every day. At this point parents can head out to explore the region or indulge in a in-room massage before lying in a cosy corner with a good book. The Grange's reputation for food is outstanding, largely thanks to the chef who creates sophisticated country house food using local farm produce and organically grown fruit and vegetables from the Victorian kitchen gardens. A children's lunch and tea are provided daily.

# WHATLEY MANOR

EASTON GREY, MALMESBURY, WILTSHIRE SN16 0RB

**Tel:** 0845 365 2801 **International:** +44 (0)1666 822888 **Fax:** 01666 826120
**Web:** www.johansens.com/whatley **E-mail:** reservations@whatleymanor.com

*Our inspector loved: The truly spoiling experience of the bedrooms, spa and food.*

**Price Guide:** (including use of spa facilities)
single from £285
superior/deluxe £335-£485
suite £650-£850

Very careful attention to detail has created this beautifully designed stylish and sophisticated retreat that never quite stops feeling like a family owned country home. The 15 bedrooms and 8 suites are furnished with Italian furniture and handmade French wallpaper, and are equipped with sound and vision systems to keep you blissfully occupied. There are 2 gastronomic experiences on offer: the intimate Dining Room, echoing the sumptuousness of the hotel, and the more informal Le Mazot with its refreshingly alternative Swiss interior. The highly acclaimed spa, Aquarias, includes one of the UK's largest hydrotherapy pools as well as a La Prairie "Art of Beauty" centre. A private cinema can accommodate up to 40 people, and the encompassing gardens have plenty of spaces for you to escape to.

**Awards/Recognition:** 1 Star Michelin 2007; Condé Nast Johansens Most Excellent Spa 2005; 3 AA Rosettes 2006-2007; Relais & Châteaux

**Location:** Off the B4040; A429, 3 miles; M4 jct 17, 8 miles; London, 75-min train

**Attractions:** The Cotswolds; Bath; Malmesbury House Abbey House Gardens; Westonbirt Arboretum

# HOWARD'S HOUSE

TEFFONT EVIAS, SALISBURY, WILTSHIRE SP3 5RJ
**Tel:** 0845 365 1905 **International:** +44 (0)1722 716392 **Fax:** 01722 716820
**Web:** www.johansens.com/howardshouse **E-mail:** enq@howardshousehotel.com

**Our inspector loved:** *Sitting on the terrace overlooking the gardens.*

**Price Guide:**
single £105
double/twin £165–£185

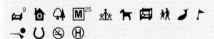

**Location:** Just off B3089; A303, 3 miles; Salisbury, 10 miles

**Attractions:** Salisbury Cathedral; Stonehenge; Stourhead Gardens; Longleat

Tucked away in the depths of rural Wiltshire you can easily be persuaded to curl up by the fire in winter with a good book and glass of port, or listen to the tinkling of the fountain in the lily pond while inhaling fragrant jasmine through open windows in summer. Howard's House in the quintessential English hamlet of Teffont Evias is a charming small country house hotel, with thoughtful touches of fresh fruit, homemade biscuits and glossy mags in the bedroom. Home-grown and local produce is transformed into modern British cuisine with flair and imagination in the award-winning restaurant. An ideal escape, the hotel is 9 miles from Stonehenge, and ideally situated for visiting Salisbury Cathedral, Wilton House and Stourhead Gardens.

# THE PEAR TREE AT PURTON

CHURCH END, PURTON, SWINDON, WILTSHIRE SN5 4ED
**Tel:** 0845 365 2635  **International:** +44 (0)1793 772100  **Fax:** 01793 772369
**Web:** www.johansens.com/peartree  **E-mail:** relax@peartreepurton.co.uk

***Our inspector loved:*** *The extensive, well-kept gardens, including a wetland area and vineyard*

**Price Guide:**
single £110
double/twin £110–£135
suite £135

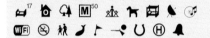

Owners Francis and Anne Young are justly proud of their achievements at this lovely honey-coloured stone hotel, nestling in the Vale of the White Horse between the Cotswolds and Marlborough Downs. It has received many awards for excellence and you will understand why as you enjoy good English food in the conservatory restaurant overlooking beautiful gardens or rest in the well-appointed bedrooms and suites with digital TV, safe and other little essential luxuries. Each bedroom is named after a character associated with the Saxon village of Purton, such as Anne Hyde, mother of Queen Mary II, and Queen Anne. Explore some of the history for yourself at the unique twin-towered Parish Church and the ancient hill fort of Ringsbury Camp.

**Awards/Recognition:** 2 AA Rosettes 2007-2008

**Location:** B4534, 2.3 miles; A3102, 3.3 miles; M4 jct 16, 3.7 miles; Swindon, 5 miles

**Attractions:** Avebury; Bowood House; Bath; Cirencester

# BISHOPSTROW HOUSE & SPA

WARMINSTER, WILTSHIRE BA12 9HH
**Tel:** 0845 365 3038  **International:** +44 (0)1985 212312  **Fax:** 01985 216769
**Web:** www.johansens.com/bishopstrowhouse  **E-mail:** info@bishopstrow.co.uk

*Our inspector loved: The peaceful setting with good service and relaxing atmosphere.*

**Price Guide:**
single from £99
double/twin £160–£245
suite from £330

**Awards/Recognition:** 2 AA Rosettes 2006-2007

**Location:** On the B3414; A303, 10 miles; Bristol International Airport, 38 miles; M3 jct 8, 40 miles

**Attractions:** Bath; Longleat; Stourhead; Stonehenge;

This ivy-clad, Grade II listed Georgian mansion is an intimate country retreat with comfortable contemporary facilities and the not to be missed luxurious Bishopstrow Spa. Attention to detail is uppermost in the library, drawing room and conservatory with their beautiful antiques and Victorian oil paintings, you should be pleased with the grandly furnished bedrooms. You can take pleasure in tasting skilfully prepared modern British food in the Mulberry Restaurant, or lighter meals in the Mulberry Bar and conservatory overlooking 27 acres of gardens. There is an indoor and outdoor heated swimming pool, gym and sauna, fly fishing on the hotel's private stretch of the River Wylye, golf at 5 nearby courses, riding, game and clay pigeon shooting.

# THE ELMS

STOCKTON ROAD, ABBERLEY, WORCESTERSHIRE WR6 6AT
**Tel:** 0845 365 2485 **International:** +44 (0)1299 896666 **Fax:** 01299 896804
**Web:** www.johansens.com/elmsworcester **E-mail:** info@theelmshotel.co.uk

*Our inspector loved:* The entrance area with rugs, flagstones and an open fire in winter.

**Price Guide:**
single £85–£275
double/twin £100–£290

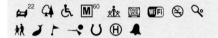

**Awards/Recognition:** 2 AA Rosettes 2006-2007

**Location:** On the A443; M5 jct 5/ 6, 11.5 miles; Birmingham International Airport, 29 miles

**Attractions:** West Midlands Safari Park; Severn Valley Railway, Cadbury World; Witley Court

Built in 1710 by a pupil of the great Sir Christopher Wren, this fine Queen Anne mansion sits between Worcester and Tenbury Wells. Surrounded by beautiful meadows, woodland, hop fields and orchards of cider apples and cherries of the Teme Valley, whose river runs crimson from red sandstone when in flood, The Elms is now a member of the Luxury Family Hotel group. Children will love it here. There is a supervised Ofsted registered crèche/playroom, babysitting services and listening devices available, and older children will be occupied with the many activities on offer including trampolining and game consoles. There are 17 bedrooms located in the main house and 5 found in the characterful coach-house, and a handsome restaurant serving sophisticated, imaginative dishes prepared by Head Chef Daren Bale alongside a well-selected fine wine list. A spa and new function room will be opening in 2008.

# DORMY HOUSE

WILLERSEY HILL, BROADWAY, WORCESTERSHIRE WR12 7LF
**Tel:** 0845 365 3269 **International:** +44 (0)1386 852711 **Fax:** 01386 858636
**Web:** www.johansens.com/dormyhouse **E-mail:** reservations@dormyhouse.co.uk

**Our inspector loved:** *The fabulous penthouse suite.*

**Price Guide:**
single from £124
double/twin from £180
suite from £230

**Awards/Recognition:** 2 AA Rosettes 2007-2008

**Location:** A44, 0.60 mile; Broadway, 3 miles; M40 jct 8 or 15, 25 miles; Birmingham International, 41 miles

**Attractions:** Cotswolds; Cheltenham; Worcester; Stratford-upon-Avon

Dormy House aims to be a home-away-from-home and with its cosy rooms, postcard pretty landscape and above all, unstuffy service and atmosphere, you might well wish this was your own abode. Its 17th-century stone walls, log fires and discreet alcoves draw you in, and quintessentially English rooms feature rich fabrics, carved headboards and plump cushions. Enjoy the locally-sourced produce served in The Dining Room or the gastropub menu in the popular Barn Owl bar. You can swing a golf club or mallet on the 9-hole putting green or croquet lawn, have a round of bar billiards in the games room and relax in the sauna and steam room. The beautiful village of Broadway and the surrounding Cotswolds are right on the doorstep.

# THE LYGON ARMS

BROADWAY, WORCESTERSHIRE WR12 7DU
**Tel:** 0845 365 2586 **International:** +44 (0)1386 852255 **Fax:** 01386 854470
**Web:** www.johansens.com/lygonarms **E-mail:** reservations@thelygonarms.co.uk

***Our inspector loved:*** *The comprehensive restoration that has brought the new Lygon back to and beyond its former glory.*

**Price Guide:**
single from £101
double/twin from £113
suite from £263

**Location:** On the B4632; A44, 1 mile; M5 jct 9, 15 miles; London, 2-hour drive

**Attractions:** Snowshill Manor; Sudeley Castle; The Cotswolds, Stratford-upon-Avon

The Lygon Arms has been welcoming travellers since the 16th century, and today, its charm and sense of occasion is as pronounced as ever. Offering the best of modern comfort, this landmark property underwent an ambitious restoration project throughout 2007 that successfully retained the very heart and sole of the hotel that continues to be synonymous with first-class, worldwide quality. With 67 rooms and 8 stunning suites, some dating back to 1532, half of the bedrooms are in the main house while the other half are located in the award-winning Garden and Orchard Wings. For a sense of sheer drama look no further than the Great Hall; this elegant dining room has been internationally recognised for its food, ambience and service, and offers flawless attention to detail that will ensure every occasion is memorable. Adjoining The Lygon Arms is Goblets, an informal brasserie serving original interpretations of traditional English fare.

# BUCKLAND MANOR

BUCKLAND, NEAR BROADWAY, WORCESTERSHIRE WR12 7LY
**Tel:** 0845 365 3210 **International:** +44 (0)1386 852626 **Fax:** 01386 853557
**Web:** www.johansens.com/bucklandmanor **E-mail:** info@bucklandmanor.co.uk

***Our inspector loved:*** *The entrancing view of the gardens from the sumptuous Fountain room.*

**Price Guide:**
single £260-£470
double £270-£470

**Awards/Recognition:** 3 AA Rosettes 2007-2008; Relais & Châteaux

**Location:** A44, 3 miles; M40 jct 8, 45 miles; Broadway, 2.5 miles; Evesham, 9 miles

**Attractions:** Sudeley Castle; Snowshill Manor; Cotswolds; Stratford-upon-Avon

You can almost feel the warm glow of Buckland Manor's golden Cotswold stone, and willl be dying to get to the luxury and history behind its weather-beaten walls. First mentioned in the records of Gloucester Abbey in 600AD, the Abbot received it as a gift from Kynred, ruler of Mercia and chief king of the 7 kingdoms of England. It remains gracious and traditional, and glorious grounds reveal small waterfalls, tennis courts, putting green and croquet lawns. Relax before log fires in 3 delightfully decorated drawing rooms, one with wood panelling and a beamed ceiling. Delightful bedrooms with lovely furnishings and bathrooms that use water from the Manor's own spring. Chef, Matt Hodgkin's cuisine is delicious and award-winning.

# BROCKENCOTE HALL

CHADDESLEY CORBETT, NR KIDDERMINSTER, WORCESTERSHIRE DY10 4PY
**Tel:** 0845 365 3204 **International:** +44 (0)1562 777876 **Fax:** 01562 777872
**Web:** www.johansens.com/brockencotehall **E-mail:** info@brockencotehall.com

*Our inspector loved:* The new bar with its striking colour scheme carried through to the conservatory.

**Price Guide:**
single from £96
double/twin from £120
four poster from £152

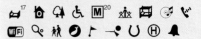

In an unspoilt corner of English countryside, the Brockencote estate reaches back over three centuries, and its gatehouse, lake, half-timbered dovecote, European and North American trees and elegant conservatory give you a flavour of the changes in fashion and taste over the years.This multi award winning hotel including 3 AA Red Stars is matched by the Hall's friendly staff. Owners Alison and Joseph Petitjean provide excellent service.In true country house style each bedroom is different, and interiors combine classical architecture with creature comforts and elaborate décor.The Hall specialises in traditional French cuisine with occasional regional and seasonal dishes.. Just to the south of Birmingham, you'll find it convenient situated whether travelling for business or pleasure, and a fine base for touring historic Worcestershire.

**Awards/Recognition:** 2 AA Rosettes 2006-2007

**Location:** on the A448; M42 jct 1, 8 miles; M5 jct 4, 12 miles; Birmingham International Airport, 28 miles

**Attractions:** Severn Valley Railway; Worcester Cathedral & Porcelain Museum; Ironbridge Gorge; Warwick Castle

# THE EVESHAM HOTEL

COOPER'S LANE, OFF WATERSIDE, EVESHAM, WORCESTERSHIRE WR11 1DA
**Tel:** 0845 365 2487 **International:** +44 (0)1386 765566 **US toll free:** Reservations: 0800 716969 **Fax:** 01386 765443
**Web:** www.johansens.com/evesham **E-mail:** reception@eveshamhotel.com

**Our inspector loved:** *Everything - and don't miss the UK's Best Loos (both!).*

**Price Guide:**
single £78–£92
double/twin £128
family suite £173

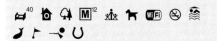

**Awards/Recognition:** 1 AA Rosette 2007-2008

**Location:** Just off B4035; A44/A46, 1 mile; M5 jct 9, 11 miles; Birmingham Airport, 34 miles

**Attractions:** The Cotswolds; Warwick; Stratford-upon-Avon; Severn Valley

It's the appealingly unconventional atmosphere at the Evesham Hotel that sticks in your mind! Combining a refreshing, award-winning welcome to families with style and efficiency, it has been very successfully run by the Jenkinsons for the past 30 years. All bedrooms come complete with a teddy bear and toy duck for the bath, and the restaurant menus are imaginative and versatile. And somewhat unique is the "Euro-sceptic" wine list - everything but French and German! However, the full drinks selection is dazzling. An indoor pool has a seaside theme, while the peace of the 2.5 acre garden belies the hotel's proximity to the town - a 5-minute walk away. In the gardens are six 300-year-old mulberry trees and a magnificent cedar of Lebanon, planted in 1809. Closed at Christmas.

# THE COTTAGE IN THE WOOD

HOLYWELL ROAD, MALVERN WELLS, WORCESTERSHIRE WR14 4LG
**Tel:** 0845 365 2431 **International:** +44 (0)1684 575859 **Fax:** 01684 560662
**Web:** www.johansens.com/cottageinthewood **E-mail:** reception@cottageinthewood.co.uk

*Our inspector loved: The secluded and well-appointed bedrooms in "The Pinnacles".*

**Price Guide:**
single £79–£109
double/twin £99–£179

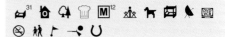

**Awards/Recognition:** Condé Nast Johansens / Taittinger Wine List Award 2006; 2 AA Rosettes 2006-2007

**Location:** A449, 0.25 mile; M5 jct 7/8, 15 miles; Birmingham Airport, 48 miles

**Attractions:** Hereford Cathedral; Three Counties Showground; The Cotswolds; Various Historic Castles & Gardens

The Malvern Hills - once home and inspiration for England's great composer, Sir Edward Elgar - provide a 30 mile Severn Valley outlook from The Cottage in the Wood. Accommodation is both in the main house, originally the Dower House to the Blackmore Park Estate, in Beech Cottage - an old scrumpy house - and the magnificent new building "The Pinnacles", whose rooms with patios or balconies boast spectacular views. Owned and run by 2 generations of the Pattin family, the hotel's atmosphere is genuinely warm and relaxing, and a regularly changing modern English menu is complemented by an almost obsessional wine list of 600 bins. If you are a little over-indulgent then take a walk to the tops of the Malvern Hills direct from the hotel grounds.

# THE DEVONSHIRE ARMS COUNTRY HOUSE HOTEL & SPA

BOLTON ABBEY, SKIPTON, NORTH YORKSHIRE BD23 6AJ
**Tel:** 0845 365 2461 **International:** +44 (0)1756 718111 **Fax:** 01756 710564
**Web:** www.johansens.com/devonshirearms **E-mail:** res@devonshirehotels.co.uk

***Our inspector loved:*** *The relaxed, informal and unstuffy ambience.*

**Price Guide:**
single £175–£370
double/twin £220–£380
suite £380-£420

**Awards/Recognition:** Condé Nast Johansens / Taittinger Wine List Award 2005; 1 Star Michelin 2007; 4 AA Rosettes 2007-2008

**Location:** On the B6160; A59, 400yds; Skipton, 6 miles; Leeds Bradford Airport, 12 miles

**Attractions:** Bolton Abbey Estate & Priory; Fountains Abbey & Studley Royal Water Garden; Fly Fishing on the River Wharfe; Harrogate for shopping and antiques

Reflecting its idyllic Yorkshire Dales setting, The Devonshire offers you a peaceful, welcome and relaxing escape, amidst 30,000 acres of rolling parkland, far from the bustling crowds. Owned by the Duke and Duchess of Devonshire the hotel features paintings from the Devonshire Collection at Chatsworth. You will be very easily enticed by the fine dishes created by Michelin Star Executive Head Chef Michael Wignall in the elegant Burlington Restaurant - allow time to peruse the wine list of over 2,500 labels - or soak up the lively décor and contemporary art of the informal Brasserie and Bar. Make the most of a full range of leisure, health and beauty therapy facilities in the Spa, housed in a converted 17th-century barn. All this on the doorstep of the Bolton Abbey Estate with its 80 miles of footpaths, nature walks and hiking trails, church and ruins of the 12th century Augustinian Priory and picturesque village.

# GRINKLE PARK HOTEL

GRINKLE LANE, EASINGTON, SALTBURN-BY-THE-SEA, CLEVELAND TS13 4UB
**Tel:** 0845 365 3421 **International:** +44 (0)1287 640515 **Fax:** 01287 641278
**Web:** www.johansens.com/grinklepark **E-mail:** info.grinklepark@classiclodges.co.uk

***Our inspector loved:*** *The peaceful setting of this traditional country house hotel.*

**Price Guide:**
single £80-£120
double £120-£175

**Location:** A171, 2 miles; Guisborough, 9 miles; Whitby, 12 miles; Teesside Airport, 22 miles

**Attractions:** North York Moors National Park; Whitby Abbey; Goathland & Heartbeat Country; North York Moors Steam Railway

Set in the North Yorkshire National Park this 1880s, impressive baronial house stands in 35 acres of parkland and flower-abundant gardens. If you are an outdoor sports enthusiast you will no doubt appreciate the surrounding 3000 acre estate which is recognised as one of the north of England's leading shooting estates. After a bracing day outside the individually furnished bedrooms offer welcome home comforts. The house retains many original features, including extensive wood panelling and high embossed ceilings. Roaring log fires warm the comfortable lounge and bar. The inviting dining room, with immaculately dressed tables, leads to the veranda with garden-views and offers a unique dining experience; the table d'Hôte and á la carte menus use only the finest, freshest local ingredients. Well-behaved dogs are welcome.

# GRANTS HOTEL

SWAN ROAD, HARROGATE, NORTH YORKSHIRE HG1 2SS
**Tel:** 0845 365 1784  **International:** +44 (0)1423 560666  **Fax:** 01423 502550
**Web:** www.johansens.com/grants  **E-mail:** enquiries@grantshotel-harrogate.com

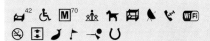

***Our inspector loved:*** *The close proximity to the centre of Harrogate.*

**Price Guide:**
single £105–£125
double/twin £110–£160
suites £168

**Location:** Harrogate Conference Centre, 5-min walk; A61, 150yds; A1M jct 46, 10 miles; Harrogate Train Station, 8-min walk

**Attractions:** Harrogate; Fountains Abbey & Studley Royal Water Gardens; Harewood House; Harlow Carr RHS Gardens

Follow in the footsteps of the fashionable 19th-century set who came to Harrogate to "take the waters" of the famous spa, and take advantage of staying at friendly, hospitable Grants Hotel. Created by Pam and Peter Grant, bedrooms are comfortable, whilst downstairs you can relax in the lounge or go for drinks in Harry Grant's Bar, or on the terrace gardens. Menus are traditional rustic, with a smattering of Oriental influence, served in the French café-style Chimney Pots Bistro, complete with brightly coloured check blinds and Beryl Cook prints. Don't miss out on mouth-watering home-made puddings. Grants also offers its own meeting and syndicate rooms, the Herriot Suite. The Royal Pump Room Museum and the Royal Baths Assembly Rooms are nearby.

# HOB GREEN HOTEL, RESTAURANT & GARDENS

MARKINGTON, HARROGATE, NORTH YORKSHIRE HG3 3PJ
**Tel:** 0845 365 1867 **International:** +44 (0)1423 770031 **Fax:** 01423 771589
**Web:** www.johansens.com/hobgreen **E-mail:** info@hobgreen.com

*Our inspector loved:* Strolling around the large, lovingly tended Victorian walled herb, vegetable and cutting flower garden.

**Price Guide:**
single £95–£118
double/twin £110–£155
suite £135–£175

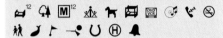

A charming "country house" set in 870 acres of farm and woodland, Hob Green gazes upon some of Yorkshire's most dramatic scenery. Bedrooms are tasteful, and the drawing room and hall, warmed by log fires in cool weather, are comfortably furnished. Sit, relax and "antique spot" the gorgeous furniture, porcelain and pictures. The restaurant's reputation is excellent, and much of its fresh produce grows in the hotel's own garden. Interesting menus are complemented by a good choice of wines, which are sensibly priced. Every whim is catered for here, so all you need to do is enjoy it! For a dose of culture and history, Fountains Abbey and Studley Royal Water Gardens are nearby, or you can ride at the Yorkshire Riding Centre.

**Location:** A61, 2.5 miles; A1 M jct 17, 7 miles; Harrogate, 4.5 miles

**Attractions:** Historic City of Ripon; Ripon Racecourse; Harrogates; Fountains Abbey and Studley Royal Water Gardens (NT)

# SIMONSTONE HALL

HAWES, NORTH YORKSHIRE DL8 3LY
**Tel:** 0845 365 2348  **International:** +44 (0)1969 667255  **Fax:** 01969 667741
**Web:** www.johansens.com/simonstonehall  **E-mail:** email@simonstonehall.demon.co.uk

*Our inspector loved:* The wonderful setting with stunning views across Upper Wensleydale.

**Price Guide:**
single £75–£120
double/twin £110–£190

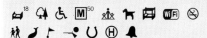

**Location:** A684, 1.5 miles; Hawes, 1.5 miles

**Attractions:** Hardraw Force; Wensleydale Creamery Cheese Factory; Yorkshire Dales; Bolton Castle

This former 18th-century hunting lodge has been lovingly restored and furnished with antiques, to create an idyllic and memorable retreat. The hall stands in a beautiful setting adjacent to 4,000 acres of grouse moors and upland grazing. Many period features have been retained such as the panelled dining room, mahogany staircase with ancestral stained glass windows and a lounge with ornamental ceilings. The bedrooms are of a high standard, 5 which offer four-poster and 2 with sleigh beds. In the restaurant, you can enjoy the freshest local produce presented most imaginatively,whilst absorbing stunning views across Upper Wensleydale. Excellent wines are available to complement any dish. Traditional country cuisine is served in the Game Tavern and The Orangery which provide a particularly warm and informal atmosphere.

# THE PHEASANT

HAROME, HELMSLEY, NORTH YORKSHIRE YO62 5JG
**Tel:** 0845 365 2641 **International:** +44 (0)1439 771241 **Fax:** 01439 771744
**Web:** www.johansens.com/pheasanthelmsley **E-mail:** reservations@thepheasanthotel.com

***Our inspector loved:*** *The friendly and relaxed ambience in this family-run hotel.*

**Price Guide:** (including 5-course dinner)
single £82–£98
double/twin £164–£178

**Location:** A170, 2 miles; Helmsley, 3 miles; York, 25 miles

**Attractions:** Rievaulx Abbeys; Castle Howard; Duncombe Park; North York Moors National Park

The Pheasant, rich in oak beams and open log fires, offers 2 types of accommodation, some in the hotel and some in a charming, 16th-century thatched cottage. The Binks family, who built the hotel have created a friendly atmosphere which is an essential part of the warm Yorkshire welcome that awaits you. The bedrooms and suites are brightly decorated in an attractive cottage style. Traditional English cooking is the speciality of the restaurant and many of the dishes are prepared using local fresh fruit and vegetables. During summer, guests may relax on the terrace overlooking the pond. An indoor heated swimming pool is an added attraction and dogs are most welcome if prior notice is given. Closed Christmas, January and February.

# JUDGES COUNTRY HOUSE HOTEL

KIRKLEVINGTON HALL, KIRKLEVINGTON, YARM, NORTH YORKSHIRE TS15 9LW
**Tel:** 0845 365 1928 **International:** +44 (0)1642 789000 **Fax:** 01642 782878
**Web:** www.johansens.com/judges **E-mail:** enquiries@judgeshotel.co.uk

***Our inspector loved:*** *The friendly, attentive staff and the pet goldfish in every bedroom.*

**Price Guide:**
single £149–£163
double/twin £179–£194

**Awards/Recognition:** 3 AA Rosettes 2007-2008

**Location:** A67, 0.1 miles; A19, 1.5 miles; Yarm, 1.5 miles

**Attractions:** Historic city of Durham; Croft Motor racing circuit; Cleveland Hills; North Yorkshire Moors

Located within 31 acres of idyllic landscaped gardens and woodlands, this charming country house hotel is an oasis of peace. The luxurious interior design makes it easy to relax and unwind from the stresses of daily life. Public rooms are elegantly decorated with fine fabrics, and you are surrounded by books, paintings and antiques. The bedrooms are very comfortable and each includes a foot spa, an iPod docking station and a pet goldfish ! Some rooms have Jacuzzi baths and all have an evening turndown service. Menus feature a 6-course meal which is served in the Conservatory Restaurant, accompanied by the finest of wines. Private dining is available, perfect for parties or the family. The hotel's location makes it ideal for exploring a host of attractions in the North East.

# THE GRANGE HOTEL

1 CLIFTON, YORK, NORTH YORKSHIRE YO30 6AA
**Tel:** 0845 365 2507 **International:** +44 (0)1904 644744 **Fax:** 01904 612453
**Web:** www.johansens.com/grangeyork **E-mail:** info@grangehotel.co.uk

*Our inspector loved: The stunning orchid arrangement in the York stone-paved front hall.*

**Price Guide:**
single £115–£190
double/twin £135–£225
suite £265

**Awards/Recognition:** 2 AA Rosettes 2006-2007

**Location:** York City Centre, 1 mile; A1237, 1.5 miles; AiM, 10 miles

**Attractions:** York Minster; Castle Howard; Yorkshire Dales and Moors; Leeds

Take a short walk from the world-famous Minster to find this sophisticated Regency town house, where beautiful stone-flagged floors lead to classic, richly decorated receptions rooms. The flower-filled Morning Room swallows you up with deep sofas and blazing fire in winter months, while antiques and English chintz reflect the proprietor's careful attention to detail in the bedrooms. Double doors between the panelled library and drawing room can be thrown open, creating a perfect venue for social and business events. Recently refurbished, the Ivy Brasserie has an excellent reputation for food, and the Cellar Bar welcomes you for lunch Monday to Saturday and dinner every night until the theatres close. York's list of attractions include the National Railway Museum and the medieval Shambles.

# MIDDLETHORPE HALL HOTEL, RESTAURANT & SPA

BISHOPTHORPE ROAD, YORK, NORTH YORKSHIRE YO23 2GB
**Tel:** 0845 365 2061 **International:** +44 (0)1904 641241 **Fax:** 01904 620176
**Web:** www.johansens.com/middlethorpehall **E-mail:** info@middlethorpe.com

***Our inspector loved:*** *The organic walled garden and the Spa in the adjacent cottages.*

**Price Guide:**
single £125–£175
double/twin £185–£330
suite from £275–£450

**Awards/Recognition:** 3 AA Rosettes 2006-2007

**Location:** A1036, 1.7 miles; A64, 3 miles; A1(M), 12.6 miles; Leeds, 23.3 miles

**Attractions:** York; York Racecourse; Castle Howard; Fountains and Rievaulx Abbey

This imposing William III house stands in 20 acres of gardens and parkland overlooking York Racecourse. Originally built in 1699 for Thomas Barlow, a wealthy merchant, Middlethorpe Hall was for a time the home of Lady Mary Wortley Montagu, the 18th-century diarist. It is now an immaculately restored example of its period renovated by Historic House Hotels. Each room is filled with period furniture and paintings, and the beautifully decorated bedrooms and suites are located in the main house and 18th-century courtyard. There is also a private cottage comprising 2 suites. The panelled dining rooms look out to the gardens and offer the best in contemporary English cooking that is rapidly gaining well-deserved recognition for its imaginative cuisine that maintains traditional brilliance. Treat yourself with a trip to the health and fitness spa with inviting pool and treatment rooms.

# THE WORSLEY ARMS HOTEL

HOVINGHAM, NEAR YORK, NORTH YORKSHIRE YO62 4LA
**Tel:** 0845 365 2746 **International:** +44 (0)1653 628234 **Fax:** 01653 628130
**Web:** www.johansens.com/worsleyarms **E-mail:** enquires@worsleyarms.co.uk

*Our inspector loved: Walking around the wine cellar choosing the wine for dinner.*

**Price Guide:**
single £85–£110
double/twin £115–£200

**Awards/Recognition:** 1 AA Rosette 2007-2008

**Location:** On the B1257; Malton, 8 miles; Helmsley, 8 miles; York, 30 miles

**Attractions:** Castle Howard; North York Moors; Yorkshire Dales; York Minster

The Worsley Arms is an attractive Georgian spa hotel in the heart of Hovingham, an unspoilt Yorkshire village dating back to Roman times. The hotel overlooks the village green and was built in 1841 by the baronet Sir William Worsley whose nearby family home, Hovingham Hall is the birthplace of the Duchess of Kent. Today the hotel is owned and run by Anthony and Sally Finn. Elegant furnishings and open fires create a welcoming atmosphere.The award-winning restaurant offers creatively prepared dishes, including game from the estate. Visit the wine cellar to choose your wine for dinner. The Cricketers bar provides a more informal setting to enjoy modern cooking at its best. The bedrooms vary in size some with views over the pretty village green.

# Monk Fryston Hall Hotel

MONK FRYSTON, NORTH YORKSHIRE LS25 5DU

**Tel:** 0845 365 2073  **International:** +44 (0)1977 682369  **Fax:** 01977 683544
**Web:** www.johansens.com/monkfrystonhall  **E-mail:** reception@monkfrystonhallhotel.co.uk

***Our inspector loved:*** *The oak-panelled front hall and bar with open fires in the winter.*

**Price Guide:**
single £85–£110
double/twin £120–£185

**Location:** A1, 3 miles; A63, 50yds; Leeds, 13 miles; York, 17 miles

**Attractions:** Leeds; York; Castle Howard; Temple Newsam

A mellow old manor house, equally close to York and Leeds, Monk Fryston is ideal if you're touring, travelling on business, or just need a secluded spot to escape. Its mullioned and transom windows and family coat of arms above the doorway will remind you of its fascinating past dating back to 1740. Bedrooms, ranging from cosy to spacious, offer a high standard of comfort. A hearty menu offers many traditional English dishes, and from the Hall you can walk from the terrace into an ornamental garden overlooking the lake - a delight at any time of year. Wedding receptions are held in the oak-panelled Haddon Room with its splendid Inglenook fireplace, and The Rutland Room is a convenient venue for meetings and private parties.

# WHITLEY HALL HOTEL

ELLIOTT LANE, GRENOSIDE, SHEFFIELD, SOUTH YORKSHIRE S35 8NR
**Tel:** 0845 365 2803 **International:** +44 (0)114 245 4444 **Fax:** 0114 245 5414
**Web:** www.johansens.com/whitleyhall **E-mail:** reservations@whitleyhall.com

*Our inspector loved: The friendly staff and the peacocks fanning their tails in the ladscaped gardens.*

**Price Guide:**
single £85–£110
double/twin £110–£140

This romantic 16th-century ivy clad manor's exterior has more than a hint of the period drama about it, and inside, its sweeping split staircase leads to recently refurbished comfortable bedrooms. You can enjoy superbly cooked food from an extensive menu using fresh local produce and imbibe in a relaxing glass of wine tucked away in the oak panelled bar and lounge next to an open fire. If you like to stretch your legs after dinner, step outside and stroll around the Hall's 20 acres of ornamental lakes, rolling lawns and mature woodland. If you should happen to find your own Jane Eyre or Mr D'Arcy, the hotel is licensed for civil weddings, and you could honeymoon amidst the stunning Peak District National Park landscapes.

**Location:** A629, 0.5 miles; M1 jct 35/36, 4 miles; Sheffield, 5 miles

**Attractions:** Holmfirth; Derbyshire Dales; Chatsworth House; Peak District National Park

# 42 THE CALLS

42 THE CALLS, LEEDS, WEST YORKSHIRE LS2 7EW
**Tel:** 0845 365 3602 **International:** +44 (0)113 244 0099 **Fax:** 0113 234 4100
**Web:** www.johansens.com/42thecalls **E-mail:** hotel@42thecalls.co.uk

***Our inspector loved:*** *The innovative design of the hotel and the privacy hatches for room service.*

**Price Guide:**
single £124–£194
double/twin £148–£255
suite from £220

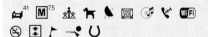

**Location:** City Centre Loop jct 15, 0.25 miles; M621 jct 3, 1.5 miles

**Attractions:** Royal Armories; Thackery Medical Museum

A former corn mill, this unique hotel makes full use of its original features and river-side setting in the heart of Leeds. Expert interior design has created imaginatively styled interiors that combine impressive beams, girders and old machinery with handmade beds and armchairs, Eastern rugs, beautiful fabrics and lavish bathrooms. The hotel does offer round the clock room service or you can conveniently dine out in some of the city's restaurants and simply sign your bill to the hotel. The stylish Brasserie 44 is just next door, and boutique shops, offices, galleries and theatres are all within a few minutes' walk. This is also a great choice for meetings and small receptions.

Insurance & Risk Management Advisors
To us, no two hotels are the same

+44 151 243 0287
Johansens@jltgroup.com

Insurance | Experience | Excellence
Preferred insurance partner of Condé Nast Johansens

JARDINE LLOYD THOMPSON
Leisure

# Ireland

For further information on Ireland, please contact:

**The Irish Tourist Board**
(Bord Fáilte Éireann)
Baggot Street Bridge
Dublin 2
Tel: +353 (0)1 602 4000 or +44 (0)1850 230 330
Internet: www.ireland.ie

**Tourism Ireland**
Tourism Centre
Suffolk Street
Dublin 2
Tel: +353 (0)1 605 7700
Internet: www.discoverireland.com

**Northern Ireland Tourist Information**
Belfast Welcome Centre
47 Donegall Place
Belfast, BT1 5AD
Tel: +44 (0)28 9024 6609
Internet: www.gotobelfast.com

or see **pages 293-296** for details of local historic houses, castles and gardens to visit during your stay.

For additional places to stay in Ireland, turn to **pages 291-292** where a listing of our Recommended Small Hotels, Inns & Restaurant Guide can be found.

# CABRA CASTLE

KINGSCOURT, CO CAVAN
**Tel:** 00 353 42 9667030 **Fax:** 00 353 429667039
**Web:** www.johansens.com/cabracastle **E-mail:** sales@cabracastle.com

***Our inspector loved:*** *The classical setting of this wonderful castle.*

**Price Guide:** (euro)
single from €128
double from €384

**Location:** N2, 7km; M1, 20km; Dublin, 80km; Dublin Airport, 72km

**Attractions:** Dun a Ri Forest Park; Carrickmacross - home of the famous lace; Kells with its high crosses and round tower

An 18th century castle which you'll find to be an oasis of sophistication and splendour. Surrounded by 100 acres of gardens and parkland there's plenty of space and opportunities for you to do the things you want to; take a stroll, go fishing, horse riding or play a round of golf on the hotel's own 9 holes. The restaurant prides itself on growing many of its own ingredients and is inspired by traditional Irish recipes. Bedrooms in the main building are individually appointed from the grandiose to the charming however most are to be found in The Courtyard. Here the design has made the most of many original features and rooms have access to the walled garden. This is a great spot for family gatherings, weddings and receptions

# LONGUEVILLE HOUSE & PRESIDENTS' RESTAURANT

MALLOW, CO CORK, IRELAND
**Tel:** 00 353 22 47156 **Fax:** 00 353 22 47459
**Web:** www.johansens.com/longuevillehouse **E-mail:** info@longuevillehouse.ie

***Our inspector loved:*** *Dinner with delicious seasonal vegetables fresh from the enchanting kitchen garden.*

**Price Guide:** (euro)
single from €110
double/twin from €235

**Location:** Mallow, 3; Cork Airport, 22; Dublin, 2-hours train

**Attractions:** Mallow Castle; Cork Racecourse; Anne's Grove Gardens

This superb listed Georgian manor will offer you a piece of early 18th century Ireland. Virtually self-sufficient - a tradition that has remained largely unaltered for almost 300 years - the hotel uses fresh produce from the estate's farm, gardens and river;including kitchen garden honey and preserves and house smoked salmon. Needless to say the daily menus under the direction of talented chef patron William O'Callaghan are a delight to the taste buds. Staying here you feel more like you are a house guest, a feeling that is aided by the attentive service and the personal touches such as O'Callaghan family photos and heir looms. The conservatory is a master piece of ironwork completed by Richard Turner, 1866 who previous works had included the Botanical Gardens at Kew and in Belfast. Fishing & shooting is available on the estate.

233

# HARVEY'S POINT

LOUGH ESKE, DONEGAL TOWN, CO DONEGAL, IRELAND
**Tel:** 00 353 74 972 2208 **Fax:** 00 353 74 972 2352
**Web:** www.johansens.com/harveyspoint **E-mail:** info@harveyspoint.com

***Our inspector loved:*** *The genuine desire of every staff member to please.*

**Price Guide:** (euro)
single €240
double/twin €290-€360
suite from €580

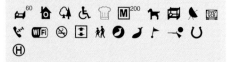

Against a backdrop of the beautiful Blue Stack Mountains, Harvey's Point Nestles on the edge of Lough Eske and has all the ingredients of a haven to which you would wish to retreat, unwind and rejuvenate. Bedrooms are spacious and all have large bathrooms with sunken baths large enough for two.Though if you really want to indulge, a penthouse suite has a lofty living-room, dressing room, bar, bath jet pool and mini-plasma in the bathroom. The restaurant delights with innovative modern celtic dishes as well as international fare worked around the seasons. Entertainment is important here and on top of the resident pianist, throughout the year on Wednesday and Friday performers from amongst Irelands most sought after and diverse perform.

**Location:** Donegal Town, 3 miles; Donegal Airport, 50 miles; Sligo Airport, 50 miles

**Attractions:** Top Championship Golf Courses; Donegal Town; Glenvagh National Park and Castle

# BROOKS HOTEL

DRURY STREET, DUBLIN 2
**Tel:** 00 353 1 670 4000 **Fax:** 00 353 1 670 4455
**Web:** www.johansens.com/brooks **E-mail:** reservations@brookshotel.ie

*Our inspector loved:* The elegant and comfortable residents lounge.

**Price Guide:** (euro, room only)
single €170–€270
double €180–€375

**Location:** Dublin Airport, 8km; Dublin Port, 2km

**Attractions:** Temple Bar; Dublin Castle; Grafton Street; Trinity College

Brooks' is a four star designer boutique hotel located in the fashionable heart of Dublin City, just two minutes stroll from Grafton Street, Temple Bar and Trinity College. Discerning travellers won't be disappointed by the contemporary design and the impressively trained staff who deliver a high level of attentive service here. Innovative Irish and International cuisine is served in Francesca's Restaurant and uses the finest of local produce cooked by an award winning team. Jasmine Bar is an upbeat and stylish meeting place which on some nights includes sounds from the resident pianist. Superb accommodation and facilities also include air-conditioning throughout, a private residents lounge and fitness suite with sauna and state of the art screening room. Drury Street car park is conveniently located directly opposite the hotel

# ABBEYGLEN CASTLE

SKY ROAD, CLIFDEN, CO GALWAY
**Tel:** 00 353 952 1201 **Fax:** 00 353 952 1797
**Web:** www.johansens.com/abbeyglen **E-mail:** info@abbeyglen.ie

**Our inspector loved:** *The truly open and genuine warmth of the proprietor's Paul and Brian.*

**Price Guide:** (euro)
single from €120
standard double from €190
superior from €340

**Awards/Recognition:** 2 AA Rosettes 2007-2008

**Location:** Sky Road (Clifden), 0.5 miles; Galway (N59), 50 miles; Galway Airport, 55 miles

**Attractions:** Connemara National Park; Kylemore Abbey & Gardens; Connemara Golf Club, the Sky Road, great walking

Perched just off the famous Sky Road near Clifden, the "capital" of Connemara, this 205-year-old castle is nestled amongst sheltered parkland and intriguing gardens. Facing Clifden Bay and with its back to the glorious rolling hills more fondly known as the Twelve Bens. Inside, large open fires and traditional furnishings provide a warm and welcoming atmosphere. For those who enjoy fishing, this hotel is ideally situated for shore angling and guests can have their catch cooked for them in the restaurant. Other activities include pony trekking, snooker, swimming, tennis and table tennis. In the evening you can curl up with a glass of fine wine in the charming Resident's lounge that often hosts spontaneous music evenings.

# CASHEL HOUSE

CASHEL, CONNEMARA, CO GALWAY, IRELAND
**Tel:** 00 353 95 31001 **Fax:** 00 353 95 31077
**Web:** www.johansens.com/cashelhouse **E-mail:** res@cashel-house-hotel.com

***Our inspector loved:*** *Being greeted by the ever-lit peat fire in the snug.*

**Price Guide:** (euro)
single €95–€135
double/twin €190–€270
suite €270–€350

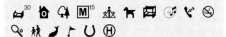

**Location:** N59, 6km; Galway, 65km; Galway Airport, 70km

**Attractions:** Connemara Loop; Connemara National Park; Private Beach; Delightful Gardens

Surrounded by exotic flowering gardens and woodland walks at the head of Cashel Bay, this pretty hotel exudes tranquility. Built by the owners' great, great grandfather for Captain Thomas Hazel, an English landowner, you will be welcomed today by proprietors Dermot and Kay McEvilly for whom nothing is too much trouble. Turf and log fires glow in public areas where the furnishings and décor reflect good taste. Bedrooms and suites are comfortable and overlook the hill or garden. In the dining room, Dermot and Kay oversee the preparation of imaginative dishes from the constantly changing menu. The emphasis is on local seafood, lamb, beef, game and home-grown vegetables, complemented by a carefully chosen wine list. Swimming from the private beach is just one of a variety of pursuits.

# RENVYLE HOUSE HOTEL

CONNEMARA, CO GALWAY, IRELAND
**Tel:** 00 353 95 43511 **Fax:** 00 353 95 43515
**Web:** www.johansens.com/renvylehouse **E-mail:** info@renvyle.com

*Our inspector loved: Delightful food in the restaurant accompanied by the attentive service.*

**Price Guide:** (euro)
single from €85
double/twin €110–€240

Set between mountains and the sea, this hardy, beautiful building has occupied it's rugged, romantic position on Ireland's unspoilt Connemara coast for over 4 centuries. Established as a hotel for more than 100 years it witnessed a procession of luminaries through its doors - Augustus John, Lady Gregory, Yeats and Churchill, drawn no doubt by an atmosphere as warm as the turf fires that glow in public areas. A very family friendly hotel and whose activities would keep even the most impatient child or adult happy. Tennis, fishing, croquet, riding, canoeing, clay pigeon shooting, bowls and golf. Beyond, you can walk in the heather-clad hills, or swim and sunbathe on empty beaches. The restaurant, a focal point in the hotel constantly changes its menu to incorporate the local catch of the day, seasonal herbs and Renvyle lamb.

**Location:** Letterfrack/N59, 4 miles; Westport, 36 miles; Galway Airport, 60 miles

**Attractions:** Connemara National Park; Kylemore Abbey; Killary Harbour Cruise; Scubadive sites

# St. Clerans Manor House

CRAUGHWELL, CO GALWAY, CO GALWAY
**Tel:** 00 353 91 846555  **Fax:** 00 353 91 846600
**Web:** www.johansens.com/stclerans  **E-mail:** info@stclerans.com

***Our inspector loved:*** *The aristocratic grandeur enhanced by the truly beautiful setting.*

**Price Guide:** (euro)
double €325-€525

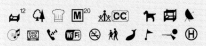

**Location:** N6, 3km; Galway City, 23km; Galway Airport, 18km

**Attractions:** Galway City; Connemara; Cliffs of Moher

Life at St Clerans Manor seems to proceed at a wonderfully leisurely pace, and present owner Merv Griffin has pulled out all the stops to create an almost magical atmosphere. You'll discover art treasures plucked from around the globe and period furnishings throughout the house, and each of the truly beautiful bedrooms offers breathtaking views of the surrounding countryside. You might be surprised to find a renowned Japanese chef in this country house 32km east of Galway, but Hisashi Kumagai, known as "Kuma", creates inspired European and Oriental dishes, served in the splendid dining room that has hosted kings, princes and Hollywood celebrities. The key is in the exceptionally fine detail and St Cleran's delivers all round.

# PARK HOTEL KENMARE & SÁMAS

KENMARE, CO. KERRY, IRELAND
**Tel:** 00 353 64 41200 **Fax:** 00 353 64 41402
**Web:** www.johansens.com/parkkenmare **E-mail:** info@parkkenmare.com

**Our inspector loved:** *The many ways to indulge at the award-winning Samas spa.*

**Price Guide:** (euro)
single €226–€280
double €452–€606
suite €696–€846

**Awards/Recognition:** 3 AA Rosettes 2006-2007

**Location:** R569; Kenmare, 0.1 mile; Kerry Airport, 28 miles

**Attractions:** The Ring of Kerry; Bantry Bay; Dingle; The Killarney National park

SÁMAS, a Deluxe Destination Spa has been added to the much applauded Park Hotel Kenmare, and the mystical magic of Ireland can certainly be found in this enchanting corner of County Kerry. Samas offers over 60 Holistic treatments combined with heat experiences and relaxation to rejuvenate body, mind and spirit. Male and female areas are on hand to spare any blushes! Park Hotel Kenmare itself is elegant with glorious country views, and holds numerous awards. Bedrooms are deeply comfortable with traditional furnishings and the hallways are filled with wonderful antiques and treasures. The restaurant over looks the terraced garden and serves acclaimed seasonal menus that lean towards local seafood. There is also a 12-seat cinema, tennis, croquet and golf next door.

# SHEEN FALLS LODGE

KENMARE, CO. KERRY, IRELAND
**Tel:** 00 353 64 41600  **Fax:** 00 353 64 41386
**Web:** www.johansens.com/sheenfallslodge  **E-mail:** info@sheenfallslodge.ie

***Our inspector loved:*** *It's elegance and sitting outside Oscar's Bistro on the banks of the falls.*

**Price Guide:** (euro)
deluxe room €310–€455

**Awards/Recognition:** Relais & Châteaux; 2 AA Rosettes 2006-2007

**Location:** Kenmare/R569, 1 mile; Killarney/N22, 19 miles; Kerry Airport, 30 miles; Cork Airport 60 miles

**Attractions:** Blarney Castle; Killarney National Park; Ring of Kerry, Beara Peninsula

You can understand why the Marquis of Lansdowne chose this idyllic location for his summer residence, flowing falls in a magical setting of 300 acres of woodlands and close by the lively coloured village of Kenmare. Sheen Falls Lodge, a sporting estate has been beautifully styled and with little expense spared was deservedly included in the 2005 Top Ten European Resort list by Condé Nast Readers. Both restaurants deserve a visit and the more informal Oscar's Bistro leads out onto a riverbank terrace. The wine cellar is immensely impressive and tastings can be arranged with the charming sommelier. Ultimate luxury can be found in the 1,350 square feet of the Presidential suite with its octagonal shaped drawing room, 20ft high ceiling and huge viewing windows. Here you really can do as much or as little as you like.

# THE BREHON

MUCKROSS ROAD, KILLARNEY, CO. KERRY CO. KERRY
**Tel:** 00 353 64 30700 **Fax:** 00 353 64 30701
**Web:** www.johansens.com/thebrehon **E-mail:** info@thebrehon.com

*Our inspector loved: The indulgent treatments using wonderfully fragrant oils at the Angsana Spa.*

**Price Guide:** (euro)
single €125-€175
double €190-€290
suite €340-€440

**Location:** Town Centre, 0.5 miles; Kerry Airport, 14 miles; Cork Airport, 54 miles

**Attractions:** Killarney National Park; Killarney Golf and Fishing Club; The Ring of Kerry; The Dingle Peninsula

A majestic hotel in "the Garden of the Blest", 25,000 acres of woodlands and mountains in the Killarney National Park. The contemporary rooms are creatively decorated in calm natural tones with bold, colourful touches. Elegant ensuite bathrooms feature an aromatic natural amenities range. All rooms enjoy far-reaching views of the national park, while Superior Deluxe rooms boast balconies or bay windows from which to savour them. Award-winning chefs create extensive and enticing of Irish and international cuisine, to be enjoyed in the contemporary Brehon restaurant. The impressive afternoon teas, served on the sun-drenched Mezzanine are not to be missed. Active guests will revel in the wealth of leisure opportunities available at the Brehon, while those seeking relaxation will visit the beautiful Angsana Spa.

# CAHERNANE HOUSE HOTEL

MUCKROSS ROAD, KILLARNEY, CO KERRY, IRELAND
**Tel:** 00 353 64 31895 **Fax:** 00 353 64 34340
**Web:** www.johansens.com/cahernane **E-mail:** info@cahernane.com

***Our inspector loved:*** *The enduring charm of this welcoming and intimate hotel.*

**Price Guide:** (euro)
single from €180
double from €200
suite from €320

**Location:** Killarney, 1 mile; Kerry Airport, 14 miles

**Attractions:** Ring of Kerry; Muckross House; Killarney Golf club; Killarney National Park

A shady tunnel of greenery frames the ¼ mile long drive to this welcoming 17th-century house, where time seems to move at a wonderfully sedate pace. The former home to the Earls of Pembroke it stands in gorgeous parklands on the edge of Killarney's National Park. You'll find the Browne family pride themselves on their hospitality and will be keen to ensure you make the most of your stay. Bedroom have plenty of individual personality and the suites are enhanced with beautiful antiques. Recipient of numerous awards, Herbert Room restaurant offers menus by chef Pat Karney, or you can eat more informally in the Cellar Bar, home to an impressive stock of wines. There's tennis and croquet or simply enjoy garden walks and views of the National Parks untamed beauty.

# HOTEL DUNLOE CASTLE

BEAUFORT, KILLARNEY, CO KERRY
**Tel:** 00 353 64 44111 **Fax:** 00 353 64 44583
**Web:** www.johansens.com/dunloecastle **E-mail:** sales.kih@liebherr.com

*Our inspector loved: The inspiring views from my room and the genuine warm service.*

**Price Guide:**
single €170-€250
double €210-€290

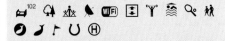

**Location:** Beaufort, 1 miles; Killarney, 6 miles; Kerry Airport, 10 miles

**Attractions:** Ring of Kerry; Dingle Bay; Gap of Dunloe

A contemporary castle build in picturesque rolling parkland, with pastures of Halfinger Ponies and views towards the breathtaking Gap of Dunloe. The grounds include the original 12th Century Dunloe Castle ruins and in whose shadow lies an historically important garden flaunting a myriad of magical plants including the Killarney strawberry tree and the rare Chinese swamp cypress. Fine cuisine and great views is complemented by an extensive selection of wines in the Oak Room Restaurant. Lighter dishes are served in the Garden Café and there are plenty of places for an after-dinner cocktail. Bedrooms feature floor to ceiling windows and most have balconies on which to relax. There's an impressive selection of activities including a 25m pool and down by the stable after breakfast you'll find the ponies saddled up to take you for a complementary gentle morning ride. Closed from 27th October 2007 to 14th April 2008.

# BALLYGARRY HOUSE

KILLARNEY ROAD, TRALEE, CO KERRY, IRELAND
**Tel:** 00 353 66 7123322 **Fax:** 00 353 66 7127630
**Web:** www.johansens.com/ballygarryhouse **E-mail:** info@ballygarryhouse.com

***Our inspector loved:*** *The new Nadur Spa with its organic products.*

**Price Guide:** (euro)
sngles €100–€160
double/ twin €150–€210
junior Suite €180–€210

**Location:** Tralee, 1 miles; Kerry Airport, 15 miles; Killarney, 20 miles; Shannon Airport, 80 miles

**Attractions:** Ring of Kerry; Dingle Peninsula; Siamsa Tire; Killarney National Park

Ballygarry House is family-run and owner Padraig McGillicudy knows how to make you feel at home. Gracious and restful, the interior is decorated with rich warm colours, antiques blended sympathetically with modern touches and fresh floral displays. There are corners to curl up in with a good book or to indulge in an afternoon Irish tea. Brooks restaurant serves modern Irish cuisine taking care to select the best of local produce and with large windows overlooking the gardens you see why this is a local favourite. On warm days lunch can be taken in the Courtyard. Really embrace the Gaelic mood in the new Nádúr spa, which offers traditional Irish seaweed soaks as well as a hot tub, thermal suite and rejuvenating mud wraps. Outside, pretty lawns look up to the majestic Kerry Mountains.

# KILLASHEE HOUSE HOTEL & VILLA SPA

KILLASHEE, NAAS, CO KILDARE, IRELAND
**Tel:** 00 353 45 879277  **Fax:** 00 353 45 879266
**Web:** www.johansens.com/killashee  **E-mail:** reservations@killasheehouse.com

*Our inspector loved:* The fun underground bar, The Nun's Kitchen.

**Price Guide:** (euro)
single €145–€175
double/twin €190–€250
suites €265–€495

A tall, slim bell tower and fancy Jacobean-style façade catch your eye as you approach this prestigious 4 Star hotel along an elegant curved driveway. Built as a hunting lodge in the 1860's, it's now found its niche as a spa and fitness retreat, just 45 minutes from Dublin. Many bedrooms and suites have four-poster beds and stunning views over the gardens and across to the Wicklow Mountains. Traditional Irish and Mediterranean cuisine can be enjoyed in the award-winning Turner's restaurant. If you want to work up an appetite or simply relax before dinner the Country Club and Villa Spa with 25m pool and 18 treatment rooms offer fitness and pampering. Several racecourses and championship golf courses are within easy reach.

**Awards/Recognition:** 1 AA Rosette 2006-2007; Condé Nast Johansens Readers Award 2007

**Location:** On the Old Kilcullen Road; Naas, 1.5 miles; Dublin, 45-min drive

**Attractions:** The Japanese Garden; The Powers Court Garden; The Wicklow Mountains; Glendalough

# MOUNT JULIET CONRAD

THOMASTOWN, CO KILKENNY, IRELAND
**Tel:** 00 353 56 777 3000 **Fax:** 00 353 56 777 3019
**Web:** www.johansens.com/mountjuliet **E-mail:** info@mountjuliet.ie

***Our inspector loved:*** *The feeling of being a welcomed house guest at an exceptional sporting estate.*

**Price Guide:** (euro)
single from €150
double/twin €210–€335
suite from €405

**Awards/Recognition:** 2 AA Rosettes 2006-2007

**Location:** Dublin Waterford Road, 2 miles; Kilkenny, 10 miles; Dublin Airport, 76 miles; Waterford Airport, 25 miles

**Attractions:** Kilkenny Castle; Waterford Crystal; The Rock of Cashel; St. Cannice Cathedral

With beautiful architectural features and at times a feeling of opulence Mount Juliet has the warmth and atmosphere of a private family home set in a wonderful 1,500 acres. 32 bedrooms in the main house are individually designed with an emphasis on country house elegance whilst those wanting to be close to the spa can chose one of 16 'club' rooms in the more informal atmosphere of Hunters Yard. Plenty of options for dining, the sophisticated Lady Helen Dining Room with panoramic views and detailed stucco work in the main house or Kendall's an informal brasserie in Hunters Yard. Synonymous with horses, riders of all standards and disciplines can enjoy the exceptional facilities here. Golfers will be challenged on the superb 72 par Jack Nicklaus Signature Course, a past Irish Open venue. Winner of The Georgina Campbell Hotel of the Year Award 2007

# ASHFORD CASTLE

CONG, CO MAYO
**Tel:** 00 353 94 95 46003  **Fax:** 00 353 94 95 46260
Web: www.johansens.com/ashfordcastle E-mail: ashford@ashford.ie

***Our inspector loved:*** *This fabulous place in a fairytale setting.*

**Price Guide:** (euro, room only)
single/twin/double €244–€590
stateroom/suite €522–€1187

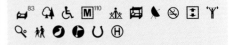

**Location:** N84, 9km; Galway City, 42km; Galway Airport, 44km

**Attractions:** Connemara Loop; Connemara National Park

Set amidst stunning surroundings and formerly the home of Lord Ardilaun and the Guinness family, this 13th-century castle became a luxury hotel in 1939. A choice of restaurants include: the award-winning George "V" dining room offering modern and traditional dishes and the elegant Connaught Room which is open from May to September, Thursday to Sunday and where menus feature the very best Irish produce. The Drawing Room serves lunch, afternoon tea and more relaxed evening dining. Take a short stroll across the River Cong to Cullen's at the Cottage, where you can enjoy a bistro-style menu and choose a lobster from the tank! Don't miss the nightly entertainment in the Dungeon Bar. Activities include; falconry, fishing, clay pigeon shooting, tennis, a 9-hole golf course, health centre and treatment rooms. Boat trips can be arranged on Lough Corrib.

# KNOCKRANNY HOUSE HOTEL & SPA

WESTPORT, CO MAYO, IRELAND
**Tel:** 00 353 98 28600 **Fax:** 00 353 98 28611
**Web:** www.johansens.com/knockranny **E-mail:** info@khh.ie

**Our inspector loved:** *The whole sense of relaxation and well-being.*

**Price Guide:** (euro)
single from €105
double/twin from €140
suite from €210

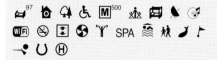

**Awards/Recognition:** 1 AA Rosette 2007-2008

**Location:** Just off the N5; Town Centre 10-min walk; Train & Bus Station 15-min walk; Knock Airport, 45-mins drive

**Attractions:** Westport House Estate & Country Gardens; Clew Bay & Islands; Croagh patrick Mountain; Blue Flag Beaches

Rising into view against Croagh Patrick Mountain this Victorian hotel and spa evokes an image of a bygone era. Knockranny has a reputation as one of Ireland's finest hotels since 1997. You have a wide choice of bedrooms with courtyard or mountain views including Grand De Luxe - De Luxe - Master Suites and Executive Suites. The new rooms are very spacious and feature king-size beds, 32" LCD TVs, surround-sound systems, free broadband Internet access, oversized bathrooms with spa bath as standard. Antique furniture features throughout the hotel and the conservatory and library look out onto magnificent scenery. You can enjoy contemporary Irish cuisine and fish dishes in the restaurant. Spa Salveo features a vitality pool, a serail mud chamber and 12 treatment rooms.

# NUREMORE HOTEL AND COUNTRY CLUB

CARRICKMACROSS, CO MONAGHAN, IRELAND
**Tel:** 00 353 42 9661438 **Fax:** 00 353 42 9661853
**Web:** www.johansens.com/nuremore **E-mail:** info@nuremore.com

***Our inspector loved:*** *The extensive sporting and health facilities.*

**Price Guide:** (Euro)
single €150–€200
double/twin €220–€280
suite from €250–€300

**Awards/Recognition:** 3 AA Rosettes 2007-2008

**Location:** N2, 1 mile; Dublin, 45-min drive; Belfast, 75-min drive

**Attractions:** Knockabbey Castle & Grounds,; Monaghan County Museum,; Carrickmacross Lace Gallery,; Mourne Clay Pigeon Shooting

Nuremore is set amidst 200 acres of rolling countryside with beautifully landscaped gardens. Its facilities include a swimming pool, treatment rooms and a health club featuring a gymnasium, spa bath, sauna and steam room. The hotel's renowned 18-hole championship golf course makes superb use of the surrounding lakes and landscape. Resident professional, Maurice Cassidy, is on hand to offer advice and tuition. All 72 bedrooms and suites are well appointed to ensure a generous sense of personal space and you can sample classic European cuisine, with Irish and French influences, prepared by award-winning Chef Raymond McArdle. The restaurant features in the Bridgestone Guide to Ireland's best 100 restaurants. Ideal for weddings and meetings, the impressive conference centre constantly evolves to ensure cutting edge facilities.

# THE HUNTING LODGE

CASTLE LESLIE ESTATE, GLASLOUGH, CO MONAGHAN
**Tel:** 00 353 4788100 **Fax:** 00 353 4788256
**Web:** www.johansens.com/castleleslie **E-mail:** info@castleleslie.com

*Our inspector loved: Relaxing in the cellar bar and its roaring log fire.*

**Price Guide:** (euro)
single from €140
double from €190

**Location:** R 185, 200yds; N2, 5 miles; Dublin Airport 90-minutes; Belfast Airport 70-minutes

**Attractions:** Castle Leslie Estate; The Equestrian Centre; The Cookery School; The Organic Victorian Spa

One of the last bastions of family-run castle hotels in Ireland, The Hunting Lodge is part of the Castle Leslie Estate, and is the home to one of Ireland's finest equestrian playgrounds. There are over 300 cross country jumps designed by the Willis Brothers of Badminton Fame and in addition, there is also a "virtual horse for the complete novice". Not only a horse-enthusiast's retreat, the Lodge offers something for everyone with the delightful bedrooms and the intimate and snug Conor's bar, that has roaring fires and cosy corners to curl up in. Try the Victorian Spa, Ireland's first truly organic spa, where hot tubs overlook the stables or sign up for a cookery course located in the restored original kitchen of Castle Leslie. There is also over 1,000 acres of the most magnificent Irish countryside, right on the doorstep to enjoy and explore!

251

# DUNBRODY COUNTRY HOUSE & COOKERY SCHOOL

ARTHURSTOWN, NEW ROSS, CO WEXFORD, IRELAND
**Tel:** 00 353 51 389 600  **Fax:** 00 353 51 389 601
**Web:** www.johansens.com/dunbrody  **E-mail:** dunbrody@indigo.ie

*Our inspector loved:* The new champagne & seafood bar and the sheer fact I was looked after so incredibly well.

**Price Guide:** (euro)
single €152–€345
double/twin €245–€345
suite €400–€430

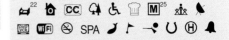

Contemporary canvases hang next to portrait oils and gives you some clue as to the ingenuity of the owners of this former home of the Marquess of Donegall. Kevin and Catherine Dundon have created a seriously good small luxury hotel. As a renowned chef Kevin oversees the cooking school and restaurant whilst Catherine is a meticulous and welcoming host. Bedrooms are spacious and delightful and many look over the garden and lawns. A lovely alternative to the excellent restaurant is the new champagne and seafood bar with impressive glass chandeliers, high wide counter, comfy stools and a menu full of local fish from the Hook Peninsula. On a short break you could fit in a cookery class, be pampered in the chic and intimate spa and tour this beautiful part of Ireland - wonderful.

**Location:** Arthurstown, 0.5km; Passage East car Ferry, 2km; Waterford, 10km; Wexford N11, 22km

**Attractions:** Hook Peninsula; Dunbrody Abbey; Waterford

# MARLFIELD HOUSE

GOREY, CO WEXFORD, IRELAND
**Tel:** 00 353 53 94 21124 **Fax:** 00 353 53 94 21572
**Web:** www.johansens.com/marlfieldhouse **E-mail:** info@marlfieldhouse.ie

*Our inspector loved:* The warm hospitality from this beautiful family run hotel

**Price Guide:** ( euro)
single from €130
double/twin from €240
state rooms from €405
( closed mid-December - 1st February)

**Awards/Recognition:** Relais & Châteaux

**Location:** N11, 0.5 miles; Gorey, 0.5 miles; Dublin Airport, 60 miles

**Attractions:** Wicklow; Kilkenny; Many Golf Courses; Glendalough

Staying at the award-winning Marlfield House is a truly memorable experience, as this former residence of the Earl of Courtown presents Regency lifestyle in all its glory. Recognised as one of the finest country houses in Ireland, its welcoming hosts Raymond and Mary Bowe, and daughters Margaret and Laura, maintain it brilliantly. Interiors abound with original antiques and period detail such as classical decoupage prints and garlands. Bedrooms are the epitome of comfort and elegance and many have views over the knot garden or lake. The entrance hall is certainly imposing however it is a house with a truly warm atmosphere and endless architectural delights including the Richard Turner conservatory. Ingredients from the kitchen garden influences the daily menus and enhance the succulent flavours of local seafood and meats.

# KELLY'S RESORT HOTEL & SPA

ROSSLARE, CO WEXFORD, IRELAND
**Tel:** 00 353 53 32114 **Fax:** 00 353 53 32222
**Web:** www.johansens.com/kellysresort **E-mail:** kellyhot@iol.ie

***Our inspector loved:*** *The numerous places to lie and relax, great staff and location on the beach.*

**Price Guide:** (euro, all inclusive, except some spa facilities and hire equipmet)
2 night break from €630
5 night breaks from €1230

**Location:** N25, 7 miles; N11/ Wexford, 17 miles; Waterford airport, 45 miles; Dublin, 94 miles

**Attractions:** Hook Lighthouse; National Heritage Park; Johnstown Castle Garden; Waterford

The long sandy beach of Rosslare fronts Kelly's in an area regarded as having the best weather in Ireland. There's a very light and fresh feel to this award-winning hotel. Walls are lined with an exceptional collection of contemporary art, many of which you can admire as you enjoy the delicious food of Beaches Restaurant. There is also the informal and buzzy atmosphere of the La Marine Bistro & Bar. Whilst you would enjoy a relaxing break here alone, Kelly's is great for families looking to have fun together yet when needed time apart. Kids have their own high-tea, crèche, entertainment and mini-activities whilst for adults, amongst other things, in & outdoor tennis, golf, aqua club and indulging at SeaSpa whose clever design using light and texture stimulates a feeling of calm. Minimum stay of 2 nights. Meals included.

# Scotland

For further information on Scotland, please contact:

**Visit Scotland**
Ocean Point 1,
94 Ocean Drive, Leith
Edinburgh EH6 6JH
Tel: +44 (0)131 472 2222 or +44 (0)1463 716 996
Internet: www.visitscotland.com

**Greater Glasgow & Clyde Valley Tourist Board**
Tel: +44 (0)141 204 4400
Internet: www.seeglasgow.com

**Edinburgh & Lothians Tourist Board**
Tel: +44 (0)845 2255 121
Internet: www.edinburgh.org

**The Scottish Borders Tourist Board**
Tel: 0870 608 0404
Internet: www.scot-borders.co.uk

or see **pages 293-296** for details of local historic
houses, castles and gardens to visit during your stay.

For additional places to stay in Scotland, turn to
**pages 291-292** where a listing of our Recommended
Small Hotels, Inns & Restaurant Guide can be found.

# DARROCH LEARG

BRAEMAR ROAD, BALLATER, ABERDEENSHIRE AB35 5UX
**Tel:** 0845 365 3263 **International:** +44 (0)13397 55443 **Fax:** 013397 55252
**Web:** www.johansens.com/darrochlearg **E-mail:** enquiries@darrochlearg.co.uk

*Our inspector loved: The individual style of the bedrooms with wonderful views to the hills.*

**Price Guide:**
single £110–£140
double/twin £180–£270

**Awards/Recognition:** 3 AA Rosettes 2007-2008

**Location:** Ballater village, 10-min walk; Aberdeen, 42 miles

**Attractions:** Balmoral; River Dee at the doorstep; Stunning countryside; Castle and Whisky Trails

Situated in 4 acres of leafy grounds Darroch Learg is situated on the side of the hill which dominates Ballater. The hotel was built in 1888 as a fashionable country residence, with panoramic views over the golf course, River Dee and Balmoral Estate to the fine peaks of the Grampian Mountains. The bedrooms are comfortable and individually furnished. The reception rooms are similarly elegant and welcoming and log fires create a particularly cosy atmosphere on chilly nights. The food is excellent and the chef was awarded Hotel Chef of the Year in 2005. The wine list has achieved 13th place in the Top 100 UK Restaurants Wine Lists guide. The views are stunning with a wonderful outlook south over the hills of Glen Muick.

# LOCH MELFORT HOTEL & RESTAURANT

ARDUAINE, BY OBAN, ARGYLL PA34 4XG
**Tel:** 0845 365 2036 **International:** +44 (0)1852 200233 **Fax:** 01852 200214
**Web:** www.johansens.com/lochmelfort **E-mail:** reception@lochmelfort.co.uk

***Our inspector loved:*** *The newly decorated dining room with stunning food and view.*

**Price Guide:** (including dinner)
double/twin £118-£178
superior £138–£218

**Awards/Recognition:** 2 AA Rosettes 2007-2008

**Location:** on the A816; Oban, 18.6 miles

**Attractions:** Arduaine Gardens; Dunstaffnage Castle; The Marine Sanctuary.; Kilchoan Castle

You can see the Islands of Jura, Shuna and Scarba from this hideaway hotel amidst the awe-inspiring mountains of Argyll in Asknish Bay,on the west coast of Scotland. Friendly staff are there to welcome you into the warm atmosphere and the award winning restaurant is perfect for a romantic meal, with breathtaking views stretching as far as the eye can see. Menus offer local fish,shellfish and meat dishes plus a mouth-watering array of home-made desserts, delicious ice creams and Scottish cheeses. Bedrooms are spacious, decorated with bold bright fabrics and feature large patio windows to take the maximum advantage of the panoramic view. The Arduaine Gardens next to the hotel are home to plants and trees from around the world.

# ARDANAISEIG

KILCHRENAN BY TAYNUILT, ARGYLL PA35 1HE
**Tel:** 0845 365 3614 **International:** +44 (0)1866 833333 **Fax:** 01866 833222
**Web:** www.johansens.com/ardanaiseig **E-mail:** ardanaiseig@clara.net

**Our inspector loved:** *A feeling of total tranquility.*

**Price Guide:** (including dinner)
double/twin £178–£388
suite £302-£438

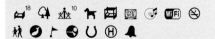

**Location:** A85, 10 miles; Oban, 26 miles

**Attractions:** The Ardanaiseig Open Air Theatre; Kilchurn Castle; Boating

The surreal feeling you get when you approach Ardanaiseig is of being suspended in time. Built in 1834 and standing in an achingly beautiful spot at the foot of Ben Cruachan, overlooking Loch Awe you get a sense of the true history and romance of the Highlands. Roaring log fires in the drawing room, bowls of fresh flowers, antiques and paintings are complemented by dreamy views of the loch and faraway mountains. Peaceful bedrooms suit the house's style, but real Scottish hospitality comes to the fore in the restaurant, where award-winning chef, Gary Goldie works miracles using largely local produce. Outside, the gardens and estate are a riot of colour, and you can enjoy fishing, tennis and exhilarating hill or lochside walks.

# CALLY PALACE HOTEL

GATEHOUSE OF FLEET, DUMFRIES & GALLOWAY DG7 2DL
**Tel:** 0845 365 2873 **International:** +44 (0)1557 814341 **Fax:** 01557 814522
**Web:** www.johansens.com/callypalace **E-mail:** info@callypalace.co.uk

*Our inspector loved:* The traditional décor and grandeur of the interior. Cally Palace attracts a more mature clientele.

**Price Guide:**
single from £94
double from £198
suite from £212

**Awards/Recognition:** 1 AA Rosette 2006-2007

**Location:** A75, 2 miles; Prestwick Airport, 75 miles

**Attractions:** Cream o' Galloway; Wigtown Book Town; Kirkcudbright for Art

Gatehouse of Fleet is a former cotton town on the Water of Fleet where Burns composed, "Scots wha hae wi' Wallace bled," on the nearby moors. Surrounded by 150 acres of superb landscaped grounds, this 18th-century mansion is a building of opulence. You will immediately feel relaxed by the comfortable ambience of a bygone age that fulfils all hopes of a welcoming retreat from modern-day life. Two huge marble pillars frame the entrance hall that leads into the lounge with impressive gilt ceiling. Bedrooms ooze character and combine traditional furnishings with modern conveniences and little touches that make all the difference to your stay. Dinner in the elegant dining room is accompanied by a pianist who will be more than happy to take requests.

# KIRROUGHTREE HOUSE

NEWTON STEWART, WIGTOWNSHIRE DG8 6AN

**Tel:** 0845 365 1962 **International:** +44 (0)1671 402141 **Fax:** 01671 402425
**Web:** www.johansens.com/kirroughtreehouse **E-mail:** info@kirroughtreehouse.co.uk

Kirroughtree House was built by the Heron family in 1719 in the foothills of the Cairnsmore of Fleet, on the edge of Galloway Forest Park. You can linger over the spectacular views from 8 acres of landscaped gardens. The original staircase in the Oak panelled lounge is where Robert Burns often recited his poems. The bedrooms are comfortable and the deluxe rooms have spectacular views over the surrounding countryside. Kirroughtree's award winning culinary reputation, ensures that only the finest produce is used to create meals of originality and finesse. This is an ideal venue for small meetings, family parties and weddings; exclusive use of the hotel can be arranged. Pitch and putt and croquet can be enjoyed in the grounds and walking expeditions are recommended.

**Our inspector loved:** *An ideal retreat, comfortable spacious bedrooms and excellent food.*

**Price Guide:**
single £95–£120
double/twin £170–£210
suite £220

**Awards/Recognition:** 2 AA Rosettes 2006-2007

**Location:** off the B7079; A75, 0.8 miles; Prestwick Airport, 58 miles

**Attractions:** Wigtown; Castle Kennedy Gardens; Whithorn Priory and Dig; Gem Rock Musuem

# CHANNINGS

12-16 SOUTH LEARMONTH GARDENS, EDINBURGH EH4 1EZ
**Tel:** 0845 365 3229 **International:** +44 (0)131 274 7401 **Fax:** 0131 274 7405
**Web:** www.johansens.com/channings **E-mail:** reserve@channings.co.uk

**Our inspector loved:** *The country-style tranquillity in a city setting charmed by attentive staff.*

**Price Guide:**
single £85–£140
double/twin £95–£185
four poster/suite £150–£285

**Awards/Recognition:** 2 AA Rosettes 2007-2008

**Location:** M9, 8 miles; Edinburgh Airport, 10 miles; Waverley Station 1.5 miles

**Attractions:** Edinburgh Castle; Princes Street; Royal Yacht Britannia; Palace of Holyrood House

A clever and delightful combination of restored Edwardian elegance complemented by contemporary furnishing. If you like to browse, there is an interesting collection of antique prints, furniture, objets d'art, periodicals and books. The oak-panelled Library or Kingsleigh room are perfect for discreet meetings and small private dinners and menus are overseen by Head Chef, Karen Mackay who creates colourful menus from local and seasonal produce. After a day exploring this vibrant city Channings is a peaceful haven in which to relax and recharge - its rather like an exclusive, tranquil club, where nothing is too much trouble for the friendly staff. Coffee shops, galleries and bars are close by and its just 10 minutes walk to Princes street.

# MAR HALL HOTEL & SPA

MAR HALL DRIVE, EARL OF MAR ESTATE, BISHOPTON, NEAR GLASGOW PA7 5NW
**Tel:** 0845 365 2054 **International:** +44 (0)141 812 9999 **Fax:** 0141 812 9997
**Web:** www.johansens.com/marhall **E-mail:** reservations@marhall.com

*Our inspector loved: The peaceful suroundings, the quality and taste of the decor.*

**Price Guide:** (room only)
double (single occupancy) £135–£190
double/twin £175–£230
suite £250–£495

Hard to believe just 20 minutes from Glasgow's thriving city centre is the Earl of Mar Estate where the impressive Mar Hall Hotel is situated. Over the years the lush surroundings and crisp air have drawn guests including Mary Queen of Scots and Robert the Bruce. Now one of Scotland's premier 5-star hotels, its lavish rooms and suites have strong individuality, a striking blend of antiquity and the contemporary. Shades of gold and cream set the tone for a relaxing dining experience in The Cristal restaurant with huge windows allowing views across the formal gardens. The menu is inspirational under the direction of award-winning Chef Jim Kerr. Lighter meals & tea can be taken down at the Spa or in the Grand Hall under its beautiful fanned ceiling. Mar Hall is a great place to spend time with yourself or with friends.

**Location:** M8 jct 30, 2 miles; Glasgow, 14 miles; Glasgow Airport, 6.2 miles

**Attractions:** Glasgow City Centre; Glasgow School of Art; Glasgow Cathedral; Kelvingrove Art Gallery

# INVERLOCHY CASTLE

TORLUNDY, FORT WILLIAM PH33 6SN
**Tel:** 0845 365 1926 **International:** +44 (0)1397 702177 **Fax:** 01397 702953
**Web:** www.johansens.com/inverlochy **E-mail:** info@inverlochy.co.uk

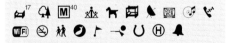

***Our inspector loved:*** *Stunning location and the attention to detail.*

**Price Guide:**
single £250-£350
double £300-£550
suite £450-£650

**Awards/Recognition:** Relais & Châteaux; 1 Michelin Star 2007; 3 AA Rosettes 20o7-2008

**Location:** On A82; Fort William Railway Station, 4 miles; Inverness Airport, 69 miles

**Attractions:** Ben Nevis; Glencoe; Glenfinnan; Loch Ness

Queen Victoria's words from 1873, "I never saw a lovelier or more romantic spot", describe Inverlochy perfectly, and the first Lord Abinger who built the castle in 1863 certainly knew how to pick a gorgeous location in the foothills of Ben Nevis. Today the castle makes a splendid hotel managed by Norbert Lieder and first impressions of the massive reception room featuring Venetian crystal chandeliers, a Michaelangelo-style ceiling and a handsome staircase leading to 3 elaborately decorated dining rooms, carry a real 'wow' factor. Bedrooms are spacious, individually furnished and offer every comfort. Michelin-starred chef Matt Gray, creates modern British cuisine using local game, hand picked wild mushrooms and scallops from the Isle of Skye. Various outdoor activities await you and stunning historical landscapes are nearby.

# BUNCHREW HOUSE HOTEL

INVERNESS IV3 8TA

**Tel:** 0845 365 3214 **International:** +44 (0)1463 234917 **Fax:** 01463 710620
**Web:** www.johansens.com/bunchrewhouse **E-mail:** welcome@bunchrew-inverness.co.uk

*Our inspector loved:* The feeling of a highland home with spectacular views from all rooms.

**Price Guide:**
single £105–£170
double/twin £150–£240

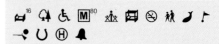

This 17th-century Scottish mansion, the "Hotel on the Shore" sits amidst 20 acres of landscaped gardens and woodlands, catching the sound of the sea lapping at its garden walls and gazes at Ben Wyvis and the Black Isle. Careful restoration has preserved it's heritage, whilst providing you with the utmost in comfort and convenience; bedrooms are furnished to enhance their natural features, and the panelled drawing room's log fires in winter lend it added appeal. Savour the candle-lit restaurant where traditional cuisine includes prime Scottish beef, fresh lobster and langoustines, locally caught game and venison and freshly grown vegetables. Local places of interest include Cawdor Castle and Loch Ness, or if you fancy brushing off your skis head to nearby Aviemore.

**Awards/Recognition:** 2 AA Rosettes 2007-2008

**Location:** Inverness, 2 miles; A9, 3 miles; Inverness Airport, 13 miles

**Attractions:** Loch Ness & Castle Urquhart; Culloden Battle Field; 25 Golf Courses Wthin 90 minutes Drive; Dolphin Watching Cruise

# DRUMOSSIE HOTEL

OLD PERTH ROAD, INVERNESS IV2 5BE
**Tel:** 0845 365 3272 **International:** +44 (0)1463 236451 **Fax:** 01463 712858
**Web:** www.johansens.com/drumossiehotel **E-mail:** stay@drumossiehotel.co.uk

***Our inspector loved:*** *Amazing 'Art Deco' facade of the building.*

**Price Guide:**
double (single occupancy) from £120
double from £150

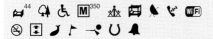

**Awards/Recognition:** 2 AA Rosettes 2006-2007

**Location:** Inverness, 4 miles; Inverness Airport, 7 miles

**Attractions:** Loch Ness; Cawdor Castle; Fort George

An art deco style gem on the edge of Scotland's newest city and in the heart of the Highlands. With warm colour schemes and romantic four posters, its 44 bedrooms are spacious and relaxed, many with views overlooking the delightful gardens. The magnificent ballroom with floor to ceiling windows can entertain up to 450 guests though those wanting a more intimate stay will enjoy the excellent service and personal attention to detail. The restaurant is notably excellent using the best local ingredients and with a fine selection of wines to complement every dish. If you're after adventure, this area plays host to a multitude of outdoor activities; from hiking, climbing and trekking, to cycling, off-road driving and monster hunting in Loch Ness.

# ROCPOOL RESERVE

CULDUTHEL ROAD, INVERNESS, IV2 4AG
**Tel:** 0845 365 2304 **International:** +44 (0)1463 240089 **Fax:** 01463 248431
**Web:** www.johansens.com/rocpool **E-mail:** info@rocpool.com

*Our inspector loved: Unique, with stylish decor and lavish accessories in all rooms including underfloor heating in tiled bathrooms.*

**Price Guide:**
single £95–£195
double £145–£250
suite £250-£280

**Location:** City Centre, 5-min walk; Inverness Airport, 10 miles

**Attractions:** Eden Court Theatre; Cairngorms National Park.; Culloden; Loch Ness

You cannot help but be bowled over by Adrian Pieraccini's boutique hotel overlooking Inverness's riverside – elegant and contemporary with bits of the classical blended in. The attention to detail is phenomenal and throughout the recurring colour scheme of red, black and white, bedrooms are fitted with plasma TVs, DVD players and iPod docking stations. Egyptian linens, king-size beds, and Italian ceramics in bathrooms, while one room even has a hot tub on the terrace! Cocktail hour amidst the bar's white leather seats and sparkling chandeliers will relax you before an indulgent, seasonal Italian dinner in the exceptional Reserve Restaurant, where a climate controlled balcony overlooks the river. All this an wonderful staff. Definitely the place to stay in Europe's fastest growing city!

# CUILLIN HILLS HOTEL

PORTREE, ISLE OF SKYE IV51 9QU
**Tel:** 0845 365 3255  **International:** +44 (0)1478 612003  **Fax:** 01478 613092
**Web:** www.johansens.com/cuillinhills  **E-mail:** info@cuillinhills-hotel-skye.co.uk

**Our inspector loved:** *Hotel of character with imposing view over bay at Portree.*

**Price Guide:**
single £70–£90
double/twin £120–£240

**Awards/Recognition:** 2 AA Rosettes 2006-2007

**Location:** A855, 500yds; Skye Bridge, 33 miles; Portree, 10-min walk

**Attractions:** Exploring Skye, Sea Trips, Excellent views from the hotel

What more could you ask for, stunning views of the majestic Cuillin Mountains and Portree Bay. Originally built in the 1870s as a hunting lodge, Cuillin Hills benefits from 15 acres of private mature grounds, which create a secluded setting and peaceful atmosphere. The bedrooms are spacious. The restaurant overlooks the bay and dishes include highland game,lobster,scallops and homemade desserts. Interesting more informal meals are served in the bar. After dinner select your favourite malt whisky and head for the lounge, on cooler evenings relax in front of the log fire. Discover the Isle of Skye's rich history through its castles, museums and visitor centres and the abundance of unspoilt coastal paths and woodland walks nearby. Portree town itself is a mere 10 minutes' walk.

# THE TORRIDON

TORRIDON, BY ACHNASHEEN, WESTER ROSS IV22 2EY
**Tel:** 0845 365 2037 **International:** +44 (0)1445 791242 **Fax:** 01445 712253
**Web:** www.johansens.com/thetorridon **E-mail:** info@thetorridon.com

*Our inspector loved: The warm atmosphere of the wood panelled bar and of course the most excellent food.*

**Price Guide:** (including dinner)
single £120–£165
double/twin £185–£465

**Awards/Recognition:** 2 AA Rosettes 2006-2007

**Location:** A896; Kinlochewe, 10 miles

**Attractions:** Torridon Activity Centre; Isle of Skye; Inverewe Gardens (NT); Eilean Donan Castle

Obviously a man with an eye for a view, the first Earl of Lovelace built this country house as a shooting lodge in 1887, and today Rohaise and Daniel Rose-Bristow continue its tradition of Highland hospitality. Some bedrooms are frankly indulgent; all are comfortable with delectable toiletries, crisp white linens and fresh fruit. The Victorian kitchen garden provides chef, Kevin Broome, with a plethora of produce to include in his world-class cuisine and serve in the beautiful dining room. The estate boasts a little sister property, The Torridon Inn, which provides a more informal alternative. Tramp out in the grounds amidst resident Highland cattle or be more adventurous with guided low and high level walks, abseiling, kayaking or mountain biking. An altogether fabulous experience!

# DALHOUSIE CASTLE AND SPA

NR EDINBURGH, BONNYRIGG EH19 3JB
**Tel:** 0845 365 3260 **International:** +44 (0)1875 820153 **Fax:** 01875 821936
**Web:** www.johansens.com/dalhousiecastle **E-mail:** info@dalhousiecastle.co.uk

***Our inspector loved:*** *The setting of this 13th century fortress within acres of wooded parkland.*

**Price Guide:**
single from £160
double from £220
suite from £280

**Awards/Recognition:** 2 AA Rosettes 2007-2008

**Location:** Off the B704; A7, 2 miles; Edinburgh, 12 miles; Edinburgh Airport, 16.4 miles

**Attractions:** Mining Museum at Newtongrange; Edinburgh Castle; Scottish Parliament; Whisky Heritage Centre

An impressive castle with plenty of reminders of its rich and turbulent 700 year history. A mews containing the castle falconry, A Vaulted Dungeon restaurant serving classical French and Scottish cuisine whilst 15 of the bedrooms are historically themed and include Mary Queen of Scots, Robert the Bruce and William Wallace. The "de Ramseia" suite houses the 500-year-old "Well". Several rooms are found in the 100-year-old Lodge and The Orangery Restaurant, overlooks the South Esk River. If you are looking for an exceptional venue to gather friends or impress clients Dalhousie should be on your list – high standards, warm hospitality and a lot of fun. Edinburgh is just 7 miles away so after a day exploring retire to the Aqueous Spa, with its hydro pool, Laconium, Rasul mud room and treatment rooms.

# THE ROYAL HOTEL

MELVILLE SQUARE, COMRIE, PERTHSHIRE PH6 2DN
**Tel:** 0845 365 2681 **International:** +44 (0)1764 679200 **Fax:** 01764 679219
**Web:** www.johansens.com/royalcomrie **E-mail:** reception@royalhotel.co.uk

**Our inspector loved:** *Walking through the door into an ambience of natural elegance and charm.*

**Price Guide:**
single £80–£120
double £130–£170

**Awards/Recognition:** 1 AA Rosettes 2006-2007

**Location:** A85, 500yds; M9, 15 miles, Perth 20 miles

**Attractions:** Famous Grouse Distillery (the oldest in Scotland); Drummond Castle Gardens; Scone Palace; Gleneagles

The very heart of Perthshire, this fabulous area was once a favourite of Rob Roy McGregor and Queen Victoria, whose visit resulted in the name given to Comrie's principal inn. She would appreciate its homely, elegant atmosphere today, and the genuine Highland hospitality provided by the Milsoms and their cheerful team. Relax in one of the elegant bedrooms or comfortable apartments, or work your way through the large selection of whiskies in the atmospheric lounge bar, unless your preference is for the wonderful real ale! With an AA Rosette under his belt, David Milsom works wonders with local produce in his restaurants. Wander in surrounding countryside moorlands, fly fishing on the River Earn or play golf on one of Comrie's excellent nearby courses.

# BALLATHIE HOUSE HOTEL

KINCLAVEN, STANLEY, PERTHSHIRE PH1 4QN
**Tel:** 0845 365 3027 **International:** +44 (0)1250 883268 **Fax:** 01250 883396
**Web:** www.johansens.com/ballathiehouse **E-mail:** email@ballathiehousehotel.com

***Our inspector loved:*** *The peaceful location, Idyllic setting, the antique details and fine touches.*

**Price Guide:**
single £85–£130
double/twin £170–£240
suite £250–£270

**Awards/Recognition:** 2 AA Rosettes 2006-2007

**Location:** A9, 8 miles; Edinburgh Airport, 52 miles; Perth, 12.8 miles

**Attractions:** Perth Racecourse; Glamis Castle; Scone Palace; Dunkeld

Overlooking the River Tay near Perth, Ballathie House Hotel offers fine Scottish hospitality. Dating from 1850, this mansion has a French baronial façade and handsome interiors. The drawing room overlooks lawns which slope down to the riverside, creating the perfect place to relax with coffee or to enjoy a malt whisky. The premier bedrooms are large and elegant, whilst the standard rooms are designed in a cosy, cottage style. On the ground floor there are several bedrooms suitable for guests with disabilities. Local ingredients such as Tay salmon, Scottish beef, seafood and piquant soft fruits are used to create menus catering for all tastes. You can participate in a diversity of outdoor pursuits or simply enjoy a walk round the estate and visit the farm shop.

# GLENAPP CASTLE

BALLANTRAE, SCOTLAND KA26 0NZ
**Tel:** 0845 365 1768 **International:** +44 (0)1465 831212 **Fax:** 01465 831000
**Web:** www.johansens.com/glenappcastle **E-mail:** enquiries@glenappcastle.com

*Our inspector loved:* This beautiful Castle with the most wonderful and peaceful surroundings.

**Price Guide:** (including dinner)
luxury double/twin from £375
suite from £445
master room from £525

With its 5 AA Red Stars, Glenapp is an experience rather than "just another hotel", thanks to owners Fay and Graham Cowan who bought it in 1994 in a state of neglect. Today you can enjoy the results of their no expense spared transformation, with flourishes such as stone fireplaces carved with the family crest and monogrammed china. Lounges, oak-panelled hallways and bedrooms with views of the garden or coastline are decorated with personally selected oil paintings and antiques. Head Chef Matt Weedon prepares 6-course dinners using local produce, and fruit, vegetables and herbs straight from the 36-acre gardens which contain rare trees and shrubs and an impressive Victorian glasshouse. Play tennis and croquet in the grounds, golf on nearby courses and there is a beautiful spa in close proximity.

**Awards/Recognition:** Relais & Châteaux ;
1 Star Michelin 2007; AA 3 Rosettes 2007-2008

**Location:** A77, 1 mile; Stranraer Ferry Port, 17 miles; Prestwick Airport, 40 miles

**Attractions:** Mull of Galloway; Galloway Forest Park; Robert Burns Country; Logan Botancial Gardens

# Wales

For further information on Wales, please contact:

**Wales Tourist Board**
Brunel House, 2 Fitzalan Road, Cardiff CF24 0UY
Tel: +44 (0)29 2049 9909
Web: www.visitwales.com

**North Wales Tourism**
77 Conway Road, Colwyn Bay, Conway LL29 7LN
Tel: +44 (0)1492 531731
Web: www.nwt.co.uk

**Mid Wales Tourism**
The Station, Machynlleth, Powys SY20 8TG
Tel: (Freephone) 0800 273747
Web: www.visitmidwales.co.uk

**South West Wales Tourism Partnership**
The Coach House, Aberglasney, Carmarthenshire SA32 8QH
Tel: +44 (0)1558 669091
Web: www.swwtp.co.uk

or see **pages 293-296** for details of local historic houses, castles and gardens to visit during your stay.

For additional places to stay in Wales, turn to
**pages 291-292** where a listing of our Recommended
Small Hotels, Inns & Restaurant Guide can be found.

# MISKIN MANOR COUNTRY HOUSE HOTEL

MISKIN, NR CARDIFF CF72 8ND
**Tel:** 0845 365 2069 **International:** +44 (0)1443 224204 **Fax:** 01443 237606
**Web:** www.johansens.com/miskinmanor **E-mail:** reservations@miskin-manor.co.uk

*Our inspector loved: The wonderful spacious reception rooms with many original features.*

**Price Guide:**
single from £105
double/twin/four poster from £130
suite from £240

**Awards/Recognition:** 1 AA Rosette 2006-2007

**Location:** Off the A4119; M4 Jct 34, 1.73 miles; Cardiff, 12 miles; Cardiff Airport, 14 miles

**Attractions:** Cardiff Bay; Swansea; Brecon Beacons; Gower Peninsula

It may be just 10 minutes' drive from Cardiff Bay but it's 22 acres of undisturbed parkland criss-crossed with streams promise seclusion. Dating back to the 11th century it exudes a sense of history and indeed amongst those who have enjoyed its charms was the Prince of Wales, later King Edward VIII in the 1920s. Unusually large reception rooms have fireplaces, panelled walls and elaborate plasterwork ceilings whilst bedrooms are rich in colour and texture. In the restaurant the chef delights in taking inspiration from local Welsh produce and is deservedly a popular local destination. Building up an appetite can be achieved at the popular health club, which includes a glass-backed squash court and badminton.

# Falcondale Mansion Hotel

LAMPETER, CEREDIGION SA48 7RX

**Tel:** 0845 365 3287  **International:** +44 (0)1570 422910  **Fax:** 01570 423559
**Web:** www.johansens.com/falcondale  **E-mail:** info@falcondalehotel.com

*Our inspector loved:* The transformation in the restaurant. Very attractive.

**Price Guide:**
single from £99
double/twin from £137

**Awards/Recognition:** 2 AA Rosettes 2007-2008

**Location:** A485, 1 mile; A40, 10 miles; Cardiff Airport, 95 miles; Severn Bridge, 95 miles

**Attractions:** Llanerchaeron (NT); Dolaucothi Gold Mines (NT); University of Wales; National Botanic Garden of Wales

Only 10 miles from Cardigan coast and the beautiful fishing village of Aberaeron, this elegant Victorian Italianate Mansion is rapidly gaining an excellent reputation and putting this charming area of Wales firmly on the map. Discover it before everyone else and stroll the grounds with their 14 acres of ornamental woods and sweeping lawns. A recent refurbishment has seen the 20 guest rooms stylishly transformed with luxurious bathrooms. You can book the entire hotel for exclusive use and tailor-made events. With a Welsh head chef, menus are traditionally Welsh with an international flavour, fresh produce of known origin including live lobster when in season and local fish, vegetarian options are excellent. Suit your mood with either fine dining or more informal eating in the Brasserie.

# YNYSHIR HALL

EGLWYSFACH, MACHYNLLETH, CEREDIGION SY20 8TA
**Tel:** 0845 365 3426 **International:** +44 (0)1654 781209 **Fax:** 01654 781366
**Web:** www.johansens.com/ynyshirhall **E-mail:** ynyshir@relaischateaux.com

**Our inspector loved:** *The zen like qualities, its very special with superb dining.*

**Price Guide:**
single from £110
superior double from £275
suite from £285

A charming country house, once owned by Queen Victoria, nestles in the heart of idyllic Welsh countryside. Artistic flair is apparent throughout, not only in the showcasing of stunning paintings of the local countryside but also in the stylish decoration of the public rooms and the naming of each uniquely styled bedroom. For example "Hogarth" is dramatically styled in red silk and midnight blue, features a four-poster bed and boasts views across the beautiful gardens. The delightful dining room, decorated in duck-egg blue, is a perfect setting in which to enjoy the imaginative cuisine of head chef Shane Hughes. Dishes can include Welsh lamb and black beef, farmhouse cheeses and locally sourced seafood, often enhanced with such wild ingredients as wood sorrel, samphire and wild garlic.

**Awards/Recognition:** 3 AA Rosettes 2006-2007; Relais & Châteaux

**Location:** A487, 1 mile; A470, 12 miles; Birmingham Airport, 88 miles; Cardif, 110 miles

**Attractions:** RSPB Ynys-hir Reserve; Glorious Beaches; Cambrian Mountains; Centre for Alternative Energy

# BODYSGALLEN HALL & SPA

LLANDUDNO, NORTH WALES LL30 1RS
**Tel:** 0845 365 3039  **International:** +44 (0)1492 584466  **Fax:** 01492 582519
**Web:** www.johansens.com/bodysgallenhall  **E-mail:** info@bodysgallen.com

***Our inspector loved:*** *The wonderfully comfortable interior with its original 17th century oak panelling and open fires.*

**Price Guide:**
single from £140
double/twin from £175
suite from £210

**Awards/Recognition:** Condé Nast Johansens Most Excellent Country Hotel 2007; 3 AA Rosettes 2005-2006

**Location:** A 470, 1 mile; A 55, 1 mile; Manchester Airport, 85 miles; London, 3 hours-train

**Attractions:** Bodnant Gardens; Conwy and Caernarfon Castles; Welsh Highland Railway, The Island of Anglesey; Snowdonia;

A place to be inspired. With spectacular views of Snowdonia and Conwy Castle this Grade I listed manor has grown from a 13th-century fortified tower into one of the finest hotels in Wales. Breathtaking gardens set within 200 acres include a 17th-century parterre of box hedges filled with scented herbs and a restored formal walled rose garden. Within the grounds is a cluster of 16 self-contained cottages, and the 17 bedrooms inside the house include brand new Principle Suites. From the moment you enter the entrance hall you are enveloped in comfort. Impressive antique furniture, splendid oak panelling and open fireplaces set the tone and the staff are impeccably discreet. The spa is complete with tranquillity room and indoor pool. Valley Airport is now open for flights from Cardiff.

# St Tudno Hotel & Restaurant

NORTH PROMENADE, LLANDUDNO, NORTH WALES LL30 2LP
**Tel:** 0845 365 2361 **International:** +44 (0)1492 874411 **Fax:** 01492 860407
**Web:** www.johansens.com/sttudno **E-mail:** sttudnohotel@btinternet.com

*Our inspector loved: The lounge of this special sea front hotel, nestling close to the Great Orme.*

**Price Guide:**
single from £75
double/twin £95–£230
suite from £260

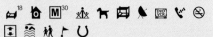

**Awards/Recognition:** 2 AA Rosettes 2006-2007; Visit Wales Gold Award

**Location:** On the A470; A55, 4 miles; Chester, 45 miles; Manchester Airport, 65 miles

**Attractions:** Great Orme Copper Mines; Theatre at Llandudno; Bodnant Gardens; Dry Ski Slope and Tobaggan run on the Great Orme

Undoubtedly one of the most delightful small hotels to be found on the coast of Britain, St Tudno now in its 36th year offers a very special experience. A former winner of the Johansen's Hotel of the Year Award for Excellence, the hotel which is elegantly and lovingly refurbished provides a particular warm welcome from Martin Bland and his staff. The individually designed bedrooms have many thoughtful extras and the Terrace Restaurant is regarded as one of Wales' leading places to eat. A little oasis of this town house is the indoor heated swimming pool and secret garden. This AA Red Star Hotel has won a host of prestigious awards: Best Seaside Resort Hotel in Great Britain (Good Hotel Guide), Welsh Hotel of the Year, 2 major wine awards and even an accolade for having the Best Hotel Loos in Britain. St Tudno is ideally situated for visits to Snowdonia, Conwy and Caernarfon Castles, World Famous Bodnant Gardens, Anglesey and glorious walks on the Great Orme.

# PALÉ HALL

PALÉ ESTATE, LLANDDERFEL, BALA, GWYNEDD LL23 7PS
**Tel:** 0845 365 2096 **International:** +44 (0)1678 530285 **Fax:** 01678 530220
**Web:** www.johansens.com/palehall **E-mail:** enquiries@palehall.co.uk

**Our inspector loved:** *The experience of another era and the space to reflect and relax. Super bathrooms.*

**Price Guide:**
single £85–£150
double/twin £115–£200

**Awards/Recognition:** 1 AA Rosette 2007-2008

**Location:** A 494, 2 miles; A 5, 6 miles; Chester, 40 miles; Liverpool Airport, 65 miles

**Attractions:** Snowdonia; Portmeirion; Lake Bala; Llechwedd Slate Mines at Blaenau Ffestiniog

Illustrious guests including Queen Victoria and Winston Churchill have stayed at Palé Hall, a beautifully preserved building with magnificent period details; galleried entrance hall, vaulted ceiling and the Boudoir with handpainted dome. Bedrooms all have their own character and many with delightful surprises. You could choose to sleep in the half tester bed enjoyed by Queen Victoria and relax in her original royal bath. Views towards the Snowdonia National Park are in abundance and there is a wonderful feeling of tranquillity. The restaurant menu has British and French dishes strongly influenced by the wealth of local produce. An inspired spot to take over for a house party of friends or colleagues.

# PENMAENUCHAF HALL

PENMAENPOOL, DOLGELLAU, GWYNEDD LL40 1YB
**Tel:** 0845 365 2104 **International:** +44 (0)1341 422129 **Fax:** 01341 422787
**Web:** www.johansens.com/penmaenuchafhall **E-mail:** relax@penhall.co.uk

**Our inspector loved:** *The special way a new restaurant and lounge have been created, still maintaining intimacy.*

**Price Guide:**
single £90–£135
double/twin £135–£210

**Awards/Recognition:** 2 AA Rosettes 2007-2008

**Location:** A493, 0.5 mile; A470, 1.5 miles; Shrewsbury, 60 miles; Chester, 64 miles

**Attractions:** Snowdonia; Narrow Guage Railways; Bodnant Garden; Portmeirion

You might want to take a moment once you've climbed Penmaenuchaf's long tree-lined driveway to fully take in its glorious setting: within the Snowdonia National Park, offering views across Mawddach Estuary and panoramic distant wooded slopes. The 21-acre grounds blend lawns, a sunken rose garden, water garden and woodland. The Victorian house is handsome, with oak and mahogany panelling, stained glass windows, polished slate floors and log fires in winter. The hotel is always discreetly evolving - this year the owners, Mark and Lorraine, have opened the new garden room restaurant and created a new bedroom with balcony to view the magnificent scenery. Dinners are imaginative and seasonal. You can fish along 10 miles of the Mawddach River, mountain bike or enjoy nearby golf courses and sandy beaches.

# HOTEL MAES-Y-NEUADD

TALSARNAU, NEAR HARLECH, GWYNEDD LL47 6YA
**Tel:** 0845 365 1902  **International:** +44 (0)1766 780200  **Fax:** 01766 780211
**Web:** www.johansens.com/maesyneuadd  **E-mail:** maes@neuadd.com

*Our inspector loved: The location with its wonderful winter walking, so relaxing and finally a delicious breakfast.*

**Price Guide:** (including dinner)
double/twin from £180–£270

**Awards/Recognition:** 2 AA Rosettes 2007-2008

**Location:** B4573, 0.5 miles; A496, 2 miles; Manchester Airport, 100 miles; Liverpool Airport, 100 miles

**Attractions:** Excellent Golf Courses; Snowdonia National Park; Harlech Castle; Welsh Mountain Railways

With spectacular views across Snowdonia National Park, this 14th-century Welsh manor, nestled into a wooded mountainside, has won numerous awards. The Jackson and Payne families own and run their country house in a comfortable and relaxed style. The bedrooms beautifully reflect the house's history, with 16th century beams, high-ceilinged Georgian rooms and two others that date all the way back to the 14th-century. The sunlit conservatory is perfect for morning coffee or afternoon tea, and the terrace offers the magnificent spectacle of the sun setting over the Lleyn Peninsula. Chef Patron, Peter Jackson creates award winning regional dishes using Welsh produce, selecting fruit and vegetables from the large, fully restored kitchen gardens. Families are welcome and early teas for young children can be arranged.

# TRE-YSGAWEN HALL COUNTRY HOUSE HOTEL & SPA

CAPEL COCH, LLANGEFNI, ISLE OF ANGLESEY LL77 7UR
**Tel:** 0845 365 2846 **International:** +44 (0)1248 750750 **Fax:** 01248 750035
**Web:** www.johansens.com/treysgawenhall **E-mail:** enquiries@treysgawen-hall.co.uk

*Our inspector loved:* The variety of facilities and quality of service that ensure you have an enjoyable and comfortable stay, whether here for business, pleasure or a day in the spa.

**Price Guide:** (including spa facilities)
deluxe single £95–£107
deluxe double/twin £132–£169
suite £250

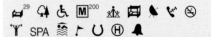

**Location:** B5111, 2 miles; A5114, 4.6 miles; A55, 6 miles Beaumaris 12.6 miles

**Attractions:** Beaumaris Castle; Anglesey Coastal Path; Anglesey Sea Zoo; Plas Newydd

At the end of a private tree-lined driveway stands the impressive Tre-Ysgawen Hall, surrounded by acres of landscaped gardens and woodland, providing guest rooms with every creature comfort and four-poster suites boasting their very own Jacuzzis. The restaurant's ever-changing menus are created from the best local, regional and seasonal produce and are served alongside a carefully chosen wine list featuring fine New and Old World selections. Noëlle's Bar also has a great selection of wines and champagnes, ranging from excellent vintages of the 1970s and '80s, to contemporary New World choices. For a more relaxed meal the Clock Tower Café Wine Bar offers both alcoholic and non-alcoholic beverages, meals, cakes and pastries. Pamper yourself in the fabulous state-of-the-art Tre-Ysgawen Spa, located in the converted Victorian stables, and choose from the hotel's exclusive "Spa Experience" or "Spa Indulgence" packages.

# THE TREARDDUR BAY HOTEL

LON ISALLT, TREARDDUR BAY, ANGLESEY LL65 2UN
**Tel:** 0845 365 3459 **International:** +44 (0)1407 860301 **Fax:** 01407 861181
**Web:** www.johansens.com/trearddurbay **E-mail:** enquiries@trearddurbayhotel.co.uk

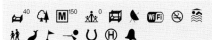

***Our inspector loved:*** *The location, its many facilities for business, pleasure or both.*

**Price Guide:**
double (single occupancy) from £96
twin from £145

**Location:** Off the B4545, 2 miles; Holyhead, 2 miles; A55 expressway, 2 miles; Valley Airport, 3 miles

**Attractions:** Anglesey Coastal Path; Beaumaris Castle; Dublin via Holyhead; Snowdonia

The Anglesey coastline is striking and with an abundance of wildlife, beaches and estuaries it most definitely is worth exploring. Trearddur Bay Hotel is a great base to do this from with its own wonderful views over the bay and a blue flag beach ideal for those who enjoy an early morning dip. Popular locally the restaurant capitalizes on the views and has recently been redecorated. A more informal meal can be enjoyed in the Inn at the Bay or there's the Snug for drinks and where on most Fridays live music is arranged. Not to disturb the whole hotel the new self-contained Venue suite has opened up plenty of flexibility for meetings and training breaks with links to several nearby golf courses and outdoor pursuit centres.

# LLANSANTFFRAED COURT HOTEL

LLANVIHANGEL GOBION, CLYTHA, ABERGAVENNY, MONMOUTHSHIRE NP7 9BA
**Tel:** 0845 365 2035 **International:** +44 (0)1873 840678 **Fax:** 01873 840674
**Web:** www.johansens.com/llansantffraedcourt **E-mail:** reception@llch.co.uk

**Our inspector loved:** *A magnificent Georgian house set in beautiful parkland.*

**Price Guide:**
single £90–£120
double/twin £120–£175
suites £175

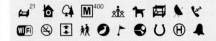

**Awards/Recognition:** 2 AA Rosettes 2006-2007

**Location:** Off the B4589; A472, 6.5 miles; M4 jct 24, 16 miles

**Attractions:** Wye Valley; Blaenavon World Heritage Site; Hay-on-Wye; Cardiff

Situated on the edge of the Brecon Beacons and the Wye Valley this award winning Georgian-style country house hotel makes a perfect retreat. The bedrooms are very comfortable and most have views over the gardens and ornamental trout lake. One room has a four-poster bed, whilst others feature oak beams and dormer windows. Restaurant menus are acclaimed and reflect the changing seasons based on the availability of fresh local produce, complemented by fine wines. You can take Afternoon tea in front of a blazing log fire during the cooler months and enjoy views of the South Wales countryside. Excellent facilities are available for private celebrations and meetings. Llansantffraed Court is also an ideal base for exploring the diverse history and beauty of the area.

# CELTIC MANOR RESORT

COLDRA WOODS, THE USK VALLEY, NEWPORT, NP18 1HQ
**Tel:** 0845 365 3297 **International:** +44 (0)1633 413000 **Fax:** 01633 412910
**Web:** www.johansens.com/celticmanor **E-mail:** postbox@celtic-manor.com

***Our inspector loved:*** *The wonderful location in vast grounds. Comfortable large bedrooms and two great spas.*

**Price Guide:**
single £165–£195
double £198–£228
suite £323–£1098

**Location:** Just off B4237; M4 Jct 24, 0.5 mile; A48, 0.5 mile; Newport, 3 miles

**Attractions:** Brecon Beacons; Roman Town of Caerleon; Chepstow Castle; Tintern Abbey

Rising majestically above the Usk Valley, Celtic Manor Resort, the host venue for the 2010 Ryder Cup has not only 3 championship courses and a world-class Golf Academy but plenty of other activities to keep the body and mind distracted. Two outstanding spa zones, tennis, shooting, mountain biking and walking trails and for young families there is a children's club and crèche, which should give plenty of quality time and space to both parents and the kids. Whilst the Resort Hotel is unashamedly modern in stature those seeking a little more tradition can stay in the Victorian Manor House hotel. Another great thing about this resort is the number of dining options from the formal to relaxed bistro and in summer The Rooftop Garden and Barbecue Terrace.

# WARPOOL COURT HOTEL

ST DAVID'S, PEMBROKESHIRE SA62 6BN
**Tel:** 0845 365 2786 **International:** +44 (0)1437 720300 **Fax:** 01437 720676
**Web:** www.johansens.com/warpoolcourt **E-mail:** info@warpoolcourthotel.com

**Our inspector loved:** *Exhilarating cliff top walks and the wonderful fish dishes on the menu.*

**Price Guide:**
single £125–£140
double/twin £180–£300

**Awards/Recognition:** 2 AA Rosettes 2007-2008

**Location:** A487, 0.5 mile; A40, 16 miles; Severn Bridge, 135 miles; Cardiff, 100 miles

**Attractions:** Pembrokeshire Heritage Coastal Walk; St David's Cathedral and Bishops Palace; Pembroke Castle; Graham Sutherland Gallery

Warpool Court was originally built as the St David's Cathedral Choir School in the 1860s, and you will feel equally inspired by the views over the coast and St Bride's Bay! Now a hotel for over 40 years with comfortable bedrooms, many overlooking the sea. The restaurant,open to non residents offers imaginative menus featuring Welsh lamb and beef whenever possible and locally caught crab, lobster, sewin and sea bass. Vegetarian dishes are also available. Stroll in the gardens, take a swim in the covered heated pool open April-October or head straight out onto the Pembrokeshire Coastal Path, with its rich variety of wildlife and scenery and the inspiration of many artists. Boat trips arranged locally. Closed in January.

# LLANGOED HALL

LLYSWEN, BRECON, POWYS LD3 0YP

**Tel:** 0845 365 2034  **International:** +44 (0)1874 754525  **Fax:** 01874 754545
**Web:** www.johansens.com/llangoedhall  **E-mail:** enquiries@llangoedhall.com

***Our inspector loved:*** *The first-class service in this relaxing treasure; a great place to stay or simply have lunch.*

**Price Guide:**
single upon request
double/twin from £210
suite from £385

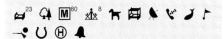

**Awards/Recognition:** 2 AA Rosettes 2006-2007

**Location:** A470, 0.75 miles; Hay-on-Wye, 9 miles; Hereford, 35 miles; Cardiff Airport, 45 miles

**Attractions:** Hay-on-Wye Specialist Book Shops; Brecon Beacons; Black Mountains; Brecon

With a spectacular location close to the Brecon Beacons, Llangoed Hall is a place where you will be treated like a king or queen. The building oozes tremendous charm and is fitted with glorious fabrics, log fires to enjoy and a fascinating collection of paintings. In the restaurant Sean Ballington and his team create sophisticated dishes with panache from local produce. General Manager, Calum Milne's keen eye for detail ensures that each guest feels special and is only too pleased to arrange any special activities at your request. The beautiful gardens, with a restored maze complement the breathtaking setting.

# LAKE VYRNWY HOTEL

LAKE VYRNWY, MONTGOMERYSHIRE SY10 0LY
**Tel:** 0845 365 1976 **International:** +44 (0)1691 870 692 **Fax:** 01691 870 259
**Web:** www.johansens.com/lakevyrnwy **E-mail:** info@lakevyrnwyhotel.co.uk

*Our inspector loved: Listening to contented diners feeling refreshed from the pure air, wondering at the location - it could be Switzerland!*

**Price Guide:**
single £90–£155
double/twin £120–£190
suite £190–£220

**Awards/Recognition:** 1 AA Rosettes 2006-2007

**Location:** A490, 8 miles; A495, 12 miles; Welshpool, 20 miles; Chester, 50 miles

**Attractions:** Powis Castle; Snowdonia; Portmeirion; Centre for Alternative Technology

The location of Lake Vyrnwy Hotel is just magical: overlooking the stunning lake and surrounded by wild moorland, forest and the rugged Berwyn Mountains. This year, an excellent extension has been added to the hotel that includes 14 bedrooms with balconies looking out to the lake and a new spa and thermal suite. An extensive conference and event suite has also been added, making this a brilliant venue for both leisure and corporate business. Sitting on the balcony prior to dinner, watching the sun go down, is a truly wonderful experience. The menus reflect a genuine enthusiasm for food and understanding of quality ingredients, and utilise as much local produce as possible. In winter there are warm welcomes with log fires and amazing local walks. Relax here for a day or two at least.

# THE LAKE COUNTRY HOUSE AND SPA

LLANGAMMARCH WELLS, POWYS LD4 4BS
**Tel:** 0845 365 2571 **International:** +44 (0)1591 620202 **Fax:** 01591 620457
**Web:** www.johansens.com/lakecountryhouse **E-mail:** info@lakecountryhouse.co.uk

*Our inspector loved:* Its charm and peace - a treasured place to be pampered whether it's business or leisure.

**Price Guide:**
single from £115
superior from £220
suite from £250

**Awards/Recognition:** Condé Nast Johansens Most Excellent Restaurant 2005; 2 AA Rosettes 2006-2007

**Location:** A 485, 3 miles; A 470, 8 miles; Hay on Wye, 21 miles; Cardiff Airport, 52 miles

**Attractions:** Brecon Beacons National Park; Aberglasney House and Gardens; Elan Valley; Raglan Castle

A trout leaping up from a serene lake, carpets of wild flowers bobbing in the breeze and badgers ambling by the woods nearby are all sights to be savoured at this glorious country house, surrounded by 50 acres of unspoilt grounds. This hidden gem is a haven for wildlife enthusiasts with over 100 bird-nesting boxes within the grounds and ample opportunities for fishing and horse riding. You can feast on traditional Welsh teas in the decadent lounges by roaring log fires in the winter or beneath the chestnut tree in the summer. Fresh produce and herbs from the garden are used in the Condé Nast Johansens award-winning restaurant whilst the superb wine list boasts over 300 choices. The lakeside spa is an inspired setting for when you totally want to unwind.

# HOLM HOUSE

MARINE PARADE, PENARTH, VALE OF GLAMORGAN CF64 3BG
**Tel:** 0845 365 2869 **International:** +44 (0)2920 701572 **Fax:** 02920 709875
**Web:** www.johansens.com/holmhouse **E-mail:** info@holmhouse.com

*Our inspector loved:* The fabulous loft suites, Chic with a capital C!

**Price Guide:** (including dinner)
single £130-£140
double £175-£260
suite £300-£350

Originally built in the 1920s, today, Holm House is cosy, quirky, eccentric, bohemian, opulent, decadent and sumptuous! Hip and funky, the brand new guest rooms, including 3 loft suites and an amazing white spa bedroom, are individually designed, beautifully decorated and warmly lit. Each is furnished to the highest standard and filled with delightful extras that will make you feel particularly spoilt and pampered. Frette bed linen, Jo Malone bathroom products, a Tassimo beverage machine and Bang & Olufsen hi-tech entertainment system are standard to each bedroom. The house is just a stone's throw from Penarth's seafront, with its smart yachts and cruisers, impressive pier and esplanade, and for those of you in need of retail therapy, Cardiff's bustling city centre is only about a 10 minutes' drive away.

**Location:** A4160, 0.5 miles; A4232, 2.2 miles; M4 jct 28, 10.5 miles; Cardiff, 5 miles

**Attractions:** Cardiff Castle; St Fagans - Museum of Welsh Life; Glamorgan Heritage Coastline; Castell Coch

# Small Hotels & Inns, Great Britain & Ireland

All the properties listed below can be found in our Recommended Small Hotels, Inns & Restaurants 2008 Guide.
More information on our portfolio of guides can be found on page 343.

## Channel Islands

| | | |
|---|---|---|
| Château La Chaire | Channel Islands | 0845 365 2863 |
| La Sablonnerie | Channel Islands | 0845 365 1972 |
| The White House | Channel Islands | 0845 365 2735 |

## England

| | | |
|---|---|---|
| Cornfields Restaurant & Hotel | Bedfordshire | 0845 365 3246 |
| Cantley House | Berkshire | 0845 365 3223 |
| The Cottage Inn | Berkshire | 0845 365 2435 |
| The Inn on the Green, Restaurant with Rooms | Berkshire | 0845 365 2547 |
| L'ortolan Restaurant | Berkshire | 0845 365 1965 |
| The Leatherne Bottel Riverside Restaurant | Berkshire | 0845 365 2578 |
| The Royal Oak Restaurant | Berkshire | 0845 365 2685 |
| Stirrups Country House Hotel | Berkshire | 0845 365 2369 |
| The Dinton Hermit | Buckinghamshire | 0845 365 2467 |
| The Crown and Punchbowl | Cambridgeshire | 0845 365 2893 |
| The Tickell Arms, Restaurant | Cambridgeshire | 0845 365 2710 |
| Broxton Hall | Cheshire | 0845 365 3208 |
| The Beeches Hotel & Elemis Day Spa | Cornwall | 0845 365 2874 |
| Cormorant Hotel & Riverside Restaurant | Cornwall | 0845 365 2875 |
| Highland Court Lodge | Cornwall | 0845 365 1852 |
| The Old Coastguard Hotel | Cornwall | 0845 365 2610 |
| Rose-In-Vale Country House Hotel | Cornwall | 0845 365 2306 |
| Tredethy House | Cornwall | 0845 365 2758 |
| Trevalsa Court Country House Hotel & Restaurant | Cornwall | 0845 365 2765 |
| Crosby Lodge Country House Hotel | Cumbria | 0845 365 3253 |
| Dale Head Hall Lakeside Hotel | Cumbria | 0845 365 3258 |
| Fayrer Garden House Hotel | Cumbria | 0845 365 3292 |
| Hipping Hall | Cumbria | 0845 365 1859 |
| Linthwaite House Hotel | Cumbria | 0845 365 2031 |
| Nent Hall Country House Hotel | Cumbria | 0845 365 2081 |
| The Pheasant | Cumbria | 0845 365 2643 |
| Temple Sowerby House Hotel and Restaurant | Cumbria | 0845 365 2389 |
| West Vale Country House & Restaurant | Cumbria | 0845 365 2795 |
| The Wheatsheaf @ Brigsteer | Cumbria | 0845 365 2734 |
| The Crown Inn | Derbyshire | 0845 365 3608 |
| Dannah Farm Country House | Derbyshire | 0845 365 3262 |
| The Wind in the Willows | Derbyshire | 0845 365 2743 |
| Combe House | Devon | 0845 365 3241 |
| Heddon's Gate Hotel | Devon | 0845 365 1834 |
| Home Farm Hotel | Devon | 0845 365 1874 |
| Kingston House | Devon | 0845 365 1937 |
| Mill End | Devon | 0845 365 2062 |
| The New Inn | Devon | 0845 365 2607 |
| Penhaven Country House Hotel | Devon | 0845 365 3745 |
| Yeoldon House Hotel | Devon | 0845 365 2837 |
| The Bridge House Hotel | Dorset | 0845 365 2408 |
| The Grange at Oborne | Dorset | 0845 365 2506 |
| The Crown House | Essex | 0845 365 2453 |
| The Swan Inn | Essex | 0845 365 2864 |
| Bibury Court | Gloucestershire | 0845 365 3035 |
| Charlton Kings Hotel | Gloucestershire | 0845 365 3230 |
| The Fleece Hotel | Gloucestershire | 0845 365 2857 |
| Lower Brook House | Gloucestershire | 0845 365 2045 |
| Lypiatt House | Gloucestershire | 0845 365 2051 |
| New Inn At Coln | Gloucestershire | 0845 365 3754 |
| Langrish House | Hampshire | 0845 365 1986 |
| The Mill At Gordleton | Hampshire | 0845 365 2597 |
| The Nurse's Cottage | Hampshire | 0845 365 2609 |
| Aylestone Court | Herefordshire | 0845 365 3022 |
| The Chase Hotel | Herefordshire | 0845 365 3741 |
| Glewstone Court | Herefordshire | 0845 365 1782 |
| Moccas Court | Herefordshire | 0845 365 2071 |
| Wilton Court Hotel | Herefordshire | 0845 365 2809 |
| Redcoats Farmhouse Hotel and Restaurant | Hertfordshire | 0845 365 2143 |
| The White House and Lion & Lamb Bar & Restaurant | Hertfordshire | 0845 365 2736 |
| The Hambrough | Isle of Wight | 0845 365 2517 |
| The Priory Bay Hotel | Isle of Wight | 0845 365 2649 |
| Rylstone Manor | Isle of Wight | 0845 365 2318 |
| Winterbourne Country House | Isle of Wight | 0845 365 2813 |
| Little Silver Country Hotel | Kent | 0845 365 2032 |
| Romney Bay House Hotel | Kent | 0845 365 2305 |
| The Royal Harbour Hotel | Kent | 0845 365 4853 |

| | | |
|---|---|---|
| **Wallett's Court Hotel & Spa** | **Kent** | **0845 365 2784** |
| Ferrari's Restaurant & Hotel | Lancashire | 0845 365 3293 |
| The Inn at Whitewell | Lancashire | 0845 365 2546 |
| Horse & Trumpet | Leicestershire | 0845 365 1879 |
| Sysonby Knoll Hotel | Leicestershire | 0845 365 2385 |
| Bailhouse Hotel | Lincolnshire | 0845 365 3024 |
| The Crown Hotel | Lincolnshire | 0845 365 2451 |
| Washingborough Hall | Lincolnshire | 0845 365 2792 |
| The Bingham Hotel | London | 0845 365 3761 |
| The Kings Arms Hotel | London | 0845 365 4857 |
| Tree Tops Country House Restaurant & Hotel | Merseyside | 0845 365 2759 |
| Beechwood Hotel | Norfolk | 0845 365 3032 |
| Broad House | Norfolk | 0845 365 4856 |
| Felbrigg Lodge | Norfolk | 0845 365 2853 |
| The Kings Head Hotel | Norfolk | 0845 365 2567 |
| The Neptune Inn & Restaurant | Norfolk | 0845 365 2604 |
| The Old Rectory | Norfolk | 0845 365 2614 |
| The Stower Grange | Norfolk | 0845 365 2701 |
| Titchwell Manor Hotel | Norfolk | 0845 365 2861 |

# Small Hotels & Inns, Great Britain & Ireland

All the properties listed below can be found in our Recommended Small Hotels, Inns & Restaurants 2008 Guide.
More information on our portfolio of guides can be found on page 343.

| | | |
|---|---|---|
| The Orchard House | Northumberland | 0845 365 3726 |
| The Otterburn Tower | Northumberland | 0845 365 3748 |
| Waren House Hotel | Northumberland | 0845 365 2785 |
| Cockliffe Country House Hotel | Nottinghamshire | 0845 365 3237 |
| Greenwood Lodge | Nottinghamshire | 0845 365 2891 |
| Langar Hall | Nottinghamshire | 0845 365 1983 |
| Burford Lodge Hotel & Restaurant | Oxfordshire | 0845 365 3215 |
| Duke Of Marlborough Country Inn | Oxfordshire | 0845 365 3784 |
| Fallowfields | Oxfordshire | 0845 365 3288 |
| The Feathers | Oxfordshire | 0845 365 2491 |
| The Jersey Arms | Oxfordshire | 0845 365 2563 |
| The Kings Head Inn & Restaurant | Oxfordshire | 0845 365 2568 |
| The Lamb Inn | Oxfordshire | 0845 365 2576 |
| The Nut Tree Inn | Oxfordshire | 0845 365 3789 |
| The Spread Eagle Hotel | Oxfordshire | 0845 365 2694 |
| Weston Manor | Oxfordshire | 0845 365 2798 |
| Barnsdale Lodge | Rutland | 0845 365 3028 |
| The Lake Isle Restaurant & Townhouse Hotel | Rutland | 0845 365 2573 |
| Pen-Y-Dyffryn Country Hotel | Shropshire | 0845 365 2106 |
| Soulton Hall | Shropshire | 0845 365 2356 |
| Bellplot House Hotel & Thomas's Restaurant | Somerset | 0845 365 3033 |
| Beryl | Somerset | 0845 365 3034 |
| Compton House | Somerset | 0845 365 3243 |
| Farthings Country House Hotel & Restaurant | Somerset | 0845 365 3290 |
| Glencot House | Somerset | 0845 365 1769 |
| Karslake Country House | Somerset | 0845 365 1935 |
| Three Acres Country House | Somerset | 0845 365 2751 |
| Woodlands Country House Hotel | Somerset | 0845 365 3242 |
| The Bildeston Crown | Suffolk | 0845 365 2860 |
| Clarice House | Suffolk | 0845 365 3235 |
| The Swan Inn | Surrey | 0845 365 3749 |
| The Hope Anchor Hotel | East Sussex | 0845 365 2519 |
| Burpham Country House | West Sussex | 0845 365 2851 |
| The Mill House Hotel | West Sussex | 0845 365 2598 |
| Beechfield House | Wiltshire | 0845 365 3031 |
| The Bell at Ramsbury | Wiltshire | 0845 365 3769 |
| The Castle Inn | Wiltshire | 0845 365 2894 |
| The Lamb at Hindon | Wiltshire | 0845 365 2574 |
| The Old Manor Hotel | Wiltshire | 0845 365 2613 |
| Stanton Manor Hotel & Gallery Restaurant | Wiltshire | 0845 365 2364 |
| Widbrook Grange | Wiltshire | 0845 365 2805 |
| Colwall Park | Worcestershire | 0845 365 3238 |
| The Old Rectory | Worcestershire | 0845 365 2615 |
| The Peacock Inn | Worcestershire | 0845 365 2634 |
| The White Lion Hotel | Worcestershire | 0845 365 2738 |
| Royal Forester Country Inn | Worcestershre | 0845 365 2865 |
| The Austwick Traddock | North Yorkshire | 0845 365 2396 |
| The Devonshire Fell | North Yorkshire | 0845 365 2462 |
| Dunsley Hall | North Yorkshire | 0845 365 3276 |
| Hob Green Hotel, Restaurant & Gardens | North Yorkshire | 0845 365 1867 |
| Marmadukes Hotel | North Yorkshire | 0845 365 4852 |
| Ox Pasture Hall Country Hotel | North Yorkshire | 0845 365 3461 |
| The Red Lion | North Yorkshire | 0845 365 2671 |
| Stow House Hotel | North Yorkshire | 0845 365 2379 |
| Hey Green Country House Hotel | West Yorkshire | 0845 365 1846 |

## Ireland

| | | |
|---|---|---|
| Ard Na Sidhe | Kerry | 00 353 66 976 9105 |
| Ballyseede Castle | Kerry | 00 353 66 712 5799 |
| Temple Country Retreat & Spa | Westmeath | 00 353 57 933 5118 |

## Scotland

| | | |
|---|---|---|
| Norwood Hall | Aberdeenshire | 0845 365 3462 |
| Highland Cottage | Argyll and Bute | 0845 365 1849 |
| Culzean Castle – The Eisenhower Apartment | South Ayrshire | 0845 365 3257 |
| Balcary Bay Hotel | Dumfries & Galloway | 0845 365 3026 |
| Corsewall Lighthouse Hotel | Dumfries & Galloway | 0845 365 2859 |
| Trigony House Hotel | Dumfries & Galloway | 0845 365 1869 |
| The Peat Inn | Fife | 0845 365 2637 |
| Forss House Hotel | Highland | 0845 365 1749 |
| Greshornish House Hotel | Highland | 0845 365 1798 |
| Ruddyglow Park | Highland | 0845 365 2315 |
| The Steadings at The Grouse & Trout | Highland | 0845 365 2698 |
| Toravaig House | Highland | 0845 365 2756 |
| Knockomie Hotel | Moray | 0845 365 1963 |
| Castle Venlaw | Scottish Borders | 0845 365 3226 |
| Cringletie House | Scottish Borders | 0845 365 3251 |

## Wales

| | | |
|---|---|---|
| Jabajak Vineyard (Restaurant with Rooms) | Carmarthenshire | 0845 365 2839 |
| Sychnant Pass House | Conwy | 0845 365 2384 |
| Tan-Y-Foel Country House | Conwy | 0845 365 2387 |
| Bae Abermaw | Gwynedd | 0845 365 3023 |
| Llwyndu Farmhouse | Gwynedd | 0845 365 3721 |
| Porth Tocyn Country House Hotel | Gwynedd | 0845 365 2136 |
| The Bell At Skenfrith | Monmouthshire | 0845 365 2403 |
| Penally Abbey | Pembrokeshire | 0845 365 2103 |
| Wolfscastle Country Hotel & Restaurant | Pembrokeshire | 0845 365 2817 |
| Glangrwyney Court | Powys | 0845 365 1764 |
| Egerton Grey | Vale of Glamorgan | 0845 365 3281 |

# Historic Houses, Castles & Gardens

We are pleased to feature over 140 places to visit during your stay at a Condé Nast Johansens Recommendation.
More information about these attractions, including opening times and entry fees, can be found on www.johansens.com

## England

### Bath & North East Somerset

**Cothay Manor**– Greenham, Wellington, Bath & North East Somerset TA21 0JR.
Tel: 01823 672 283

**Great House Farm** – Wells Rd, Theale, Wedmore, Bath & North East Somerset
BS28 4SJ. Tel: 01934 713133

**Orchard Wyndham** – Williton, Taunton, Bath & North East Somerset TA4 4HH.
Tel: 01984 632309

### Bedfordshire

**Woburn Abbey** – Woburn, Bedfordshire MK17 9WA.
Tel: 01525 290666

**Moggerhanger Park**  – Park Road, Moggerhanger, Bedfordshire  MK44 3RW .
Tel: 01767 641007

### Buckinghamshire

**Doddershall Park** – Quainton, Buckinghamshire HP22 4DF.
Tel: 01296 655238

**Nether Winchendon House** – Nr Aylesbury, Buckinghamshire HP18 0DY.
Tel: 01844 290199

**Stowe Landscape Gardens** – Stowe, Buckingham, Buckinghamshire MK18 5EH.
Tel: 01280 822850

**Waddesdon Manor** – Waddesdon, Nr Aylesbury, Buckinghamshire HP18 0JH.
Tel: 01296 653211

### Cambridgeshire

**The Manor**  – Hemingford Grey, Huntingdon, Cambridgeshire PE28 9BN.
Tel: 01480 463134

### Cheshire

**Cholmondeley Castle Gardens** – Malpas, Cheshire SY14 8AH.
Tel: 01829 720383

**Dorfold Hall** – Nantwich, Cheshire CW5 8LD. Tel: 01270 625245

**Rode Hall and Gardens** – Scholar Green, Cheshire ST7 3QP.
Tel: 01270 882961

### Co Durham

**The Bowes Museum** – Barnard Castle, Co Durham DL12 8NP.
Tel: 01833 690606

### Cumbria

**Holker Hall and Gardens** – Cark-in-Cartmel, nr Grange-over-Sands,
Cumbria LA11 7PL. Tel: 015395 58328

**Isel Hall** – Cockermouth, Cumbria CA13 OQG.
Tel: 01900 821778

**Muncaster Castle, Gardens & Owl Centre** – Ravenglass, Cumbria CA18 1RQ.
Tel: 01229 717 614

### Derbyshire

**Haddon Hall** – Bakewell, Derbyshire DE45 1LA. Tel: 01629 812855

**Melbourne Hall & Gardens** – Melbourne, Derbyshire DE73 1EN.
Tel: 01332 862502

**Renishaw Hall Gardens** – Nr Sheffield, Derbyshire S21 3WB.
Tel: 01246 432310

### Devon

**Anderton House** – Goodleigh, Devon. Tel: 01628 825920

**Bowringsleigh** – Kingsbridge, Devon TQ7 3LL. Tel: 01548 852014

**Downes** – Crediton, Devon EX17 3PL. Tel: 01392 439046

### Dorset

**Mapperton Gardens** – Mapperton, Beaminster, Dorset DT8 3NR.
Tel: 01308 862645

**Minterne Gardens** – Minterne Magna, Nr Dorchester, Dorset DT2 7AU.
Tel: 01300 341 370

**Moignes Court** – Owermoigne, Dorchester, Dorset DT2 8HY. Tel: 01305 853300

### Durham

**Auckland Castle** – Bishop Auckland, Durham DL14 7NR. Tel: 01388 601627

### East Yorkshire

**Burton Agnes Hall & Gardens** – Burton Agnes, Diffield,
East Yorkshire YO25 4NB. Tel: 01262 490 324

### Essex

**The Gardens of Easton Lodge** – Warwick House, Easton Lodge, Great Dunmow,
Essex CM6 2BB. Tel: 01371 876979

**Ingatestone** – Hall Lane, Ingatestone, Essex CM4 9NR. Tel: 01277 353010

# Historic Houses, Castles & Gardens

We are pleased to feature over 140 places to visit during your stay at a Condé Nast Johansens Recommendation. More information about these attractions, including opening times and entry fees, can be found on www.johansens.com

## Gloucestershire

**Cheltenham Art Gallery & Museum** – Clarence Street, Cheltenham, Gloucestershire GL50 3JT. Tel: 01242 237431

**Frampton Court** – Frampton-on-Severn, Gloucester, Gloucestershire GL2 7DY. Tel: 01452 740267

**Hardwicke Court** – Nr Gloucester, Gloucestershire GL2 4RS. Tel: 01452 720212

**Old Campden House** – Chipping Campden, Gloucestershire. Tel: 01628 825920

**Sezincote House & Garden** – Moreton-in-Marsh, Gloucestershire GL56 9AW. Tel: 01386 700444

**Sudeley Castle Gardens and Exhibitions** – Winchcombe, Gloucestershire GL54 5JP. Tel: 01242 602308

## Hampshire

**Avington Park** – Winchester, Hampshire SO21 1DB. Tel: 01962 779260

**Beaulieu** – Beaulieu Enterprises Ltd, John Montagu Bldg, Hampshire SO42 7ZN. Tel: 01590 612345

**Broadlands** – Romsey, Hampshire SO51 9ZD. Tel: 01794 505055

**Buckler's Hard** – Beaulieu, Brockenhurst, Hampshire. Tel: 01590 614641

**Gilbert White's House & The Oates Museum** – Selborne, Nr. Alton, Hampshire GU34 3JH. Tel: 01420 511275

**Greywell Hill House** – Greywell, Hook, Hampshire RG29 1DG.

**Pylewell Park Gardens** – South Baddesley, Lymington, Hampshire SO41 55J. Tel: 1725513004

## Hertfordshire

**Ashridge** – Berkhamsted, Hertfordshire HP4 1NS. Tel: 01442 841027

**Hatfield House** – Hatfield, Hertfordshire AL9 5NQ. Tel: 01707 287010

## Isle of Wight

**Deacons Nursery (H.H)** – Moor View, Godshill, Isle of Wight PO38 3HW. Tel: 01983 840 750 or 522

## Kent

**Cobham Hall** – Cobham, Nr Gravesend, Kent DA12 3BL. Tel: 01474 823371

**The Grange** – Ramsgate, Kent. Tel: 01628 825925

**Groombridge Place Gardens & Enchanted Forest** – Groombridge, Tunbridge Wells, Kent TN3 9QG. Tel: 01892 863999

**Hever Castle and Gardens** – Nr Edenbridge, Kent TN8 7NG. Tel: 01732 865224

**Marle Place Gardens** – Marle Place Road, Brenchley, Kent TN12 7HS. Tel: 01892 722304

**The New College of Cobham** – Cobhambury Road, Cobham, Nr Gravesend, Kent DA12 3BG. Tel: 01474 812503

**Penshurst Place and Gardens** – Penshurst, Nr Tonbridge, Kent TN11 8DG. Tel: 01892 870307

## Lancashire

**Stonyhurst College** – Stonyhurst, Clitheroe, Lancashire BB7 9PZ. Tel: 01254 826345

**Townhead House** – Slaidburn, via Clitheroe, Lancashire BBY 3AG. Tel: 01772 421566

## London

**Handel House Museum** – 25 Brook Street, London W1K 4HB. Tel: 020 7495 1685

**Pitzhanger Manor House** – Walpole Park, Mattock Lane, Ealing, London W5 5EQ. Tel: 020 8567 1227

**St Paul's Cathedral** – The Chapter House, St Paul's Churchyard, London EC4M 8AD. Tel: 020 7246 8350

**Sir John Soane's Museum** – 13 Lincoln's Inn Fields, London WC2A 3BP. Tel: 020 7405 2107

**Syon House** – Syon Park, Brentford, London TW8 8JF. Tel: 0208 560 0881

## Norfolk

**Walsingham Abbey Grounds** – Little Walsingham, Norfolk NR22 6BP. Tel: 01328 820259

## Northamptonshire

**Cottesbrooke Hall and Gardens** – Nr Northampton, Northamptonshire NN6 8PF. Tel: 01604 505808

**Haddonstone Show Gardens** – The Forge House, Church Lane, Northamptonshire NN6 8DB. Tel: 01604 770711

## Northumberland

**Chipchase Castle & Gardens** – Wark on Tyne, Hexham, Northumberland NE48 3NT. Tel: 01434 230203

## Oxfordshire

**Kingston Bagpuize House** – Abingdon, Oxfordshire OX13 5AX. Tel: 01865 820259

**Mapledurham House** – Nr Reading, Oxfordshire RG4 7TR. Tel: 01189 723 350

**Stonor Park** – Nr Henley-on-Thames, Oxfordshire RG9 6HF. Tel: 01491 638587

**Sulgrave Manor** – Manor Road, Sulgrave, Banbury, Oxfordshire OX17 2SD. Tel: 01295 760205

# Historic Houses, Castles & Gardens

We are pleased to feature over 140 places to visit during your stay at a Condé Nast Johansens Recommendation.
More information about these attractions, including opening times and entry fees, can be found on www.johansens.com

**Wallingford Castle Gardens** – Castle Street, Wallingford, Oxfordshire OX10 0AL.
Tel: 01491 835 373

## Shropshire

**Weston Park** – Weston-under-Lizard, Nr Shifnal, Shropshire TF11 8LE.
Tel: 01952 852100

## Somerset

**Hestercombe Gardens** – Cheddon Fitzpaine, Taunton, Somerset TA2 8LG.
Tel: 01823 413923
**Number One Royal Crescent** – Bath Preservation Trust, Bath,
Somerset BA1 2LR. Tel: (01225) 428126
**Robin Hood's Hut** – Halswell, Goathurst, Somerset. Tel: 01628 825925

## Staffordshire

**Ancient High House** – Greengate Street, Stafford, Staffordshire ST16 2JA.
Tel: 01785 619 131
**Izaak Walton's Cottage** – Worston Lane, Shallowford, Staffordshire ST15 0PA.
Tel: 01785 760 278
**Stafford Castle & Visitor Centre** – Newport Road, Stafford,
Staffordshire ST16 1DJ. Tel: 01785 257 698
**Whitmore Hall** – Whitmore, Nr Newcastle-under-Lyme, Staffordshire ST5 5HW.
Tel: 01782 680478

## Suffolk

**Ancient House** – Clare, Suffolk CO10 8NY. Tel: 01628 825920
**Freston Tower** – Near Ipswich, Suffolk. Tel: 01628 825920
**Kentwell Hall** – Long Melford, Sudbury, Suffolk CO10 9BA. Tel: 01787 310207
**Newbourne Hall** – Newbourne, Nr Woodbridge, Suffolk IP12 4NP.
Tel: 01473 736764

## Surrey

**Claremont House** – Claremont Drive, Esher, Surrey KT10 9LY.
Tel: 01372 473623
**Goddards** – Abinger Common, Dorking, Surrey RH5 6TH. Tel: 01628 825920
**Guildford House Gallery** – 155 High Street, Guildford, Surrey GU1 3AJ.
Tel: 01483 444740
**Loseley Park** – Guildford, Surrey GU3 1HS. Tel: 01483 304 440

## East Sussex

**Anne of Cleves House** – 52 Southover High Street, Lewes, East Sussex BN7 1JA.
Tel: 01273 474610
**Bentley Wildfowl & Motor Museum** – Halland, Nr Lewes, East Sussex BN8 5AF.
Tel: 01825 840573
**Charleston** – Firle, Nr Lewes, East Sussex BN8 6LL. Tel: 01323 811626
**Gardens and Grounds of Herstmonceux Castle** – Hailsham,
East Sussex BN27 1RN. Tel: 01323 833816
**Michelham Priory** – Upper Dicker, Hailsham, East Sussex BN27 3QS.
Tel: 01323 844 224

**Wilmington Priory** – Wilmington, Nr Eastbourne, East Sussex BN26 5SW.
Tel: 01628 825920

## West Sussex

**Denmans Garden** – Denmans Lane, Fontwell, West Sussex BN18 0SU.
Tel: 01243 542808

**Firle Place** – Nr Lewes, West Sussex BN8 6LP. Tel: 01273 8583
**Fishbourne Roman Palace** – Salthill Road, Fishbourne, Chichester, West Sussex
PO19 3QR. Tel: 01243 785859
**Goodwood House** – Goodwood, Chichester, West Sussex PO18 0QP.
Tel: 01243 538449
**High Beeches Gardens** – Handcross, West Sussex RH17 6HQ. Tel: 01444 400589
**Leonardslee Lakes and Gardens** – Lower Beeding, West Sussex RH13 6PP.
**Lewes Castle** – Barbican House, 169 High Street, Lewes,
West Sussex BN7 1YE. Tel: 01273 486 290
**Marlipins Museum** – High Street, Shoreham-by-Sea, West Sussex BN43 5DA.
Tel: 01273 462994
**Parham House & Gardens** – Parham Park, Nr Pulborough,
West Sussex RH20 4HS. Tel: 01903 742021
**The Priest House** – North Lane, West Hoathly, West Sussex RH19 4PP.
Tel: 01342 810479
**West Dean Gardens** – The Edward James Foundation, Estate Office West Dean,
Chichester, West Sussex PO18 0QZ. Tel: 01243 818210
**Worthing Museum & Art Gallery** – Chapel Road, Worthing,
West Sussex BN11 1HP. Tel: 01903 239999

## Warwickshire

**Arbury Hall** – Nuneaton, Warwickshire CV10 7PT. Tel: 02476 382804
**Kenilworth Castle** – Kenilworth, Warwickshire CV8 1NE. Tel: 01926 852078
**Shakespeare Houses** – The Shakespeare Centre, Henley Street, Stratford-upon-
Avon, Warwickshire CV37 6QW. Tel: 01789 204016

## West Midlands

**The Barber Institute of Fine Arts** – University of Birmingham, Edgbaston,
Birmingham, West Midlands B15 2TS. Tel: 0121 414 7333
**The Birmingham Botanical Gardens & Glasshouses** – Westbourne Road,
Edgbaston, Birmingham, West Midlands B15 3TR. Tel: 0121 454 1860

# Historic Houses, Castles & Gardens

We are pleased to feature over 140 places to visit during your stay at a Condé Nast Johansens Recommendation.
More information about these attractions, including opening times and entry fees, can be found on www.johansens.com

## Worcestershire

**Harvington Hall** – Harvington, Kidderminster, Worcestershire DY10 4LR.
Tel: 01562 777846
**Little Malvern Court** – Nr Malvern, Worcestershire WR14 4JN.
Tel: 01684 892988
**Witley Court and Gardens** – Witley Court, Great Witley, Worcestershire WR6 6JT.

## North Yorkshire

**Castle Howard** – Nr York, North Yorkshire YO60 7DA. Tel: 01653 648333
**Duncombe Park** – Helmsley, Ryedale, York, North Yorkshire YO62 5EB.
Tel: 01439 770213
**Forbidden Corner** – Tupgill Park Estate, Coverham, Nr Middleham,
North Yorkshire DL8 4TJ. Tel: 01969 640638

**Fountains Abbey and Studley Royal Water Garden** – Ripon Nr Harrogate,
North Yorkshire HG4 3DY. **Tel: 01765 608888**
**Ripley Castle** – Ripley Castle Estate, Harrogate, North Yorkshire HG3 3AY.
Tel: 01423 770152
**Skipton Castle** – Skipton, North Yorkshire BD23 1AW. Tel: 01756 792442

## West Yorkshire

**Bramham Park** – The Estate Office, Bramham Park, Wetherby,
West Yorkshire LS23 6ND. Tel: 01937 846000
**Bronte Parsonage Museum** – Church Street, Haworth, West Yorkshire.
Tel: 01535 642323

## N. Ireland

**North Down Museum** – Town Hall, Bangor, Down BT20 4BT, N. Ireland.
Tel: 02891 271200
**Seaforde Gardens** – Seaforde, Downpatrick, Down BT30 8PG, N. Ireland.
Tel: 028 4481 1225

## Ireland

**Bantry House & Gardens** – Bantry, Cork, Ireland. Tel: 00 353 2 750 047
**Blarney Castle , House and Gardens** – Blarney, Co. Cork, Ireland.
Tel: 00 353 21 385252

**Dunloe Castle Hotel Gardens** – Gap of Dunloe, Beaufort, Killarney, Co Kerry,
Ireland. Tel: 00 353 64 44111
**Kilmokea Country Manor and Gardens** – Great Island, Campile, Wexford,
Ireland. Tel: 00 35351 388109
**Lismore Castle Gardens & Art Gallery** – Lismore, Waterford, Ireland.
Tel: 00 353 (0)5854424

## Scotland

**Ardwell Gardens** – Ardwell House, Ardwell, Stranraer, Dumfries & Galloway
DG9 9LY. Tel: 01776 860 227
**Auchinleck House** – Ochiltree, North Ayrshire. Tel: 01628 825920
**Balfour Castle** – Shapinsay, Orkney KW17 2DY. Tel: 01856 711282
**Bowhill House & Country Park** – Bowhill, Selkirk, Scottish Borders TD7 5ET.
Tel: 01750 22204
**Callendar House** – Callendar Park, Falkirk FK1 1YR. Tel: 01324 503770
**Castle Kennedy Gardens** – The Estates Office, Rephad, Stranraer, Dumfries &
Galloway DG9 8BX. Tel: (01776) 702024
**Drumlanrig Castle, Gardens & Country Park** – Thornhill, Dumfriesshire,
Dumfries & Galloway DG3 4AQ. Tel: 01848 331555
**Floors Castle** – Kelso, Borders TD5 7SF. Tel: 01573 223333
**Golden Grove** – Llanasa, Nr Holywell, Flintshire CH8 9NA. Tel: 01745 854452
**Inveraray Castle** – Cherry Park, Inveraray, Highland PA32 8XF.
Tel: 01499 302 203
**Kelburn Castle and Country Centre** – Kelburn, Fairlie (Nr Largs),
Ayrshire KA29 0BE. Tel: 01475 568685
**Manderston** – Duns, Berwickshire, Scottish Borders TD11 3PP.
Tel: 01361 883 450
**Newliston** – Kirkliston, West Lothian EH29 9EB.
Tel: 0131 333 3231
**Paxton House & Country Park** – Paxton, Nr Berwick upon Tweed, Scottish
Borders TD15 1SZ. Tel: 01289 386291
**Traquair House** – Innerleithen, Peebles, Scottish Borders EH44 6PW.
Tel: 01896 830 323

## Wales

**Bodnant Garden** – Tal Y Cafn, Conwy LL28 5RE. Tel: 01492 650460
**Dolbelydr** – Trefnant, Denbighshire. Tel: 01628 825920
**Llanvihangel Court** – Nr Abergavenny, Monmouthshire NP7 8DH.
Tel: 01873 890 217
**Plas Brondanw Gardens** – Llanfrothen, Nr Penrhyndeudraeth,
Gwynedd LL48 6ET. Tel: 01743 241181
**St Davids Cathedral** – The Deanery, The Close, St Davids,
Pembrokeshire SA62 6RH. Tel: 01437 720 199
**Usk Castle** – Castle House, Monmouth Rd, Usk, Monmouthshire NP15 1SD.
Tel: 01291 672563

## France

**Château de Chenonceau** – 37150 Chenonceaux, France 37150, France.
Tel: 00 33 2 47 23 90 07

## The Netherlands

**Het Loo Palace National Museum** – Koninklijk Park 1, NL–7315 JA Apeldoorn,
The Netherlands. Tel: 00 31 55 577 2400

# Individuality Matters to our Partnership

# We recognise that every client is individual and has particular legal requirements.

## Our approach

We seek to anticipate your legal needs by understanding your business and by developing a close working relationship with you.

We aim to reduce the burden of the legal aspects of decision making, enabling you to maximize opportunities whilst limiting your business, financial and legal risks.

We structure our services with a view to saving expensive management time, thereby producing cost effective decision making.

## Our expertise

Since the firm was founded over 50 years ago, we have developed an acknowledged expertise in the areas of corporate & commercial law, litigation, property, employment and franchising law. We also have a leading reputation as legal advisors in the media and hotels sectors.  For personal matters, we also have a dedicated Private Client Group which provides a comprehensive and complementary range of services to the individual and their families.

We take pride in watching our clients' businesses grow and assisting them in that process wherever we can.

**For more information about how we can help you or your business visit www.gdlaw.co.uk or contact Belinda Copland bcopland@gdlaw.co.uk tel: +44 (0)20 7404 0606**

**GOODMAN** DERRICK LLP

Condé Nast Johansens Preferred Legal Partner

# Hotels, Europe & The Mediterranean

All the properties listed below can be found in our Recommended Hotels & Spas, Europe & The Mediterranean 2008 Guide. More information on our portfolio of guides can be found on page 343.

## Andorra

Sport Hotel Hermitage & Spa ..............Soldeu .................................+376 870 670

## Austria

Palais Coburg Residenz .........................Vienna .................................+43 1 518 180

## Belgium

| | | |
|---|---|---|
| Firean Hotel | Antwerp | +32 3 237 02 60 |
| Hotel Die Swaene | Bruges | +32 50 34 27 98 |
| Romantik Hotel Manoir du Dragon | Knokke~Heist | +32 50 63 05 80 |
| Grand Hotel Damier | Kortrijk | +32 56 22 15 47 |
| Hostellerie Ter Driezen | Turnhout | +32 14 41 87 57 |

## Croatia

| | | |
|---|---|---|
| Stancija Meneghetti | Bale | +385 52 528 816 |
| Grand Villa Argentina | Dubrovnik | +385 20 44 0555 |

## Czech Republic

| | | |
|---|---|---|
| Alchymist Grand Hotel and Spa | Prague | +420 257 286 011 |
| Aria Hotel Prague | Prague | +420 225 334 111 |
| Bellagio Hotel Prague | Prague | +420 221 778 999 |
| Golden Well Hotel | Prague | +420 257 011 213 |
| The Iron Gate Hotel & Suites | Prague | +420 225 777 777 |
| Nosticova Residence | Prague | +420 257 312 513 |
| Hotel Nautilus | Tábor | +420 380 900 900 |

## Estonia

| | | |
|---|---|---|
| Ammende Villa | Pärnu | +372 44 73 888 |
| The Three Sisters Hotel | Tallinn | +372 630 6300 |

## France

| | | |
|---|---|---|
| Château d'Isenbourg | Alsace~Lorraine | +33 3 89 78 58 50 |
| Château de L'Ile | Alsace~Lorraine | +33 3 88 66 85 00 |
| Domaine de la Grange de Condé | Alsace~Lorraine | +33 3 87 79 30 50 |
| Hostellerie les Bas Rupts | | |
| Le Chalet Fleuri | Alsace~Lorraine | +33 3 29 63 09 25 |
| Hôtel à la Cour d'Alsace | Alsace~Lorraine | +33 3 88 95 07 00 |
| Hôtel Les Têtes | Alsace~Lorraine | +33 3 89 24 43 43 |
| Romantik Hôtel le Maréchal | Alsace~Lorraine | +33 3 89 41 60 32 |
| Château de Bonaban | Brittany | +33 2 99 58 24 50 |
| Domaine de Bodeuc | Brittany | +33 2 99 90 89 63 |
| Domaine de Rochevilaine | Brittany | +33 2 97 41 61 61 |
| Hôtel et Spa de La Bretesche | Brittany | +33 2 51 76 86 96 |
| Hôtel l'Agapa & Spa | Brittany | +33 2 96 49 01 10 |
| Manoir de Kertalg | Brittany | +33 2 98 39 77 77 |
| Ti al Lannec | Brittany | +33 2 96 15 01 01 |

| | | |
|---|---|---|
| Château Hôtel André Ziltener | Burgandy | |
| | - Franche~Comte | +33 3 80 62 41 62 |
| Abbaye de la Bussière | Burgundy | |
| | - Franche~Comté | +33 3 80 49 02 29 |
| Château de Gilly | Burgundy | |
| | - Franche~Comté | +33 3 80 62 89 98 |
| Château de Vault de Lugny | Burgundy | |
| | - Franche~Comté | +33 3 86 34 07 86 |
| Château les Roches | Burgundy | |
| | - Franche~Comté | +33 3 80 84 32 71 |
| Hostellerie des Monts de Vaux | Burgundy | |
| | - Franche~Comté | +33 3 84 37 12 50 |
| Château d'Etoges | Champagne~Ardennes | +33 3 26 59 30 08 |
| Château de Fère | Champagne~Ardennes | +33 3 23 82 21 13 |
| Domaine du Château de Barive | Champagne~Ardennes | +33 3 23 22 15 15 |
| Le Moulin du Landion | Champagne~Ardennes | +33 3 25 27 92 17 |
| Alain Llorca - Le Moulin de Mougins | Côte d'Azur | +33 4 93 75 78 24 |

| | | |
|---|---|---|
| **Château Eza** | **Côte d'Azur** | **+33 4 93 41 12 24** |
| La Ferme d'Augustin | Côte d'Azur | +33 4 94 55 97 00 |
| La Villa Mauresque | Côte d'Azur | +33 494 83 02 42 |
| Le Bailli de Suffren | Côte d'Azur | +33 4 98 04 47 00 |
| Le Mas d'Artigny & Spa | Côte d'Azur | +33 4 93 32 84 54 |
| Château d'Artigny | Loire Valley | +33 2 47 34 30 30 |
| Château de la Barre | Loire Valley | +33 2 43 35 00 17 |
| Château de Pray | Loire Valley | +33 247 57 23 67 |
| Domaine de Beauvois | Loire Valley | +33 2 47 55 50 11 |
| Domaine de la Tortinière | Loire Valley | +33 2 47 34 35 00 |
| Hostellerie des Hauts | | |
| de Sainte~Maure | Loire Valley | +33 2 47 65 50 65 |
| Le Choiseul | Loire Valley | +33 2 47 30 45 45 |
| Le Manoir les Minimes | Loire Valley | +33 2 47 30 40 40 |
| Le Prieuré | Loire Valley | +33 2 41 67 90 14 |
| Château de Floure | Midi~Pyrénées | +33 4 68 79 11 29 |
| Hôtel Lous Grits | Midi~Pyrénées | +33 562 283 710 |
| Relais Royal | Midi~Pyrénées | +33 5 61 60 19 19 |
| Château la Chenevière | Normandy | +33 2 31 51 25 25 |
| Château les Bruyères | Normandy | +33 2 31 32 22 45 |
| Domaine Saint~Clair, Le Donjon | Normandy | +33 2 35 27 08 23 |
| Le Castel | Normandy | +33 2 33 17 00 45 |
| Manoir de la Poterie, | | |
| Spa "Les Thermes" | Normandy | +33 2 31 88 10 40 |
| Manoir de Mathan | Normandy | +33 2 31 22 21 73 |
| Carlton Hôtel | North - Picardy | +33 3 20 13 33 13 |
| Château de Cocove | North - Picardy | +33 3 21 82 68 29 |
| La Chartreuse du Val Saint~Esprit | North - Picardy | +33 3 21 62 80 00 |
| La Howarderie | North - Picardy | +33 3 20 10 31 00 |

# Hotels, Europe & The Mediterranean

All the properties listed below can be found in our Recommended Hotels & Spas, Europe & The Mediterranean 2008 Guide. More information on our portfolio of guides can be found on page 343.

| | | |
|---|---|---|
| Hospes Lancaster | Paris | +33 1 40 76 40 76 |
| Hôtel Balzac | Paris | +33 1 44 35 18 00 |
| Hôtel de Sers | Paris | +33 1 53 23 75 75 |
| Hôtel du Petit Moulin | Paris | +33 1 42 74 10 10 |
| Hôtel Duc de Saint~Simon | Paris | +33 1 44 39 20 20 |
| Hôtel Duret | Paris | +33 1 45 00 42 60 |
| Hôtel le Tourville | Paris | +33 1 47 05 62 62 |
| Hôtel Opéra Richepanse | Paris | +33 1 42 60 36 00 |
| Hôtel San Régis | Paris | +33 1 44 95 16 16 |
| La Trémoille | Paris | +33 1 56 52 14 00 |
| La Villa Maillot | Paris | +33 1 53 64 52 52 |
| Le Sainte~Beuve | Paris | +33 1 45 48 20 07 |
| Cazaudehore "La Forestière" | Paris Region | +33 1 30 61 64 64 |
| Château d'Esclimont | Paris Region | +33 2 37 31 15 15 |
| Hostellerie du Bas-Breau | Paris Region | +33 1 60 66 40 05 |
| Le Manoir de Gressy | Paris Region | +33 1 60 26 68 00 |
| Château de L'Yeuse | Poitou~Charentes | +33 5 45 36 82 60 |
| Hôtel "Résidence de France" | Poitou~Charentes | +33 5 46 28 06 00 |
| Hôtel de Toiras | Poitou~Charentes | +33 546 35 40 32 |
| Relais de Saint~Preuil | Poitou~Charentes | +33 5 45 80 80 08 |
| Bastide du Calalou | Provence | +33 4 94 70 17 91 |
| Château de Massillan | Provence | +33 4 90 40 64 51 |
| Château de Montcaud | Provence | +33 4 66 89 60 60 |
| Château des Alpilles | Provence | +33 4 90 92 03 33 |
| Domaine le Hameau des Baux | Provence | +33 4 90 54 10 30 |
| L'Estelle en Camargue | Provence | +33 4 90 97 89 01 |
| Le Mas de la Rose | Provence | +33 4 90 73 08 91 |
| Le Spinaker | Provence | +33 4 66 53 36 37 |
| Les Mas des Herbes Blanches | Provence | +33 4 90 05 79 79 |
| Manoir de la Roseraie | Provence | +33 4 75 46 58 15 |
| Chalet Hôtel La Marmotte | Rhône~Alpes | +33 4 50 75 80 33 |
| Château de Bagnols | Rhône~Alpes | +33 4 74 71 40 00 |
| Château de Coudrée | Rhône~Alpes | +33 4 50 72 62 33 |
| Château de Divonne | Rhône~Alpes | +33 4 50 20 00 32 |
| Domaine de Divonne | Rhône~Alpes | +33 4 50 40 34 34 |
| Le Beau Rivage | Rhône~Alpes | +33 4 74 56 82 82 |
| Le Fer à Cheval | Rhône~Alpes | +33 4 50 21 30 39 |
| Château de Sanse | South West | +33 5 57 56 41 10 |
| Château Le Mas de Montet | South West | +33 5 53 90 08 71 |
| Hôtel du Palais | South West | +33 5 59 41 64 00 |
| Le Relais du Château Franc Mayne | South West | +33 5 57 24 62 61 |
| Château des Briottières | Western Loire | +33 2 41 42 00 02 |

## Great Britain

| | | |
|---|---|---|
| Luton Hoo Hotel, Golf & Spa | Bedfordshire | +44 1582 734437 |
| The French Horn | Berkshire | +44 1189 692 204 |
| Soar Mill Cove Hotel | Devon | +44 1548 561 566 |
| Ashdown Park Hotel | East Sussex | +44 1342 824 988 |
| The Grand Hotel | East Sussex | +44 1323 412345 |
| Rye Lodge | East Sussex | +44 1797 223838 |
| Tylney Hall | Hampshire | +44 1256 764881 |
| Jumeirah Carlton Tower | London | +44 20 7235 1234 |
| Jumeirah Lowndes Hotel | London | +44 20 7823 1234 |
| The Mayflower Hotel | London | +44 20 7370 0991 |
| Twenty Nevern Square | London | +44 20 7565 9555 |
| Hoar Cross Hall Spa Resort | Staffordshire | +44 1283 575671 |
| Nailcote Hall | Warwickshire | +44 2476 466 174 |

## Greece

| | | |
|---|---|---|
| Hotel Pentelikon | Athens | +30 2 10 62 30 650 |
| Argentikon Luxury Suites | Chios | +30 227 10 33 111 |
| Villa de Loulia | Corfu | +30 266 30 95 394 |
| Elounda Gulf Villas & Suites | Crete | +30 28410 90300 |
| Elounda Peninsula All Suite Hotel | Crete | +30 28410 68250 |

| | | |
|---|---|---|
| **Paradise Island Villas** | **Crete** | **+30 289 702 2893** |
| Pleiades Luxurious Villas | Crete | +30 28410 90450 |
| St Nicolas Bay Resort Hotel & Villas | Crete | +30 2841 025041 |
| Imaret | Kavala | +30 2510 620 151 |
| Pavezzo Country Retreat | Lefkada | +30 26450 71782 |
| Apanema | Mykonos | +30 22890 28590 |
| Tharroe of Mykonos | Mykonos | +30 22890 27370 |
| Nikos Takis Fashion Hotel | Rhodes | +30 22410 70773 |
| Alexander's Boutique Hotel | Santorini | +30 22860 71818 |
| Canaves Oia | Santorini | +30 22860 71453 |
| Xenon Estate | Spetses | +30 22980 74120 |

## Hungary

| | | |
|---|---|---|
| Allegro Hotel - Tihany Centrum | Tihany - Lake Balaton | +36 87 448 456 |

## Italy

| | | |
|---|---|---|
| Furore Inn Resort & Spa | Campania | +39 089 830 4711 |
| Hotel Villa Maria | Campania | +39 089 857255 |
| Maison La Minervetta | Campania | +39 081 877 4455 |
| Manzi Terme Hotel & Spa | Campania | +39 081994722 |
| Hotel des Nations | Emilia Romagna | +39 0541 647 878 |
| Hotel Posta (Historical Residence) | Emilia Romagna | +39 05 22 43 29 44 |
| Hotel Villa Roncuzzi | Emilia Romagna | +39 0544 534776 |
| Palazzo Dalla Rosa Prati | Emilia Romagna | +39 0521 386 429 |
| Torre di San Martino | | |
| - Historical Residence | Emilia Romagna | +39 0523 972002 |
| Urban Hotel Design | Friuli Venezia | +39 040 302065 |
| Buonanotte Garibaldi | Lazio | +390 658 330 733 |
| Hotel dei Borgognoni | Lazio | +39 06 6994 1505 |
| Hotel dei Consoli | Lazio | +39 0668 892 972 |
| Hotel Fenix | Lazio | +39 06 8540 741 |
| Hotel Villa Clementina | Lazio | +39 06 9986268 |
| La Locanda della Chiocfciola | Lazio | +39 0761 402 734 |
| La Posta Vecchia Hotel Spa | Lazio | +39 0699 49501 |
| Relais Falisco | Lazio | +39 0761 54 98 |
| Relais Le Torrette | Lazio | +39 0763 726009 |

# Hotels, Europe & The Mediterranean

All the properties listed below can be found in our Recommended Hotels & Spas, Europe & The Mediterranean 2008 Guide. More information on our portfolio of guides can be found on page 343.

Villa Spalletti Trivelli ...................Lazio .........................+39 06 48907934
Abbadia San Giorgio
  - Historical Residence ..............Liguria ......................+39 0185 491119
Grand Hotel Diana Majestic...........Liguria ......................+39 0183 402 727
Grand Hotel Miramare.................Liguria ......................+39 0185 287013
Hotel Punta Est ......................Liguria ......................+39 019 600611
Hotel San Giorgio
  - Portofino House ..................Liguria ......................+39 0185 26991
Hotel Vis à Vis .......................Liguria ......................+39 0185 42661
Bagni di Bormio Spa Resort .........Lombardy ...................+39 0342 910131
Grand Hotel Gardone Riviera ........Lombardy ...................+39 0365 20261
Grand Hotel Villa Serbelloni .........Lombardy ...................+39 031 950 216450
Hotel Bellerive ......................Lombardy ...................+39 0365 520 410
Hotel de la Ville ....................Lombardy ...................+39 039 3942 1
I Due Roccoli Relais .................Lombardy ...................+39 030 9822 977
L'Albereta ...........................Lombardy ...................+39 030 7760 550
Petit Palais maison de charme .......Lombardy ...................+39 02 584 891
THE PLACE
  - Luxury serviced apartments .......Lombardy ...................+39 02 76026633
Albergo L'Ostelliere .................Piemonte ....................+39 0143 607 801
Foresteria dei Poderi Einaudi ........Piemonte ....................+39 0173 70414
Hotel Cristallo .......................Piemonte ....................+39 0163 922 822
Hotel Pironi ..........................Piemonte ....................+39 0323 70624
Hotel Principi di Piemonte ...........Piemonte ....................+39 011 55151
Hotel Villa Aminta ..................Piemonte ....................+39 0323 933 818
Relais Il Borgo .......................Piemonte ....................+39 0141 921272
Villa dal Pozzo d'Annone ............Piemonte ....................+39 0322 7255
Country House Cefalicchio ..........Puglia .......................+39 0883 662 736
Hotel Titano ........................San Marino Republic..........+378 991007
Grand Hotel in Porto Cervo .........Sardinia ....................+39 0789 91533
Tartheshotel ........................Sardinia ....................+39 070 97 29000

**Villa del Parco and Spa,**
  **Forte Village....................Sardinia ...........................+39 070 92171**
Villa Las Tronas .....................Sardinia ....................+39 079 981 818
Baia Taormina Grand Palace
  Hotels & Spa ......................Sicily .......................+39 0942 756292
Grand Hotel Arciduca.................Sicily .......................+39 090 9812136
Grand Hotel Atlantis Bay.............Sicily .......................+39 0942 618011
Grand Hotel Mazzarò Sea Palace .....Sicily .......................+39 0942 612111
Hotel Signum........................Sicily .......................+39 090 9844222
Locanda Don Serafino ..............Sicily .......................+39 0932 220065
Palazzo Failla Hotel .................Sicily .......................+39 0932 941059
Poggio del Sole Resort...............Sicily .......................+39 0932 666 452
Therasia Resort .....................Sicily .......................+39 090 9852555

Castel Fragsburg ....................Trentino - Alto Adige /
                                    Dolomites ...................+39 0473 244071
Du Lac et du Parc Grand Resort.......Trentino - Alto Adige /
                                    Dolomites ...................+39 0464 566600
Hotel Gardena Grödnerhof ..........Trentino - Alto Adige /
                                    Dolomites ...................+39 0471 796 315
Posthotel Cavallino Bianco .........Trentino - Alto Adige /
                                    Dolomites ...................+39 0471 613113
Romantik Hotel Art Hotel Cappella ..Trentino - Alto Adige /
                                    Dolomites ...................+39 0471 836183
Albergo Pietrasanta
  - Palazzo Barsanti Bonetti ........Tuscany ....................+39 0584 793 727
Albergo Villa Marta .................Tuscany ....................+39 0583 37 01 01
Borgo La Bagnaia Resort,
  Spa and Events Venue .............Tuscany ....................+39 0577 813000
Casa Howard Guest Houses
  - Rome and Florence ..............Tuscany ....................+39 066 992 4555
Castello Banfi - Il Borgo ............Tuscany ....................+39 0577 877 700
Country House Casa Cornacchi ......Tuscany ....................+39 055 998229
Hotel Byron ........................Tuscany ....................+39 0584 787 052
Hotel Plaza e de Russie .............Tuscany ....................+39 0584 44449
Hotel Villa Ottone ..................Tuscany ....................+39 0565 933 042
Il Pellicano Hotel & Spa .............Tuscany ....................+39 0564 858111
L'Andana ...........................Tuscany ....................+39 0564 944 800
Lucignanello Bandini ................Tuscany ....................+39 0577 803 068
Marignolle Relais & Charme ........Tuscany ....................+39 055 228 6910
Monsignor Della Casa
  Country Resort ....................Tuscany ....................+39 055 840 821
Pieve di Caminino
  (Historical Residence) .............Tuscany ....................+39 0564 569 736
Relais la Suvera (Dimora Storica)......Tuscany ....................+39 0577 960 300
Relais Piazza Signoria ...............Tuscany ....................+39 055 3987239
Relais Villa Belpoggio
  (Historical House) .................Tuscany ....................+39 055 9694411
Residenza del Moro .................Tuscany ....................+39 055 290884
Tombolo Talasso Resort .............Tuscany ....................+39 0565 74530
Villa Bordoni........................Tuscany ....................+39 055 884 0004
Villa le Piazzole ....................Tuscany ....................+39 055 223520
Villa Marsili .........................Tuscany ....................+39 0575 605 252
Villa Poggiano ......................Tuscany ....................+39 0578 758292
Abbazia San Faustino
  - Luxury Country House ..........Umbria .....................+39 0720 1717
Castello di Petroia ..................Umbria .....................+39 075 92 02 87
I Casali di Monticchio ...............Umbria .....................+39 0763 62 83 65
L'Antico Forziere ...................Umbria .....................+39 075 972 4314
La Preghiera ........................Umbria .....................+39 075 9302428
Le Torri di Bagnara
  (Medieval Historical Residences) ....Umbria .....................+39 075 579 2001
Relais Alla Corte del Sole ...........Umbria .....................+39 075 9689 008
Relais Todini .......................Umbria .....................+39 075 887521
Romantik Hotel
  le Silve di Armenzano .............Umbria .....................+39 075 801 9000
San Crispino Resort & Spa .........Umbria .....................+39 075 804 3257
Hotel Jolanda Sport ................Valle d'Aosta ...............+39 0125 366 140
Mont Blanc Hotel Village ...........Valle d'Aosta ...............+39 0165 864 111
Ai Capitani Hotel ..................Veneto .....................+39 045 6400782
Albergo Quattro Fontane
  - Residenza d'Epoca .............Veneto .....................+39 041 526 0227
Ca Maria Adele ....................Veneto .....................+39 041 52 03 078

# Hotels, Europe & The Mediterranean

All the properties listed below can be found in our Recommended Hotels & Spas, Europe & The Mediterranean 2008 Guide. More information on our portfolio of guides can be found on page 343.

| | | |
|---|---|---|
| Ca' Nigra Lagoon Resort | Veneto | +39 041 2750047 |
| Ca' Sagredo Hotel | Veneto | +39 041 2413111 |
| Charming House DD724 | Veneto | +39 041 277 0262 |
| Color Hotel | Veneto | +39 045 621 0857 |
| Hotel Flora | Veneto | +39 041 52 05 844 |
| Hotel Gabbia d'Oro (Historical Residence) | Veneto | +39 045 8003060 |
| Hotel Giorgione | Veneto | +39 041 522 5810 |
| Hotel Sant' Elena Venezia | Veneto | +39 041 27 17 811 |
| Hotel Villa Ca' Sette | Veneto | +39 0424 383 350 |
| Locanda San Verolo | Veneto | +39 045 720 09 30 |
| Locanda San Vigilio | Veneto | +39 045 725 66 88 |
| Londra Palace | Veneto | +39 041 5200533 |
| Methis Hotel | Veneto | +39 049 872 5555 |
| Novecento Boutique Hotel | Veneto | +39 041 24 13 765 |
| Park Hotel Brasilia | Veneto | +39 0421 380851 |
| Relais Duca di Dolle | Veneto | +39 0438 975 809 |
| Relais la Magioca | Veneto | +39 045 600 0167 |

## Latvia

| | | |
|---|---|---|
| TB Palace Hotel & Spa | Jūrmala | +371 714 7094 |
| Hotel Bergs | Riga | +371 6777 0900 |

## Lithuania

| | | |
|---|---|---|
| Grotthuss Hotel | Vilnius | +370 5 266 0322 |
| The Narutis Hotel | Vilnius | +370 5 2122 894 |

## Luxembourg

| | | |
|---|---|---|
| Hotel Saint~Nicolas | Remich | +35 226 663 |

## The Netherlands

| | | |
|---|---|---|
| Ambassade Hotel | Amsterdam | +31 20 5550 222 |
| Duin & Kruidberg Country Estate | Santpoort | +31 23 512 1800 |
| Auberge de Campveerse Toren | Veere | +31 0118 501 291 |

## Portugal

| | | |
|---|---|---|
| Quinta Jacintina | Almancil | +351 289 350 090 |
| Ria Park Hotel & Spa | Almancil | +351 289 359 800 |
| Casa do Terreiro do Poço | Borba | +351 917 256077 |
| Albatroz Palace, Luxury Suites | Cascais | +351 21 484 73 80 |
| Hotel Cascais Mirage | Cascais | +351 210 060 600 |
| Quinta de San José | Ervedosa Do Douro | +351 254 420000 |
| Hotel Palacio Estoril Hotel and Golf | Estoril | +351 21 468 0400 |
| Convento do Espinheiro Heritage Hotel & Spa | Evora | +351 266 788 200 |
| Quinta da Bela Vista | Funchal | +351 291 706 400 |
| Quinta das Vistas Palace Gardens | Funchal | +351 291 750 000 |
| Hotel Lusitano | Golegã | +351 249 979 170 |
| As Janelas Verdes | Lisbon | +351 21 39 68 143 |

| | | |
|---|---|---|
| Heritage Av Liberdade | Lisbon | +351 213 404 040 |
| Hotel Aviz | Lisbon | +351 210 402 000 |
| Hotel Britania | Lisbon | +351 21 31 55 016 |
| Casas do Côro | Marialva - Mêda | +351 91 755 2020 |
| Vintage House | Pinhão | +351 254 730 230 |
| Estalagem da Ponta do Sol | Ponta do Sol | +351 291 970 200 |
| Hotel Quinta do Lago | Quinta do Lago - Almancil | +351 289 350 350 |
| Convento de São Paulo | Redondo | +351 266 989 160 |

## Slovenia

| | | |
|---|---|---|
| **Hotel Golf Bled** | **Bled** | **+386 4579 1700** |

## Spain

| | | |
|---|---|---|
| Barceló la Bobadilla | Andalucía | +34 958 32 18 61 |
| Casa de los Bates | Andalucía | +34 958 349 495 |
| Casa No 7 | Andalucía | +34 954 221 581 |
| Casa Romana Hotel Boutique | Andalucía | +34 954 915 170 |
| Casa Viña de Alcantara | Andalucía | +34 956 393 010 |
| Cortijo Soto Real | Andalucía | +34 955 869 200 |
| El Ladrón de Agua | Andalucía | +34 958 21 50 40 |
| El Molino de Santillán | Andalucía | +34 952 40 09 49 |
| Fairplay Golf Hotel & Spa | Andalucía | +34 956 429100 |
| Gran Hotel Elba Estepona & Thalasso Spa | Andalucía | +34 952 809 200 |
| Hacienda Benazuza el Bulli Hotel | Andalucía | +34 955 70 33 44 |
| Hacienda La Boticaria | Andalucía | +34 955 69 88 20 |
| Hospes las Casas del Rey de Baeza | Andalucía | +34 954 561 496 |
| Hospes Palacio de los Patos | Andalucía | +34 958 535 790 |
| Hospes Palacio del Bailío | Andalucía | +34 957 498 993 |
| Hotel Almenara | Andalucía | +34 956 58 20 00 |
| Hotel Casa Morisca | Andalucía | +34 958 221 100 |
| Hotel Cortijo Faín | Andalucía | +34 956 704 131 |
| Hotel La Fuente del Sol | Andalucía | +34 95 12 39 823 |
| Hotel La Viñuela | Andalucía | +34 952 519 193 |
| Hotel Molina Lario | Andalucía | +34 952 06 002 |
| Hotel Palacio de Los Granados | Andalucía | +34 955 905 344 |
| Hotel Palacio de Santa Inés | Andalucía | +34 958 22 23 62 |
| La Posada del Torcal | Andalucía | +34 952 03 11 77 |
| Los Castaños | Andalucía | +34 952 180 778 |
| Mikasa Suites Resort | Andalucía | +34 950 138 073 |
| Palacio de los Navas | Andalucía | +34 958 21 57 60 |

# Hotels, Europe & The Mediterranean

All the properties listed below can be found in our Recommended Hotels & Spas, Europe & The Mediterranean 2008 Guide. More information on our portfolio of guides can be found on page 343.

Palacio de San Benito ......................Andalucía ...................+34 954 88 33 36
Posada de Palacio .........................Andalucía ...................+34 956 36 4840
Santa Isabel la Real ......................Andalucía ...................+34 958 294 658
Hotel el Privilegio de Tena .............Aragón .......................+34 974 487 206
Hotel La Cepada ...........................Asturias......................+34 985 84 94 45
Palacio de Cutre ...........................Asturias......................+34 985 70 80 72
Atzaró Agroturismo ......................Balearic Islands ..........+34 971 33 88 38
Blau Porto Petro Beach
   Resort & Spa .............................Balearic Islands..........+34 971 648 282
Can Lluc .....................................Balearic Islands...........+34 971 198 673
Can Simoneta ..............................Balearic Islands...........+34 971 816 110
Cas Gasi .....................................Balearic Islands...........+34 971 197 700

**Hospes Maricel...............................Balearic Islands ...............+34 971 707 744**
Hotel Aimia.................................Balearic Islands..................+34 971 631 200
Hotel Cala Sant Vicenç .................Balearic Islands..................+34 971 53 02 50
Hotel Dalt Murada .......................Balearic Islands..................+34 971 425 300
Hotel Hacienda Na Xamena ..........Balearic Islands..................+34 971 334 500
Hotel La Moraleja ........................Balearic Islands..................+34 971 534 010
Hotel Migjorn...............................Balearic Islands..................+34 971 650 668
Hotel Tres ...................................Balearic Islands..................+34 971 717 333
Palacio Ca Sa Galesa ....................Balearic Islands..................+34 971 715 400
Read's Hotel & Vespasian Spa........Balearic Islands..................+34 971 14 02 61
Son Brull Hotel & Spa ..................Balearic Islands..................+34 971 53 53 53
Valldemossa Hotel & Restaurant....Balearic Islands..................+34 971 61 26 26
Abama .......................................Canary Islands ..................+34 902 105 600
Hotel Elba Palace Golf ..................Canary Islands ..................+34 928 16 39 22
Hotel Jardín Tropical.....................Canary Islands ..................+34 922 74 60 00
Hotel las Madrigueras ..................Canary Islands ..................+34 922 77 78 18
Jardín de la Paz ...........................Canary Islands ..................+34 922 578 818
Kempinski Atlantis Bahía Real ........Canary Islands ..................+34 928 53 64 44
Princesa Yaiza Suite Hotel Resort ...Canary Islands ..................+34 928 519 222
Posada Los Nogales ......................Cantabria ........................+34 942 589 222
Castillo de Buen Amor ..................Castilla y León..................+34 923 355 002
Hacienda Zorita ...........................Castilla y León..................+34 923 129 400
Hotel Rector ...............................Castilla y León..................+34 923 21 84 82
Posada de la Casa
   del Abad de Ampudia.................Castilla y León..................+34 979 768 008
Finca Canturias ...........................Castilla~La Mancha............+34 925 59 41 08
Hotel Palacio de la Serna ..............Castilla~La Mancha............+34 926 842413
Can Bonastre Wine Resort ............Cataluña...........................+34 91 772 87 67
Dolce Sitges Hotel .......................Cataluña...........................+34 938 109 000
El Convent Begur .........................Cataluña...........................+34 972 62 30 91
Gallery Hotel...............................Cataluña...........................+34 934 15 99 11
Grand Hotel Central .....................Cataluña...........................+34 93 295 79 00
Hospes Villa Paulita ......................Cataluña...........................+34 972 884 662
Hotel Casa Fuster .........................Cataluña...........................+34 93 255 30 00

Hotel Claris .................................Cataluña...........................+34 93 487 62 62
Hotel Cram .................................Cataluña...........................+34 93 216 77 00
Hotel Duquesa de Cardona ...........Cataluña...........................+34 93 268 90 90
Hotel Gran Derby .........................Cataluña...........................+34 93 445 2544
Hotel Granados 83........................Cataluña...........................+34 93 492 96 70
Hotel Omm .................................Cataluña...........................+34 93 445 40 00
Hotel Rigat Park & Spa Beach Hotel ..Cataluña.......................+34 972 36 52 00
Hotel Santa Marta .......................Cataluña...........................+34 972 364 904
Le Meridien Ra Beach Hotel & Spa ....Cataluña.......................+34 977 694 200
Mas Passamaner...........................Cataluña...........................+34 977 766 333
Romantic Villa - Hotel Vistabella ......Cataluña.........................+34 972 25 62 00
San Sebastian Playa Hotel .............Cataluña...........................+34 93 894 86 76
Casa Palacio Conde de la Corte ........Extremadura ...................+34 924 563 311
Antiguo Convento........................Madrid .............................+34 91 632 22 20
Gran Meliá Fénix ..........................Madrid .............................+34 91 431 67 00
Hospes Madrid ............................Madrid .............................+34 902 254 255
Hotel Orfila ................................Madrid .............................+34 91 702 77 70
Hotel Quinta de los Cedros ...........Madrid .............................+34 91 515 2200
Hotel Urban ...............................Madrid .............................+34 91 787 77 70
Hotel Villa Real............................Madrid .............................+34 914 20 37 67
Hotel Etxegana ...........................País Vasco.........................+34 946 338 448
Casa Lehmi .................................Valencia............................+34 96 588 4018
Hospes Amérigo...........................Valencia............................+34 965 14 65 70
Hospes Palau de la Mar .................Valencia............................+34 96 316 2884
Hotel Marisol Park .......................Valencia............................+34 965875700
Hotel Mont Sant ..........................Valencia............................+34 962 27 50 81
Hotel Neptuno ............................Valencia............................+34 963 567 777
Hotel Sidi Saler & Spa ..................Valencia............................+34 961 61 04 11
Hotel Sidi San Juan & Spa .............Valencia............................+34 96 516 13 00
Hotel Termas Marinas el Palaiset .....Valencia..........................+34 964 300 250
Ibb Masia de Lacy........................Valencia............................+34 96 144 0567
Mas de Canicattí..........................Valencia............................+34 96 165 05 34
Torre la Mina ..............................Valencia............................+34 964 57 1746

## Switzerland

Park Hotel Weggis .......................Weggis .............................+41 41 392 05 05
Alden Hotel Splügenschloss ...........Zurich ..............................+41 44 289 99 99

## Turkey

The Marmara Antalya.....................Antalya.............................+90 242 249 36 00
Tuvana Residence ........................Antalya.............................+90 242 247 60 15
Sungate Port Royal
   Deluxe Resort Hotel...................Antalya - Kemer.................+90 242 824 9750
Turkiz Hotel
   Thalasso Centre & Marina ..........Antalya - Kemer .................+90 242 8144100
Divan Bodrum Palmira ..................Bodrum............................+90 252 377 5601
The Marmara Bodrum ..................Bodrum............................+90 252 313 8130
Oyster Residence .........................Fethiye - Ölüdeniz .............+90 252 617 0765
Cappadocia Cave Suites .................Göreme - Cappadocia ......+90 384 271 2800
A'jia Hotel ..................................Istanbul............................+90 216 413 9300
The Marmara Istanbul ..................Istanbul............................+90 212 251 4696
The Marmara Pera .......................Istanbul............................+90 212 251 4646
Sumahan On The Water ...............Istanbul............................+90 216 422 8000
Villa Mahal..................................Kalkan..............................+90 242 844 32 68
Richmond Nua Wellness - Spa .........Sapanca - Adapazarı .........+90 264 582 2100

# Hotels - The Americas

Properties listed below can be found in our Recommended Hotels, Inns, Resorts & Spas - The Americas, Atlantic, Caribbean & Pacific 2008 Guide. More information on our portfolio of guides can be found on page 343.

## Recommendations in Canada

CANADA - BRITISH COLUMBIA (VICTORIA)

**Fairholme Manor**

638 Rockland Place, Victoria, British Columbia V8S 3R2

Tel: +1 250 598 3240
www.johansens.com/fairholme

CANADA - BRITISH COLUMBIA (SALT SPRING ISLAND)

**Hastings House Country Estate**

160 Upper Ganges Road, Salt Spring Island, British Columbia V8K 2S2

Tel: +1 250 537 2362
www.johansens.com/hastingshouse

CANADA - BRITISH COLUMBIA (VICTORIA)

**Villa Marco Polo Inn**

1524 Shasta Place, Victoria, British Columbia V8S 1X9

Tel: +1 250 370 1524
www.johansens.com/villamarcopolo

CANADA - BRITISH COLUMBIA (SOOKE)

**Sooke Harbour House**

1528 Whiffen Spit Road, Sooke, British Columbia V0S 1N0

Tel: +1 250 642 3421
www.johansens.com/sookeharbour

CANADA - BRITISH COLUMBIA (WHISTLER)

**Adara Hotel**

4122 Village Green, Whistler, British Columbia V0N 1B4

Tel: +1 604 905 4009
www.johansens.com/adara

CANADA - BRITISH COLUMBIA (VANCOUVER)

**Pan Pacific Vancouver**

300-999 Canada Place, Vancouver, British Columbia V6C 3B5

Tel: +1 604 662 8111
www.johansens.com/panpacific

CANADA - NEW BRUNSWICK (ST. ANDREWS BY-THE-SEA)

**Kingsbrae Arms**

219 King Street, St. Andrews By-The-Sea, New Brunswick E5B 1Y1

Tel: +1 506 529 1897
www.johansens.com/kingsbraearms

CANADA - BRITISH COLUMBIA (VANCOUVER)

**The Sutton Place Hotel Vancouver**

845 Burrard Street, Vancouver, British Columbia V6Z 2K6

Tel: +1 604 682 5511
www.johansens.com/suttonplacebc

CANADA - ONTARIO (NIAGARA-ON-THE-LAKE)

**Riverbend Inn & Vineyard**

16104 Niagara River Parkway, Niagara-on-the-Lake, Ontario L0S 1J0

Tel: +1 905 468 8866
www.johansens.com/riverbend

CANADA - BRITISH COLUMBIA (TOFINO)

**Wickaninnish Inn**

Osprey Lane at Chesterman Beach, Tofino, British Columbia V0R 2Z0

Tel: +1 250 725 3100
www.johansens.com/wickaninnish

CANADA - ONTARIO (TORONTO)

**Windsor Arms**

18 St. Thomas Street, Toronto, Ontario M5S 3E7

Tel: +1 416 971 9666
www.johansens.com/windsorarms

CANADA - BRITISH COLUMBIA (VANCOUVER)

**Wedgewood Hotel & Spa**

845 Hornby Street, Vancouver, British Columbia V6Z 1V1

Tel: +1 604 689 7777
www.johansens.com/wedgewoodbc

CANADA - QUÉBEC (LA MALBAIE)

**La Pinsonnière**

124 Saint-Raphaël, La Malbaie, Québec G5A 1X9

Tel: +1 418 665 4431
www.johansens.com/lapinsonniere

CANADA - BRITISH COLUMBIA (VICTORIA)

**Brentwood Bay Lodge**

849 Verdier Avenue, Victoria, British Columbia V8M 1C5

Tel: +1 250 544 2079
www.johansens.com/brentwood

CANADA - QUÉBEC (MONT-TREMBLANT)

**Hôtel Quintessence**

3004 chemin de la chapelle, Mont-Tremblant, Québec J8E 1E1

Tel: +1 819 425 3400
www.johansens.com/quintessence

# Hotels - The Americas

Properties listed below can be found in our Recommended Hotels, Inns, Resorts & Spas - The Americas, Atlantic, Caribbean & Pacific 2008 Guide. More information on our portfolio of guides can be found on page 343.

### CANADA - QUÉBEC (MONTRÉAL)

**Hôtel Nelligan**

106 rue Saint-Paul Ouest, Montréal, Québec H2Y 1Z3

Tel: +1 514 788 2040
www.johansens.com/nelligan

### CANADA - QUÉBEC (MONTRÉAL)

**Le Place d'Armes Hôtel & Suites**

55 rue Saint-Jacques Ouest, Montréal, Québec H2Y 3X2

Tel: +1 514 842 1887
www.johansens.com/hotelplacedarmes

## Recommendations in Mexico

### MEXICO - BAJA CALIFORNIA NORTE (TECATE)

**Rancho La Puerta**

Tecate, Baja California Norte

Tel: +1 877 440 7778
www.johansens.com/rancholapuerta

### MEXICO - BAJA CALIFORNIA SUR (CABO SAN LUCAS)

**Esperanza**

Km. 7 Carretera Transpeninsular, Punta Ballena, Cabo San Lucas, Baja California Sur 23410

Tel: +52 624 145 6400
www.johansens.com/esperanza

### MEXICO - BAJA CALIFORNIA SUR (LOS CABOS)

**Marquis Los Cabos Beach Resort & Spa**

Lote 74, Km. 21.5 Carretera Transpeninsular, Fraccionamiento Cabo Real, Los Cabos, Baja California Sur 23400

Tel: +52 624 144 2000
www.johansens.com/marquisloscabos

### MEXICO - BAJA CALIFORNIA SUR (SAN JOSÉ DEL CABO)

**Casa Del Mar Spa Resort**

KM 19.5 Carretera Transpeninsular, San José del Cabo, Baja California Sur 23400

Tel: +52 624 145 7700
www.johansens.com/casadelmar

### MEXICO - BAJA CALIFORNIA SUR (SAN JOSÉ DEL CABO)

**Casa Natalia**

Blvd. Mijares 4, San José Del Cabo, Baja California Sur 23400

Tel: +52 624 146 7100
www.johansens.com/casanatalia

### MEXICO - COLIMA (COLIMA)

**Hacienda de San Antonio**

Municipio de Comala, Colima, Colima 28450

Tel: +52 312 316 0300
www.johansens.com/sanantonio

### MEXICO - DISTRITO FEDERAL (MEXICO CITY)

**Casa Vieja**

Eugenio Sue 45 (Colonia Polanco), Mexico Distrito Federal 11560

Tel: +52 55 52 82 0067
www.johansens.com/casavieja

### MEXICO - GUANAJUATO (GUANAJUATO)

**Quinta Las Acacias**

Paseo de la Presa 168, Guanajuato, Guanajuato 36000

Tel: +52 473 731 1517
www.johansens.com/acacias

### MEXICO - JALISCO (COSTA ALEGRE)

**El Tamarindo Beach & Golf Resort**

Km 7.5 Highway 200, Carretera Barra de Navidad - Puerto Vallarta, Cihuatlan, Jalisco 48970

Tel: +52 315 351 5031 ext. 204
www.johansens.com/eltamarindo

### MEXICO - JALISCO (COSTA ALEGRE / MANZANILLO)

**Cuixmala**

Costa Cuixmala, Carretera Melaque - Puerto Vallarta Km 46.2, La Huerta, Jalisco 48893

Tel: +52 315 351 0044
www.johansens.com/cuixmala

### MEXICO - JALISCO (PUERTO VALLARTA)

**Casa Velas Hotel Boutique**

Pelicanos 311, Fracc. Marina Vallarta, Puerto Vallarta, Jalisco 48354

Tel: +52 322 226 6688
www.johansens.com/casavelas

### MEXICO - JALISCO (PUERTA VALLARTA / COSTA ALEGRE)

**Las Alamandas Resort**

Carretera Barra de Navidad - Puerto Vallarta km 83.5, Col. Quemaro, Jalisco 48850

Tel: +52 322 285 5500
www.johansens.com/lasalamandas

### MEXICO - MICHOACÁN (MORELIA)

**Hotel Los Juaninos**

Morelos Sur 39, Centro, Morelia, Michoacán 58000

Tel: +52 443 312 00 36
www.johansens.com/juaninos

# Hotels - The Americas

Properties listed below can be found in our Recommended Hotels, Inns, Resorts & Spas - The Americas, Atlantic, Caribbean & Pacific 2008 Guide. More information on our portfolio of guides can be found on page 343.

MEXICO - MICHOACÁN (MORELIA)

**Hotel Virrey de Mendoza**

Av. Madero Pte. 310, Centro Histórico, Morelia, Michoacán 58000

Tel: +52 44 33 12 06 33
www.johansens.com/hotelvirrey

MEXICO - MICHOACÁN (MORELIA)

**Villa Montaña Hotel & Spa**

Patzimba 201, Vista Bella, Morelia, Michoacán 58090

Tel: +52 443 314 02 31
www.johansens.com/montana

MEXICO - NAYARIT (NUEVO VALLARTA)

**Grand Velas All Suites & Spa Resort**

Av. Cocoteros 98 Sur, Nuevo Vallarta, Nayarit 63735

Tel: +52 322 226 8000
www.johansens.com/grandvelas

MEXICO - OAXACA (OAXACA)

**Casa Oaxaca**

Calle García Vigil 407, Centro, Oaxaca, Oaxaca 68000

Tel: +52 951 514 4173
www.johansens.com/oaxaca

MEXICO - OAXACA (OAXACA)

**Hotel la Provincia**

Porfirio Diaz #108 Centro Historico, Oaxaca, Oaxaca 68000, Mexico

Tel: +52 951 51 40999
www.johansens.com/hotellaprovicia

MEXICO - PUEBLA (CHOLULA)

**La Quinta Luna**

3 sur 702, San Pedro Cholula, Puebla 72760

Tel: +52 222 247 8915
www.johansens.com/quintaluna

MEXICO - QUINTANA ROO (ISLA MUJERES)

**Casa De Los Sueños**

Lote 9A y 9B, A 200 MTS de Garrafon, Fracc Turquesa, Isla Mujeres, Quintana Roo 77400

Tel: +52 998 877 0651
www.johansens.com/lossuenos

MEXICO - QUINTANA ROO (PUERTO MORELOS)

**Ceiba del Mar Spa Resort**

Costera Norte Lte. 1, S.M. 10, MZ. 26, Puerto Morelos, Quintana Roo 77580

Tel: +52 998 872 8060
www.johansens.com/ceibademar

MEXICO - QUINTANA ROO (TULUM)

**Casa Nalum**

Sian Ka'an Biosphere Reserve, Quintana Roo

Tel: +52 19991 639 510
www.johansens.com/casanalum

MEXICO - YUCATÁN (MÉRIDA)

**Hacienda Xcanatun - Casa de Piedra**

Carretera Mérida - Progreso, Km 12, Mérida, Yucatán 97302

Tel: +52 999 941 0273
www.johansens.com/xcanatun

## Recommendations in U.S.A

U.S.A. - ALABAMA (PISGAH)

**Lodge on Gorham's Bluff**

101 Gorham Drive, Pisgah, Alabama 35765

Tel: +1 256 451 8439
www.johansens.com/gorhamsbluff

U.S.A. - ARIZONA (GREER)

**Hidden Meadow Ranch**

620 Country Road 1325, Greer, Arizona 85927

Tel: +1 928 333 1000
www.johansens.com/hiddenmeadow

U.S.A. - ARIZONA (PARADISE VALLEY / SCOTTSDALE)

**Sanctuary on Camelback Mountain**

5700 East McDonald Drive, Scottsdale, Arizona 85253

Tel: +1 480 948 2100
www.johansens.com/sanctuarycamelback

U.S.A. - ARIZONA (SEDONA)

**Sedona Rouge Hotel & Spa**

2250 West Highway 89A, Sedona, Arizona 86336

Tel: +1 928 203 4111
www.johansens.com/sedonarouge

U.S.A. - ARIZONA (TUCSON)

**Arizona Inn**

2200 East Elm Street, Tucson, Arizona 85719

Tel: +1 520 325 1541
www.johansens.com/arizonainn

# Hotels - The Americas

Properties listed below can be found in our Recommended Hotels, Inns, Resorts & Spas - The Americas, Atlantic, Caribbean & Pacific 2008 Guide. More information on our portfolio of guides can be found on page 343.

U.S.A. - ARIZONA (TUCSON)

**Tanque Verde Ranch**

14301 East Speedway Boulevard, Tucson, Arizona 85748

Tel: +1 520 296 6275
www.johansens.com/tanqueverde

U.S.A. - CALIFORNIA (GLEN ELLEN)

**The Gaige House**

13540 Arnold Drive, Glen Ellen, California 95442

Tel: +1 707 935 0237
www.johansens.com/gaige

U.S.A. - ARIZONA (WICKENBURG)

**Rancho de los Caballeros**

1551 South Vulture Mine Road, Wickenburg, Arizona 85390

Tel: +1 928 684 5484
www.johansens.com/caballeros

U.S.A. - CALIFORNIA (HEALDSBURG)

**The Grape Leaf Inn**

539 Johnson Street, Healdsburg, California 95448

Tel: +1 707 433 8140
www.johansens.com/grapeleaf

U.S.A. - CALIFORNIA (CARMEL-BY-THE-SEA)

**L'Auberge Carmel**

Monte Verde at Seventh, Carmel-by-the-Sea, California 93921

Tel: +1 831 624 8578
www.johansens.com/laubergecarmel

U.S.A. - CALIFORNIA (HEALDSBURG)

**Hotel Healdsburg**

25 Matheson St, Healdsburg, California 95448

Tel: +1 707 431 2800
www.johansens.com/healdsburg

U.S.A. - CALIFORNIA (CARMEL-BY-THE-SEA)

**Tradewinds Carmel**

Mission Street at Third Avenue, Carmel-by-the-Sea, California 93921

Tel: +1 831 624 2776
www.johansens.com/tradewinds

U.S.A. - CALIFORNIA (INDIAN WELLS)

**Miramonte Resort and Spa**

45-000 Indian Wells Lane, Indian Wells, California 92210

Tel: +1 760 341 2200
www.johansens.com/miramonte

U.S.A. - CALIFORNIA (CARMEL VALLEY)

**Bernardus Lodge**

415 Carmel Valley Road, Carmel Valley, California 93924

Tel: +1 831 658 3400
www.johansens.com/bernardus

U.S.A. - CALIFORNIA (KENWOOD)

**The Kenwood Inn and Spa**

10400 Sonoma Highway, Kenwood, California 95452

Tel: +1 707 833 1293
www.johansens.com/kenwoodinn

U.S.A. - CALIFORNIA (BIG SUR)

**Post Ranch Inn**

Highway 1, P.O. Box 219, Big Sur, California 93920

Tel: +1 831 667 2200
www.johansens.com/postranchinn

U.S.A. - CALIFORNIA (LA JOLLA)

**Estancia La Jolla Hotel & Spa**

9700 North Torrey Pines Road, La Jolla, California 92037

Tel: +1 858 550 1000
www.johansens.com/estancialajolla

U.S.A. - CALIFORNIA (BIG SUR)

**Ventana Inn and Spa**

Highway 1, Big Sur, California 93920

Tel: +1 831 667 2331
www.johansens.com/ventana

U.S.A. - CALIFORNIA (LITTLE RIVER)

**Stevenswood Spa Resort**

8211 North Highway 1, Little River, CALIFORNIA 95456

Tel: +1 800 421 2810
www.johansens.com/stevenswood

U.S.A. - CALIFORNIA (EUREKA)

**The Carter House Inns**

301 L Street, Eureka, California 95501

Tel: +1 707 444 8062
www.johansens.com/carterhouse

U.S.A. - CALIFORNIA (LOS ANGELES)

**Hotel Bel-Air**

701 Stone Canyon Road, Los Angeles, California 90077

Tel: +1 310 472 1211
www.johansens.com/belair

# Hotels - The Americas

Properties listed below can be found in our Recommended Hotels, Inns, Resorts & Spas - The Americas, Atlantic, Caribbean & Pacific 2008 Guide. More information on our portfolio of guides can be found on page 343.

U.S.A. - CALIFORNIA (MENDOCINO)

### The Stanford Inn By The Sea

Coast Highway One & Comptche-Ukiah Road, Mendocino, California 95460

Tel: +1 707 937 5615
www.johansens.com/stanford

U.S.A. - CALIFORNIA (SAN DIEGO)

### Tower23 Hotel

4551 Ocean Blvd., San Diego, California 92109

Tel: +1 858 270 2323
www.johansens.com/tower23

U.S.A. - CALIFORNIA (MILL VALLEY)

### Mill Valley Inn

165 Throckmorton Avenue, Mill Valley, California 94941

Tel: +1 415 389 6608
www.johansens.com/millvalleyinn

U.S.A. - CALIFORNIA (SAN FRANCISCO)

### The Union Street Inn

2229 Union Street, San Francisco, California 94123

Tel: +1 415 346 0424
www.johansens.com/unionstreetsf

U.S.A. - CALIFORNIA (MONTEREY)

### Old Monterey Inn

500 Martin Street, Monterey, California 93940

Tel: +1 831 375 8284
www.johansens.com/oldmontereyinn

U.S.A. - CALIFORNIA (SAN FRANCISCO BAY AREA)

### Inn Above Tide

30 El Portal, Sausalito, California 94965

Tel: +1 415 332 9535
www.johansens.com/innabovetide

U.S.A. - CALIFORNIA (NAPA)

### 1801 First Inn

1801 First Street, Napa, California 94559

Tel: +1 707 224 3739
www.johansens.com/1801inn

U.S.A. - CALIFORNIA (SANTA BARBARA)

### Harbor View Inn

28 West Cabrillo Boulevard, Santa Barbara, California 93101

Tel: +1 805 963 0780
www.johansens.com/harborview

U.S.A. - CALIFORNIA (NAPA)

### Milliken Creek Inn & Spa

1815 Silverado Trail, Napa, California 94558

Tel: +1 707 255 1197
www.johansens.com/milliken

U.S.A. - CALIFORNIA (SANTA YNEZ)

### The Santa Ynez Inn

3627 Sagunto Street, Santa Ynez, California 93460-0628

Tel: +1 805 688 5588
www.johansens.com/santaynez

U.S.A. - CALIFORNIA (NEWPORT BEACH)

### The Island Hotel Newport Beach

690 Newport Center Drive, Newport Beach, California 92660

Tel: +1 949 759 0808
www.johansens.com/newportbeach

U.S.A. - CALIFORNIA (SONOMA)

### Ledson Hotel & Harmony Lounge

480 First Street East, Sonoma, California 95476

Tel: +1 707 996 9779
www.johansens.com/ledsonhotel

U.S.A. - CALIFORNIA (OAKHURST)

### Château du Sureau & Spa

48688 Victoria Lane, Oakhurst, California 93644

Tel: +1 559 683 6860
www.johansens.com/chateausureau

U.S.A. - CALIFORNIA (ST. HELENA)

### Meadowood

900 Meadowood Lane, St. Helena, California 94574

Tel: +1 707 963 3646
www.johansens.com/meadowood

U.S.A. - CALIFORNIA (RANCHO SANTA FE)

### The Inn at Rancho Santa Fe

5951 Linea del Cielo, Rancho Santa Fe, California 92067

Tel: +1 858 756 1131
www.johansens.com/ranchosantafe

U.S.A. - COLORADO (BOULDER)

### The Bradley Boulder Inn

2040 16th Street, Boulder, Colorado 80302

Tel: +1 303 545 5200
www.johansens.com/bradleyboulderinn

# Hotels - The Americas

Properties listed below can be found in our Recommended Hotels, Inns, Resorts & Spas - The Americas, Atlantic, Caribbean & Pacific 2008 Guide. More information on our portfolio of guides can be found on page 343.

U.S.A. - COLORADO (CRAWFORD)

**Smith Fork Ranch**

45362 Needlerock Road, Crawford, Colorado 81415

Tel: +1 970 921 3454
www.johansens.com/smithfork

U.S.A. - COLORADO (TELLURIDE)

**The Hotel Telluride**

199 North Cornet Street, Telluride, Colorado 81435

Tel: +1 970 369 1188
www.johansens.com/telluride

U.S.A. - COLORADO (DENVER)

**Castle Marne Bed & Breakfast Inn**

1572 Race Street, Denver, Colorado 80206

Tel: +1 303 331 0621
www.johansens.com/castlemarne

U.S.A. - COLORADO (VAIL)

**The Tivoli Lodge at Vail**

386 Hanson Ranch Road, Vail, Colorado 81657

Tel: +1 970 476 5615
www.johansens.com/tivoli

U.S.A. - COLORADO (DENVER)

**Hotel Monaco**

1717 Champa Street at 17th, Denver, Colorado 80202

Tel: +1 303 296 1717
www.johansens.com/monaco

U.S.A. - COLORADO (VAIL)

**Vail Mountain Lodge & Spa**

352 East Meadow Drive, Vail, Colorado 81657

Tel: +1 970 476 0700
www.johansens.com/vailmountain

U.S.A. - COLORADO (ESTES PARK)

**Taharaa Mountain Lodge**

3110 So. St. Vrain, Estes Park, Colorado 80517

Tel: +1 970 577 0098
www.johansens.com/taharaa

U.S.A. - CONNECTICUT (GREENWICH)

**Delamar Greenwich Harbor**

500 Steamboat Road, Greenwich, Connecticut 06830

Tel: +1 203 661 9800
www.johansens.com/delamar

U.S.A. - COLORADO (MANITOU SPRINGS)

**The Cliff House at Pikes Peak**

306 Cañon Avenue, Manitou Springs, Colorado 80829

Tel: +1 719 685 3000
www.johansens.com/thecliffhouse

U.S.A. - CONNECTICUT (WESTPORT)

**The Inn at National Hall**

2 Post Road West, Westport, Connecticut 06880

Tel: +1 203 221 1351
www.johansens.com/nationalhall

U.S.A. - COLORADO (MONTROSE)

**Elk Mountain Resort**

97 Elk Walk, Montrose, Colorado 81401

Tel: +1 970 252 4900
www.johansens.com/elkmountain

U.S.A. - DELAWARE (REHOBOTH BEACH)

**The Bellmoor**

Six Christian Street, Rehoboth Beach, Delaware 19971

Tel: +1 302 227 5800
www.johansens.com/thebellmoor

U.S.A. - COLORADO (STEAMBOAT SPRINGS)

**Vista Verde Guest Ranch**

P.O. Box 770465, Steamboat Springs, Colorado 80477

Tel: +1 970 879 3858
www.johansens.com/vistaverderanch

U.S.A. - DELAWARE (REHOBOTH BEACH)

**Boardwalk Plaza Hotel**

Olive Avenue & The Boardwalk, Rehoboth Beach, Delaware 19971

Tel: +1 302 227 7169
www.johansens.com/boardwalkplaza

U.S.A. - COLORADO (TELLURIDE)

**Fairmont Heritage Place Franz Klammer Lodge**

567 Mountain Village Boulevard, Telluride, Colorado 81436

Tel: +1 970 728 4239
www.johansens.com/fairmont

U.S.A. - DELAWARE (WILMINGTON)

**Inn at Montchanin Village**

Route 100 & Kirk Road, Montchanin, Delaware 19710

Tel: +1 302 888 2133
www.johansens.com/montchanin

# Hotels - The Americas

Properties listed below can be found in our Recommended Hotels, Inns, Resorts & Spas - The Americas, Atlantic, Caribbean & Pacific 2008 Guide. More information on our portfolio of guides can be found on page 343.

U.S.A. - DISTRICT OF COLUMBIA (WASHINGTON)

**The Hay-Adams**

Sixteenth & H. Streets N.W., Washington D.C. 20006

Tel: +1 202 638 6600
www.johansens.com/hayadams

U.S.A. - FLORIDA (COCONUT GROVE)

**Grove Isle Hotel & Spa**

Four Grove Isle Drive, Coconut Grove, Florida 33133

Tel: +1 305 858 8300
www.johansens.com/groveisle

U.S.A. - FLORIDA (FISHER ISLAND)

**Fisher Island Hotel & Resort**

One Fisher Island Drive, Fisher Island, Florida 33109

Tel: +1 305 535 6000
www.johansens.com/fisherisland

U.S.A. - FLORIDA (JUPITER BEACH)

**Jupiter Beach Resort & Spa**

5 North A1A, Jupiter, Florida 33477-5190

Tel: +1 561 746 2511
www.johansens.com/jupiterbeachresort

U.S.A. - FLORIDA (KEY WEST)

**Ocean Key Resort**

Zero Duval Street, Key West, Florida 33040

Tel: +1 305 296 7701
www.johansens.com/oceankey

U.S.A. - FLORIDA (KEY WEST)

**Simonton Court Historic Inn & Cottages**

320 Simonton Street, Key West, Florida 33040

Tel: +1 305 294 6386
www.johansens.com/simontoncourt

U.S.A. - FLORIDA (KEY WEST)

**Sunset Key Guest Cottages**

245 Front Street, Key West, Florida 33040

Tel: +1 305 292 5300
www.johansens.com/sunsetkey

U.S.A. - FLORIDA (MIAMI BEACH)

**Hotel Victor**

1144 Ocean Drive, Miami Beach, Florida 33139

Tel: +1 305 428 1234
www.johansens.com/hotelvictor

U.S.A. - FLORIDA (MIAMI BEACH)

**The Setai Hotel & Resort**

2001 Collins Ave., Miami Beach, Florida 33139, U.S.A.

Tel: +1 305 520 6000
www.johansens.com/setai

U.S.A. - FLORIDA (MIAMI BEACH)

**Casa Tua**

1700 James Avenue, Miami Beach, Florida 33139

Tel: +1 305 673 0973
www.johansens.com/casatua

U.S.A. - FLORIDA (NAPLES)

**LaPlaya Beach & Golf Resort**

9891 Gulf Shore Drive, Naples, Florida 34108

Tel: +1 239 597 3123
www.johansens.com/laplaya

U.S.A. - FLORIDA (SANTA ROSA BEACH)

**WaterColor Inn and Resort**

34 Goldenrod Circle, Santa Rosa Beach, Florida 32459

Tel: +1 850 534 5000
www.johansens.com/watercolor

U.S.A. - FLORIDA (ST. PETE BEACH)

**Don CeSar Beach Resort**

3400 Gulf Boulevard, St. Pete Beach, Florida 33706

Tel: +1 727 360 1881
www.johansens.com/doncesar

U.S.A. - GEORGIA (ADAIRSVILLE)

**Barnsley Gardens Resort**

597 Barnsley Gardens Road, Adairsville, Georgia 30103

Tel: +1 770 773 7480
www.johansens.com/barnsleygardens

U.S.A. - GEORGIA (CUMBERLAND ISLAND)

**Greyfield Inn**

Cumberland Island, Georgia

Tel: +1 904 261 6408
www.johansens.com/greyfieldinn

U.S.A. - GEORGIA (MADISON)

**The James Madison Inn**

260 West Washington Street, Madison, Georgia 30650

Tel: +1 706 342 7040
www.johansens.com/jamesmadison

# Hotels - The Americas

Properties listed below can be found in our Recommended Hotels, Inns, Resorts & Spas - The Americas, Atlantic, Caribbean & Pacific 2008 Guide. More information on our portfolio of guides can be found on page 343.

### U.S.A. - GEORGIA (SAVANNAH)

**The Gastonian**

220 East Gaston Street, Savannah, Georgia 31401

Tel: +1 912 232 2869
www.johansens.com/gastonian

### U.S.A. - LOUISIANA (NEW ORLEANS)

**The St. James Hotel**

330 Magazine Street, New Orleans, Louisiana 70130

Tel: +1 504 304 4000
www.johansens.com/stjamesno

### U.S.A. - HAWAII (BIG ISLAND)

**The Palms Cliff House**

28-3514 Mamalahoa Highway 19, P.O. Box 189, Honomu, Hawaii 96728-0189

Tel: +1 808 963 6076
www.johansens.com/palmscliff

### U.S.A. - MAINE (GREENVILLE)

**The Lodge At Moosehead Lake**

368 Lily Bay Road, P.O. Box 1167, Greenville, Maine 04441

Tel: +1 207 695 4400
www.johansens.com/lodgeatmooseheadlake

### U.S.A. - HAWAII (MAUI)

**Hotel Hana-Maui and Honua Spa**

5031 Hana Highway, Hana, Maui, Hawaii 96713

Tel: +1 808 248 8211
www.johansens.com/hanamaui

### U.S.A. - MAINE (KENNEBUNKPORT)

**The White Barn Inn**

37 Beach Avenue, Kennebunkport, Maine 04043

Tel: +1 207 967 2321
www.johansens.com/whitebarninn

### U.S.A. - HAWAII (BIG ISLAND)

**Shipman House**

131 Ka'iulani Street, Hilo, Hawaii 96720

Tel: +1 808 934 8002
www.johansens.com/shipman

### U.S.A. - MAINE (PORTLAND)

**Portland Harbor Hotel**

468 Fore Street, Portland, Maine 04101

Tel: +1 207 775 9090
www.johansens.com/portlandharbor

### U.S.A. - IDAHO (KETCHUM)

**Knob Hill Inn**

960 North Main Street, P.O. Box 800, Ketchum, Idaho 83340

Tel: +1 208 726 8010
www.johansens.com/knobhillinn

### U.S.A. - MARYLAND (FROSTBURG)

**Savage River Lodge**

1600 Mt. Aetna Road, Frostburg, Maryland 21532

Tel: +1 301 689 3200
www.johansens.com/savageriver

### U.S.A. - KANSAS (LAWRENCE)

**The Eldridge**

701 Massachusetts, Lawrence, Kansas 66044

Tel: +1 785 749 5011
www.johansens.com/eldridge

### U.S.A. - MASSACHUSETTS (BOSTON)

**The Charles Street Inn**

94 Charles Street, Boston, Massachusetts 02114

Tel: +1 617 314 8900
www.johansens.com/charlesstreetinn

### U.S.A. - LOUISIANA (NEW ORLEANS)

**Hotel Maison de Ville**

727 Rue Toulouse, New Orleans, Louisiana 70130

Tel: +1 504 561 5858
www.johansens.com/maisondeville

### U.S.A. - MASSACHUSETTS (BOSTON)

**Fifteen Beacon**

15 Beacon Street, Boston, Massachusetts 2108

Tel: +1 617 670 1500
www.johansens.com/fifteenbeacon

### U.S.A. - LOUISIANA (NEW ORLEANS)

**The Lafayette Hotel**

600 St. Charles Avenue, New Orleans, Louisiana 70130

Tel: +1 504 524 4441
www.johansens.com/lafayette

### U.S.A. - MASSACHUSETTS (BOSTON)

**Hotel Commonwealth**

500 Commonwealth Avenue, Boston, Massachusetts 02215

Tel: +1 617 933 5000
www.johansens.com/commonwealth

# Hotels - The Americas

Properties listed below can be found in our Recommended Hotels, Inns, Resorts & Spas - The Americas, Atlantic, Caribbean & Pacific 2008 Guide. More information on our portfolio of guides can be found on page 343.

U.S.A. - MASSACHUSETTS (BOSTON)

**The Lenox**

61 Exeter Street at Boylston, Boston, Massachusetts 02116

Tel: +1 617 536 5300
www.johansens.com/lenox

U.S.A. - MASSACHUSETTS (MARTHA'S VINEYARD)

**Winnetu Oceanside Resort at South Beach**

31 Dunes Road, Edgartown, Massachusetts 02539

Tel: +1 508 310 1733
www.johansens.com/winnetu

U.S.A. - MASSACHUSETTS (BOSTON)

**The Liberty Hotel**

215 Charles Street, Boston, Massachusetts 02114

Tel: +1 617 224 4000
www.johansens.com/liberty

U.S.A. - MISSISSIPPI (JACKSON)

**Fairview Inn & Restaurant**

734 Fairview Street, Jackson, Mississippi 39202

Tel: +1 601 948 3429
www.johansens.com/fairviewinn

U.S.A. - MASSACHUSETTS (CAPE COD)

**Wequassett Resort and Golf Club**

On Pleasant Bay, Chatham, Cape Cod, Massachusetts 02633

Tel: +1 508 432 5400
www.johansens.com/wequassett

U.S.A. - MISSISSIPPI (NATCHEZ)

**Monmouth Plantation**

36 Melrose Avenue, Natchez, Mississippi 39120

Tel: +1 601 442 5852
www.johansens.com/monmouthplantation

U.S.A. - MASSACHUSETTS (CAPE COD)

**The Crowne Pointe Historic Inn & Spa**

82 Bradford Street, Provincetown, Cape Cod, Massachusetts 02657

Tel: +1 508 487 6767
www.johansens.com/crownepointe

U.S.A. - MISSISSIPPI (NESBIT)

**Bonne Terre Country Inn**

4715 Church Road West, Nesbit, Mississippi 38651

Tel: +1 662 781 5100
www.johansens.com/bonneterre

U.S.A. - MASSACHUSETTS (IPSWICH)

**The Inn at Castle Hill**

280 Argilla Road, Ipswich, Massachusetts 01938

Tel: +1 978 412 2555
www.johansens.com/castlehill

U.S.A. - MISSOURI (KANSAS CITY)

**The Raphael Hotel**

325 Ward Parkway, Kansas City, Missouri 64112

Tel: +1 816 756 3800
www.johansens.com/raphael

U.S.A. - MASSACHUSETTS (LENOX)

**Blantyre**

16 Blantyre Road, P.O. Box 995, Lenox, Massachusetts 01240

Tel: +1 413 637 3556
www.johansens.com/blantyre

U.S.A. - MISSOURI (RIDGEDALE)

**Big Cedar Lodge**

612 Devil's Pool Road, Ridgedale, Missouri 65739

Tel: +1 417 335 2777
www.johansens.com/bigcedar

U.S.A. - MASSACHUSETTS (LENOX)

**Cranwell Resort, Spa & Golf Club**

55 Lee Road, Route 20, Lenox, Massachusetts 01240

Tel: +1 413 637 1364
www.johansens.com/cranwell

U.S.A. - MONTANA (BIG SKY)

**The Big EZ Lodge**

7000 Beaver Creek Road, Big Sky, Montana 59716

Tel: +1 406 995 7000
www.johansens.com/bigez

U.S.A. - MASSACHUSETTS (MARTHA'S VINEYARD)

**The Charlotte Inn**

27 South Summer Street, Edgartown, Massachusetts 02539

Tel: +1 508 627 4151
www.johansens.com/charlotte

U.S.A. - MONTANA (DARBY)

**Triple Creek Ranch**

5551 West Fork Road, Darby, Montana 59829

Tel: +1 406 821 4600
www.johansens.com/triplecreek

# Hotels - The Americas

Properties listed below can be found in our Recommended Hotels, Inns, Resorts & Spas - The Americas, Atlantic, Caribbean & Pacific 2008 Guide. More information on our portfolio of guides can be found on page 343.

U.S.A. - NEW HAMPSHIRE (WHITEFIELD / WHITE MOUNTAINS)

**Mountain View Grand Resort & Spa**

Mountain View Road, Whitefield, New Hampshire 03598

Tel: +1 603 837 2100
www.johansens.com/mountainview

U.S.A. - NEW YORK (LAKE PLACID)

**Whiteface Lodge**

7 Whiteface Inn Lane, Lake Placid, New York 12946

Tel: +1 518 523 0500
www.johansens.com/whiteface

U.S.A. - NEW MEXICO (ESPAÑOLA)

**Rancho de San Juan**

P.O. Box 4140, Highway 285, Española, New Mexico 87533

Tel: +1 505 753 6818
www.johansens.com/ranchosanjuan

U.S.A. - NEW YORK (NEW YORK CITY)

**Hotel Plaza Athénée**

37 East 64th Street, New York City, New York 10021

Tel: +1 212 734 9100
www.johansens.com/athenee

U.S.A. - NEW MEXICO (SANTA FE)

**The Bishop's Lodge Resort & Spa**

1297 Bishop's Lodge Road, Santa Fe, New Mexico 87501

Tel: +1 505 983 6377
www.johansens.com/bishopslodge

U.S.A. - NEW YORK (NEW YORK CITY)

**The Inn at Irving Place**

56 Irving Place, New York, New York City 10003

Tel: +1 212 533 4600
www.johansens.com/irvingplace

U.S.A. - NEW MEXICO (TAOS)

**El Monte Sagrado Living Resort & Spa**

317 Kit Carson Road, Taos, New Mexico 87571

Tel: +1 505 758 3502
www.johansens.com/elmontesagrado

U.S.A. - NEW YORK (NEW YORK CITY)

**Jumeirah Essex House**

160 Central Park South, New York City, New York 10019

Tel: +1 212 247 0300
www.johansens.com/essexhouse

U.S.A. - NEW YORK (BUFFALO)

**The Mansion on Delaware Avenue**

414 Delaware Avenue, Buffalo, New York 14202

Tel: +1 716 886 3300
www.johansens.com/mansionondelaware

U.S.A. - NEW YORK (TARRYTOWN)

**Castle On The Hudson**

400 Benedict Avenue, Tarrytown, New York 10591

Tel: +1 914 631 1980
www.johansens.com/hudson

U.S.A. - NEW YORK (EAST AURORA)

**The Roycroft Inn**

40 South Grove Street, East Aurora, New York 14052

Tel: +1 716 652 5552
www.johansens.com/roycroftinn

U.S.A. - NEW YORK (VERONA)

**The Lodge at Turning Stone**

5218 Patrick Road, Verona, New York 13478

Tel: +1 315 361 8525
www.johansens.com/turningstone

U.S.A. - NEW YORK (HUNTINGTON)

**OHEKA Castle Hotel & Estate**

135 West Gate Drive, Huntington, New York 11743

Tel: +1 631 659 1400
www.johansens.com/oheka

U.S.A. - NEW YORK/LONG ISLAND (EAST HAMPTON)

**The Baker House 1650**

181 Main Street, East Hampton, New York 11937

Tel: +1 631 324 4081
www.johansens.com/bakerhouse

U.S.A. - NEW YORK (LAKE PLACID)

**Mirror Lake Inn Resort & Spa**

77 Mirror Lake Drive, Lake Placid, New York

Tel: +1 518 523 2544
www.johansens.com/mirrorlake

U.S.A. - NEW YORK/LONG ISLAND (EAST HAMPTON)

**The Mill House Inn**

31 North Main Street, East Hampton, New York 11937

Tel: +1 631 324 9766
www.johansens.com/millhouse

# Hotels - The Americas

Properties listed below can be found in our Recommended Hotels, Inns, Resorts & Spas - The Americas, Atlantic, Caribbean & Pacific 2008 Guide. More information on our portfolio of guides can be found on page 343.

U.S.A. - NEW YORK/LONG ISLAND (SOUTHAMPTON)

**1708 House**

126 Main Street, Southampton, New York 11968

Tel: +1 631 287 1708
www.johansens.com/1708house

U.S.A. - NORTH CAROLINA (NEW BERN)

**The Aerie Inn**

509 Pollock Street, New Bern, North Carolina 28562

Tel: +1 252 636 5553
www.johansens.com/aerieinn

U.S.A. - NORTH CAROLINA (ASHEVILLE)

**Haywood Park Hotel**

One Battery Park Avenue, Asheville, North Carolina 28801

Tel: +1 828 252 2522
www.johansens.com/haywoodpark

U.S.A. - NORTH CAROLINA (RALEIGH - DURHAM)

**The Siena Hotel**

1505 E. Franklin Street, Chapel Hill, North Carolina 27514

Tel: +1 919 929 4000
www.johansens.com/siena

U.S.A. - NORTH CAROLINA (ASHEVILLE)

**Inn on Biltmore Estate**

One Antler Hill Road, Asheville, North Carolina 28803

Tel: +1 828 225 1600
www.johansens.com/biltmore

U.S.A. - OKLAHOMA (OKLAHOMA CITY)

**Colcord Hotel**

15 North Robinson, Oklahoma City, Oklahoma 73102

Tel: +1 405 601 4300
www.johansens.com/colcord

U.S.A. - NORTH CAROLINA (BLOWING ROCK)

**Gideon Ridge Inn**

202 Gideon Ridge Road, Blowing Rock, North Carolina 28605

Tel: +1 828 295 3644
www.johansens.com/gideonridge

U.S.A. - OKLAHOMA (TULSA)

**Hotel Ambassador**

1324 South Main Street, Tulsa, Oklahoma 74119

Tel: +1 918 587 8200
www.johansens.com/ambassador

U.S.A. - NORTH CAROLINA (CHARLOTTE)

**Ballantyne Resort**

10000 Ballantyne Commons Parkway, Charlotte, North Carolina 28277

Tel: +1 704 248 4000
www.johansens.com/ballantyneresort

U.S.A. - OREGON (PORTLAND)

**The Heathman Hotel**

1001 S.W. Broadway, Portland, Oregon 97205

Tel: +1 503 241 4100
www.johansens.com/heathman

U.S.A. - NORTH CAROLINA (DUCK)

**The Sanderling Resort & Spa**

1461 Duck Road, Duck, North Carolina 27949

Tel: +1 252 261 4111
www.johansens.com/sanderling

U.S.A. - OREGON (PORTLAND)

**The Benson Hotel**

309 Southwest Broadway, Portland, Oregon 97205

Tel: +1 503 228 2000
www.johansens.com/benson

U.S.A. - NORTH CAROLINA (HIGHLANDS)

**Inn at Half Mile Farm**

P.O. Box 2769, 214 Half Mile Drive, Highlands, North Carolina 28741

Tel: +1 828 526 8170
www.johansens.com/halfmilefarm

U.S.A. - OREGON (EUGENE)

**The Campbell House**

252 Pearl Street, Eugene, Oregon 97401

Tel: +1 541 343 1119
www.johansens.com/campbell

U.S.A. - NORTH CAROLINA (HIGHLANDS)

**Old Edwards Inn and Spa**

445 Main Street, Highlands, North Carolina 28741

Tel: +1 828 526 8008
www.johansens.com/oldedwards

U.S.A. - PENNSYLVANIA (BRADFORD)

**Glendorn**

1000 Glendorn Drive, Bradford, Pennsylvania 16701

Tel: +1 814 362 6511
www.johansens.com/glendorn

# Hotels - The Americas

Properties listed below can be found in our Recommended Hotels, Inns, Resorts & Spas - The Americas, Atlantic, Caribbean & Pacific 2008 Guide. More information on our portfolio of guides can be found on page 343.

U.S.A. - PENNSYLVANIA (HERSHEY)

### The Hershey Hotel & Spa

100 Hotel Road, Hershey, Pennsylvania 17033

Tel: +1 717 533 2171
www.johansens.com/hershey

U.S.A. - SOUTH CAROLINA (CHARLESTON)

### The Boardwalk Inn at Wild Dunes Resort

5757 Palm Boulevard, Isle of Palms, South Carolina 29451

Tel: +1 843 886 6000
www.johansens.com/boardwalk

U.S.A. - PENNSYLVANIA (NEW HOPE)

### The Inn at Bowman's Hill

518 Lurgan Road, New Hope, Pennsylvania 18938

Tel: +1 215 862 8090
www.johansens.com/bowmanshill

U.S.A. - SOUTH CAROLINA (CHARLESTON)

### Charleston Harbor Resort & Marina

20 Patriots Point Road, Charleston, South Carolina 29464

Tel: +1 843 856 0028
www.johansens.com/charlestonharbor

U.S.A. - PENNSYLVANIA (PHILADELPHIA)

### Rittenhouse 1715, A Boutique Hotel

1715 Rittenhouse Square, Philadelphia, Pennsylvania 19103

Tel: +1 215 546 6500
www.johansens.com/rittenhouse

U.S.A. - SOUTH CAROLINA (CHARLESTON)

### Woodlands Resort & Inn

125 Parsons Road, Summerville, South Carolina 29483

Tel: +1 843 875 2600
www.johansens.com/woodlandssc

U.S.A. - PENNSYLVANIA (SKYTOP)

### Skytop Lodge

One Skytop, Skytop, Pennsylvania 18357

Tel: +1 570 595 7401
www.johansens.com/skytop

U.S.A. - SOUTH CAROLINA (KIAWAH ISLAND)

### The Sanctuary at Kiawah Island Golf Resort

One Sanctuary Beach Drive, Kiawah Island, South Carolina 29455

Tel: +1 843 768 6000
www.johansens.com/sanctuary

U.S.A. - RHODE ISLAND (NEWPORT)

### Chanler at Cliff Walk

117 Memorial Boulevard, Newport, Rhode Island 02840

Tel: +1 401 847 1300
www.johansens.com/chanler

U.S.A. - SOUTH CAROLINA (MYRTLE BEACH)

### Marina Inn at Grande Dunes

8121 Amalfi Place, Myrtle Beach, South Carolina 29572

Tel: +1 843 913 1333
www.johansens.com/marinainn

U.S.A. - RHODE ISLAND (NEWPORT)

### La Farge Perry House

24 Kay Street, Newport, Rhode Island 02840

Tel: +1 401 847 2223
www.johansens.com/lafargeperry

U.S.A. - SOUTH CAROLINA (TRAVELERS REST)

### La Bastide

10 Road Of Vines, Travelers Rest, South Carolina 29210

Tel: +1 864 836 8463
www.johansens.com/labastide

U.S.A. - RHODE ISLAND (PROVIDENCE)

### Hotel Providence

311 Westminster Street, Providence, Rhode Island 02903

Tel: +1 401 861 8000
www.johansens.com/providence

U.S.A. - TENNESSEE (MEMPHIS)

### Madison Hotel Memphis

79 Madison Avenue, Memphis, Tennessee 38103

Tel: +1 901 333 1200
www.johansens.com/madisonmemphis

U.S.A. - SOUTH CAROLINA (BLUFFTON)

### The Inn at Palmetto Bluff

476 Mount Pelia Road, Bluffton, South Carolina 29910

Tel: +1 843 706 6500
www.johansens.com/palmettobluff

U.S.A. - TENNESSEE (NASHVILLE)

### The Hermitage Hotel

231 Sixth Avenue North, Nashville, Tennessee 37219

Tel: +1 615 244 3121
www.johansens.com/hermitagetn

Properties listed below can be found in our Recommended Hotels, Inns, Resorts & Spas - The Americas, Atlantic, Caribbean & Pacific 2008 Guide. More information on our portfolio of guides can be found on page 343.

U.S.A. - TEXAS (AUSTIN)

### The Mansion at Judges' Hill

1900 Rio Grande, Austin, Texas 78705

Tel: +1 512 495 1800
www.johansens.com/judgeshill

U.S.A. - VERMONT (WOODSTOCK)

### The Jackson House Inn

114-3 Senior Lane, Woodstock, Vermont 05091

Tel: +1 802 457 2065
www.johansens.com/jacksonhouse

U.S.A. - TEXAS (GRANBURY)

### The Inn on Lake Granbury

205 West Doyle Street, Granbury, Texas 76048

Tel: +1 817 573 0046
www.johansens.com/lakegranbury

U.S.A. - VIRGINIA (ABINGDON)

### The Martha Washington Inn

150 West Main Street, Abingdon, Virginia 24210

Tel: +1 276 628 3161
www.johansens.com/themartha

U.S.A. - TEXAS (HOUSTON)

### Hotel Granduca

1080 Uptown Park Boulevard, Houston, Texas 77056

Tel: +1 713 418 1000
www.johansens.com/granduca

U.S.A. - VIRGINIA (CHARLOTTESVILLE)

### Boar's Head Inn

200 Ednam Drive, Charlottesville, Virginia 22903

Tel: +1 434 972 2232
www.johansens.com/boarsheadusa

U.S.A. - TEXAS (HOUSTON)

### Hotel ICON

220 Main, Houston, Texas 77002

Tel: +1 713 224 4266
www.johansens.com/hotelicon

U.S.A. - VIRGINIA (GLOUCESTER)

### The Inn at Warner Hall

4750 Warner Hall Road, Gloucester, Virginia 23061

Tel: +1 804 695 9565
www.johansens.com/warnerhall

U.S.A. - UTAH (MOAB)

### Sorrel River Ranch Resort & Spa

Mile 17 Scenic Byway 128, H.C. 64 BOX 4000, Moab, Utah 84532

Tel: +1 435 259 4642
www.johansens.com/sorrelriver

U.S.A. - VIRGINIA (IRVINGTON)

### Hope and Glory Inn

65 Tavern Road, Irvington, Virginia 22480

Tel: +1 804 438 6053
www.johansens.com/hopeandglory

U.S.A. - UTAH (SUNDANCE)

### Sundance Resort

RR#3 Box A-1, Sundance, Utah 84604

Tel: +1 801 225 4107
www.johansens.com/sundance

U.S.A. - VIRGINIA (MIDDLEBURG)

### The Goodstone Inn & Estate

36205 Snake Hill Road, Middleburg, Virginia 20117

Tel: +1 540 687 4645
www.johansens.com/goodstoneinn

U.S.A. - VERMONT (LUDLOW/OKEMO)

### Castle Hill Resort & Spa

Jct. Routes 103 and 131, Cavendish, Vermont 05142

Tel: +1 802 226 7361
www.johansens.com/castlehillvt

U.S.A. - VIRGINIA (STAUNTON)

### Frederick House

28 North New Street, Staunton, Virginia 24401

Tel: + 1 540 885 4220
www.johansens.com/frederickhouse

U.S.A. - VERMONT (WARREN)

### The Pitcher Inn

275 Main Street, P.O. Box 347, Warren, Vermont 05674

Tel: +1 802 496 6350
www.johansens.com/pitcherinn

U.S.A. - VIRGINIA (WASHINGTON METROPOLITAN AREA)

### Morrison House

116 South Alfred Street, Alexandria, Virginia 22314

Tel: +1 703 838 8000
www.johansens.com/morrisonhouse

# Hotels - The Americas

Properties listed below can be found in our Recommended Hotels, Inns, Resorts & Spas - The Americas, Atlantic, Caribbean & Pacific 2008 Guide. More information on our portfolio of guides can be found on page 343.

U.S.A. - VIRGINIA (WILLIAMSBURG)

**Wedmore Place**

5810 Wessex Hundred, Williamsburg, Virginia 23185

Tel: +1 757 476 5885
www.johansens.com/wedmore

U.S.A. - WYOMING (GRAND TETON NATIONAL PARK)

**Jenny Lake Lodge**

Inner Park Loop Road, Grand Teton National Park, Wyoming 83013

Tel: +1 307 543 3300
www.johansens.com/jennylake

U.S.A. - WASHINGTON (BELLEVUE)

**The Bellevue Club Hotel**

11200 S.E. 6th Street, Bellevue, Washington 98004

Tel: +1 425 455 1616
www.johansens.com/bellevue

## Recommendations in Central America

U.S.A. - WASHINGTON (BELLINGHAM)

**The Chrysalis Inn and Spa**

804 10th Street, Bellingham, Washington 98225

Tel: +1 360 756 1005
www.johansens.com/chrysalis

BELIZE - AMBERGRIS CAYE (SAN PEDRO)

**Victoria House**

P.O. Box 22, San Pedro, Ambergris Caye

Tel: +501 226 2067
www.johansens.com/victoriahouse

U.S.A. - WASHINGTON (SEATTLE)

**Hotel Ändra**

2000 Fourth Avenue, Seattle, Washington 98121

Tel: +1 206 448 8600
www.johansens.com/hotelandra

BELIZE - CAYO (SAN IGNACIO)

**The Lodge at Chaa Creek**

P.O. Box 53, San Ignacio, Cayo

Tel: +501 824 2037
www.johansens.com/chaacreek

U.S.A. - WASHINGTON (SPOKANE)

**The Davenport Hotel and Tower**

10 South Post Street, Spokane, Washington 99201

Tel: +1 509 455 8888
www.johansens.com/davenport

COSTA RICA - ALAJUELA (BAJOS DEL TORO)

**El Silencio Lodge & Spa**

Bajos del Toro, Alajuela

Tel: +506 291 3044
www.johansens.com/elsilencio

U.S.A. - WASHINGTON (WINTHROP)

**Sun Mountain Lodge**

P.O. Box 1,000, Winthrop, Washington 98862

Tel: +1 509 996 2211
www.johansens.com/sunmountain

COSTA RICA - ALAJUELA (LA FORTUNA DE SAN CARLOS)

**Tabacón Grand Spa Thermal Resort**

La Fortuna de San Carlos, Arenal

Tel: +506 519 1900
www.johansens.com/tabacon

U.S.A. - WASHINGTON (WOODINVILLE)

**The Herbfarm**

14590 North East 145th Street, Woodinville, Washington 98072

Tel: +1 425 485 5300
www.johansens.com/herbfarm

COSTA RICA - GUANACASTE (ISLITA)

**Hotel Punta Islita**

Guanacaste

Tel: +506 231 6122
www.johansens.com/hotelpuntaislita

U.S.A. - WYOMING (CHEYENNE)

**Nagle Warren Mansion**

222 East 17Th Street, Cheyenne, Wyoming 82001

Tel: +1 307 637 3333
www.johansens.com/naglewarrenmansion

COSTA RICA - GUANACASTE (PLAYA CONCHAL)

**Paradisus Playa Conchal**

Bahía Brasilito, Playa Conchal, Santa Cruz, Guanacaste

Tel: +506 654 4123
www.johansens.com/paradisusplayaconchal

# Hotels - The Americas

Properties listed below can be found in our Recommended Hotels, Inns, Resorts & Spas - The Americas, Atlantic, Caribbean & Pacific 2008 Guide. More information on our portfolio of guides can be found on page 343.

### COSTA RICA - OSA PENISULA (PUERTO JIMENEZ)

**Lapa Rios Eco Lodge**

Puerto Jimenez, Osa Penisula

Tel: +506 735 5130
www.johansens.com/laparios

### ARGENTINA - BUENOS AIRES (CIUDAD DE BUENOS AIRES)

**Moreno Hotel Buenos Aires**

Moreno 376, Ciudad de Buenos Aires, Buenos Aires C1091AAH

Tel: +54 11 6091 2000
www.johansens.com/moreno

### COSTA RICA - PUNTARENAS (MANUEL ANTONIO)

**Gaia Hotel & Reserve**

Km 2.7 Carretera Quepos, Manuel Antonio

Tel: +506 777 9797
www.johansens.com/gaiahr

### ARGENTINA - NEUQUÉN (VILLA LA ANGOSTURA)

**Correntoso Lake & River Hotel**

Av. Siete Lagos 4505, Villa La Angostura, Patagonia

Tel: +54 11 4803 0030
www.johansens.com/correntoso

### GUATEMALA - ANTIGUA GUATEMALA

**Filadelfia Coffee Resort & Spa**

150 meters North of the San Felipe Chapel, Antigua Guatemala

Tel: +502 7728 0800
www.johansens.com/filadelfia

### ARGENTINA - NEUQUÉN (VILLA LA ANGOSTURA)

**Hotel Las Balsas**

Bahía Las Balsas s/n, Villa La Angostura, Neuquén 8407

Tel: +54 2944 494308
www.johansens.com/lasbalsas

### HONDURAS - ATLÁNTIDA (LA CEIBA)

**The Lodge at Pico Bonito**

A. P. 710, La Ceiba, Atlántida, C. P. 31101

Tel: +504 440 0388
www.johansens.com/picobonito

### ARGENTINA - RIO NEGRO (SAN CARLOS BARILOCHE)

**Isla Victoria Lodge**

Isla Victoria, Parque Nacional Nahuel Huapi, C.C. 26 (R8401AKU)

Tel: +54 43 94 96 05
www.johansens.com/islavictoria

### ARGENTINA - SANTA CRUZ (EL CALAFATE)

**Los Sauces Casa Patagónica**

Los Gauchos 1352/70, CP9405, El Calafate, Santa Cruz

Tel: +54 2902 495854
www.johansens.com/lossauces

# Recommendations in South America

### ARGENTINA - BUENOS AIRES (CIUDAD DE BUENOS AIRES)

**1555 Malabia House**

Malabia 1555, C1414DME Ciudad de Buenos Aires, Buenos Aires

Tel: +54 11 4832 3345
www.johansens.com/malabiahouse

### BRAZIL - ALAGOAS (SÃO MIGUEL DOS MILAGRES)

**Pousada do Toque**

Rua Felisberto de Ataide, Povoado do Toque, São Miguel dos Milagres, 57940-000 Alagoas

Tel: +55 82 3295 1127
www.johansens.com/pousadadotoque

### ARGENTINA - BUENOS AIRES (CIUDAD DE BUENOS AIRES)

**Home Buenos Aires**

Honduras 5860, Ciudad de Buenos Aires, Buenos Aires 1414

Tel: +54 11 4778 1008
www.johansens.com/homebuenosaires

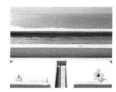

### BRAZIL - BAHIA (ARRAIAL D'ÁJUDA)

**Maitei Hotel**

Estrada do Mucugê, 475, Arraial D'Ájuda, Porto Seguro, Bahia 45816-000

Tel: +55 73 3575 3877
www.johansens.com/maitei

### ARGENTINA - BUENOS AIRES (CIUDAD DE BUENOS AIRES)

**LoiSuites Recoleta Hotel**

Vicente López 1955 – C1128ACC, Ciudad de Buenos Aires, Buenos Aires

Tel: +54 11 5777 8950
www.johansens.com/loisuites

### BRAZIL - BAHIA (CORUMBAU)

**Fazenda São Francisco**

Ponta do Corumbau s/n, Prado, Bahia

Tel: +55 11 3078 4411
www.johansens.com/fazenda

# Hotels - The Americas

Properties listed below can be found in our Recommended Hotels, Inns, Resorts & Spas - The Americas, Atlantic, Caribbean & Pacific 2008 Guide. More information on our portfolio of guides can be found on page 343.

BRAZIL - BAHIA (CORUMBAU)

**Tauana**

Corumbau, Prado, Bahia

Tel: +55 73 3668 5172
www.johansens.com/tauana

BRAZIL - BAHIA (CORUMBAU)

**Vila Naiá - Paralelo 17°**

Ponta do Corumbau s/n, Corumbau, Prado, Bahia

Tel: +55 73 3573 1006
www.johansens.com/vilanaia

BRAZIL - BAHIA (ITACARÉ)

**Txai Resort**

Rod. Ilhéus-Itacaré km 48, Itacaré, Bahia 45530-000

Tel: +55 73 2101 5000
www.johansens.com/txairesort

BRAZIL - BAHIA (MARAU)

**Kiaroa Eco-Luxury Resort**

Loteamento da Costa, área SD6, Distrito de barra grande, Município de Maraú, Bahia, CEp 45 520-000

Tel: +55 71 3272 1320
www.johansens.com/kiaroa

BRAZIL - BAHIA (PRAIA DO FORTE)

**Praia do Forte EcoResort & Thalasso Spa**

Avenida do Farol, Praia do Forte - Mata de São João, Bahia

Tel: +55 71 36 76 40 00
www.johansens.com/praiadoforte

BRAZIL - BAHIA (TRANCOSO)

**Estrela d'Agua**

Estrada Arraial d'Ajuda, Trancoso S/N, Trancoso Porto Seguro, Bahia 45818-000

Tel: +55 73 3668 1030
www.johansens.com/estreladagua

BRAZIL - BAHIA (TRANCOSO)

**Etnia Pousada and Boutique**

Trancoso, Bahia 45818-000

Tel: +55 73 3668 1137
www.johansens.com/etnia

BRAZIL - MINAS GERAIS (TIRADENTES)

**Pousada dos Inconfidentes**

Rua João Rodrigues Sobrinho 91, 36325-000, Tiradentes, Minas Gerais

Tel: +55 32 3355 2135
www.johansens.com/inconfidentes

BRAZIL - MINAS GERAIS (TIRADENTES)

**Solar da Ponte**

Praça das Mercês S/N, Tiradentes, Minas Gerais 36325-000

Tel: +55 32 33 55 12 55
www.johansens.com/solardaponte

BRAZIL - PERNAMBUCO (FERNANDO DE NORONHA)

**Pousada Maravilha**

Rodovia BR-363, s/n, Sueste, Ilha de Fernando de Noronha, Pernambuco 53990-000

Tel: +55 81 3619 0028
www.johansens.com/maravilha

BRAZIL - PERNAMBUCO (PORTO DE GALINHAS)

**Nannai Beach Resort**

Rodovia PE-09, acesso à Muro Alto, Km 3, Ipojuca, Pernambuco 55590-000

Tel: +55 81 3552 0100
www.johansens.com/nannaibeach

BRAZIL - RIO DE JANEIRO (ANGRA DOS REIS)

**Sítio do Lobo**

Ponta do Lobo, Ilha Grande, Angra dos Reis, Rio de Janeiro

Tel: +55 21 2227 4138
www.johansens.com/sitiodolobo

BRAZIL - RIO DE JANEIRO (BÚZIOS)

**Casas Brancas Boutique-Hotel & Spa**

Alto do Humaitá 10, Armação dos Búzios, Rio de Janeiro 28950-000

Tel: +55 22 2623 1458
www.johansens.com/casasbrancas

BRAZIL - RIO DE JANEIRO (BÚZIOS)

**Pérola Búzios Design Hotel**

Av. José Bento Ribeiro Dantas, 222, Armação dos Búzios, Rio de Janeiro 28950-000

Tel: +55 22 2620 8507
www.johansens.com/perolabuzios

BRAZIL - RIO DE JANEIRO (BÚZIOS)

**Portobay Glenzhaus**

Rua dos Coqueiros, 10, Armação dos Búzios, Rio de Janeiro 28950-000

Tel: +55 22 2623 2823
www.johansens.com/glenzhaus

BRAZIL - RIO DE JANEIRO (PETRÓPOLIS)

**Parador Santarém Marina**

Estrada Correia da Veiga, 96, Petrópolis, Rio de Janeiro 25745-260

Tel: +55 24 2222 9933
www.johansens.com/paradorsantarem

# Hotels - The Americas

Properties listed below can be found in our Recommended Hotels, Inns, Resorts & Spas - The Americas, Atlantic, Caribbean & Pacific 2008 Guide. More information on our portfolio of guides can be found on page 343.

BRAZIL - RIO DE JANEIRO (PETRÓPOLIS)

### Solar do Império

Koeler Avenue, 376- Centro, Petrópolis, Rio de Janeiro

Tel: +55 24 2103 3000
www.johansens.com/solardoimperio

BRAZIL - SANTA CATARINA (PALHOÇA)

### Ilha do Papagaio

Ilha do Papagaio, Palhoça, Santa Catarina 88131-970

Tel: +55 48 3286 1242
www.johansens.com/ilhadopapagaio

BRAZIL - RIO DE JANEIRO (PETRÓPOLIS)

### Tankamana EcoResort

Estrada Júlio Cápua, S/N Vale Do Cuiabá, Itaipava - Petrópolis, Rio De Janeiro 25745-050

Tel: +55 24 2222 9181
www.johansens.com/tankamana

BRAZIL - SANTA CATARINA (PRAIA DO ROSA)

### Pousada Solar Mirador

Estrada Geral do Rosa s/n, Praia do Rosa, Imbituba, Santa Catarina 88780-000

Tel: +55 48 3355 6144
www.johansens.com/solarmirador

BRAZIL - RIO DE JANEIRO (RIO DE JANEIRO)

### Hotel Marina All Suites

Av. Delfim Moreira, 696, Praia do Leblon, Rio de Janeiro 22441-000

Tel: +55 21 2172 1001
www.johansens.com/marinaallsuites

BRAZIL - SANTA CATARINA (PRAIA DO ROSA)

### Quinta do Bucanero

Estrada Geral do Rosa s/n, Praia do Rosa, Imbituba, Santa Catarina 88780-000

Tel: +55 48 3355 6056
www.johansens.com/bucanero

BRAZIL - RIO GRANDE DO NORTE (PRAIA DA PIPA)

### Toca da Coruja

Av. Baia dos Golfinhos, 464, Praia da Pipa, Tibau do Sul, Rio Grande do Norte 59178-000

Tel: +55 84 3246 2226
www.johansens.com/rocadacoruja

BRAZIL - SÃO PAULO (CAMPOS DO JORDÃO)

### Hotel Frontenac

Av. Dr. Paulo Ribas, 295 Capivari, Campos do Jordão 12460-000

Tel: +55 12 3669 1000
www.johansens.com/frontenac

BRAZIL - RIO GRANDE DO SUL (GRAMADO)

### Estalagem St. Hubertus

Rua Carrieri, 974, Gramado, Rio Grande do Sul 95670-000, Brazil

Tel: +55 54 3286 1273
www.johansens.com/sthubertus

BRAZIL - SÃO PAULO (ILHABELA)

### DPNY Beach Hotel Boutique

Av. Pacheco do Nascimento, 7668, Praia do Curral , Ilhabela, São Paulo 11630-000

Tel: +55 12 3894 2121
www.johansens.com/dpnybeach

BRAZIL - RIO GRANDE DO SUL (GRAMADO)

### Kurotel

Rua Nacões Unidas 533, P.O. Box 65, Gramado, Rio Grande do Sul 95670-000

Tel: +55 54 3295 9393
www.johansens.com/kurotel

BRAZIL - SÃO PAULO (MAIRIPORÃ)

### Spa Unique Garden

Estrada Laramara, 3500, Mairiporã, São Paulo 07600-970

Tel: +55 11 4486 8700
www.johansens.com/uniquegarden

BRAZIL - RIO GRANDE DO SUL (SÃO FRANCISCO DE PAULA)

### Pousada Do Engenho

Rua Odon Cavalcante, 330, São Francisco de Paula 95400-000, Rio Grande do Sul

Tel: +55 54 3244 1270
www.johansens.com/pousadadoengenho

BRAZIL - SÃO PAULO (SÃO PAULO)

### Hotel Unique

Av. Brigadeiro Luis Antonio, 4.700, São Paulo, São Paulo 01402-002

Tel: +55 11 3055 4710
www.johansens.com/hotelunique

BRAZIL - SANTA CATARINA (GOVERNADOR CELSO RAMOS)

### Ponta dos Ganchos

Rua Eupídio Alves do Nascimento, 104, Governador Celso Ramos, Santa Catarina 88190-000

Tel: +55 48 3262 5000
www.johansens.com/pontadosganchos

CHILE - PATAGONIA (PUERTO GUADAL)

### Hacienda Tres Lagos

Carretera Austral Sur Km 274, Localidad Lago Negro, Puerto Guadal, Patagonia

Tel: +56 2 333 4122
www.johansens.com/treslagos

# Hotels - The Americas, Atlantic & Caribbean

All the properties listed below can be found in our Recommended Hotels, Inns, Resorts & Spas - The Americas, Atlantic, Caribbean & Pacific 2008 Details of this Guide and others in our portfolio can be found on page 343.

CHILE - ARAUCANIA (PUCON)

**Hotel Antumalal**

Carretera Pucon - Villarica Highway at km 2 from Pucon, Pucon, Araucania

Tel: +56 45 441 011
www.johansens.com/antumalal

ATLANTIC - BERMUDA (HAMILTON)

**Rosedon Hotel**

P.O. Box Hm 290, Hamilton Hmax

Tel: +1 441 295 1640
www.johansens.com/rosedonhotel

CHILE - SANTIAGO (SAN FELIPE)

**Termas de Jahuel Hotel & Spa**

Jahuel, San Felipe, Santiago

Tel: +56 2 411 1720
www.johansens.com/jahuel

ATLANTIC - BERMUDA (HAMILTON)

**Waterloo House**

P.O. Box H.M. 333, Hamilton H.M. B.X.

Tel: +1 441 295 4480
www.johansens.com/waterloohouse

CHILE - ARAUCANÍA (VILLARRICA)

**Villarrica Park Lake Hotel**

Camino a Villarrica km.13, Araucanía, Villarrica

Tel: +56 2 207 7070
www.johansens.com/villarrica

ATLANTIC - BERMUDA (PAGET)

**Horizons and Cottages**

33 South Shore Road, Paget, P.G. 04

Tel: +1 441 236 0048
www.johansens.com/horizonscottages

PERU - LIMA PROVINCIAS (YAUYOS)

**Refugios Del Peru - Viñak Reichraming**

Santiago de Viñak, Yauyos, Lima

Tel: +51 1 421 6952
www.johansens.com/refugiosdelperu

ATLANTIC - BERMUDA (SOMERSET)

**Cambridge Beaches Resort & Spa**

Kings Point, Somerset

Tel: +1 441 234 0331
www.johansens.com/cambridgebeaches

ATLANTIC - BERMUDA (SOUTHAMPTON)

**The Reefs**

56 South Shore Road, Southampton

Tel: +1 441 238 0222
www.johansens.com/thereefs

## Recommendations in the Atlantic

ATLANTIC - BAHAMAS (ANDROS)

**Kamalame Cay**

Staniard Creek, Andros

Tel: +1 242 368 6281
www.johansens.com/kamalamecay

## Recommendations in the Caribbean

ATLANTIC - BAHAMAS (GRAND BAHAMA ISLAND)

**Old Bahama Bay at Ginn Sur Mer**

West End, Grand Bahama Island

Tel: +1 242 350 6500
www.johansens.com/oldbahamabay

CARIBBEAN - ANGUILLA (RENDEZVOUS BAY)

**CuisinArt Resort & Spa**

P.O. Box 2000, Rendezvous Bay

Tel: +1 264 498 2000
www.johansens.com/cuisinartresort

ATLANTIC - BAHAMAS (HARBOUR ISLAND)

**Pink Sands**

Chapel Street, Harbour Island

Tel: +1 242 333 2030
www.johansens.com/pinksands

CARIBBEAN - ANTIGUA (ST. JOHN'S)

**Blue Waters**

P.O. Box 257, St. John's

Tel: +44 870 360 1245
www.johansens.com/bluewaters

# Hotels - Caribbean

All the properties listed below can be found in our Recommended Hotels, Inns, Resorts & Spas - The Americas, Atlantic, Caribbean & Pacific 2008
Details of this Guide and others in our portfolio can be found on page 343.

CARIBBEAN - ANTIGUA (ST. JOHN'S)

**Curtain Bluff**

P.O. Box 288, St. John's

Tel: +1 268 462 8400
www.johansens.com/curtainbluff

CARIBBEAN - BARBUDA (PALMETTO POINT)

**The Beach House**

Palmetto Point

Tel: +1 516 767 3057
www.johansens.com/beachbarbuda

CARIBBEAN - ANTIGUA (ST. JOHN'S)

**Galley Bay**

Five Islands, St. John's

Tel: +1 954 481 8787
www.johansens.com/galleybay

CARIBBEAN - BRITISH VIRGIN ISLANDS (PETER ISLAND)

**Peter Island Resort**

Peter Island

Tel: +1 770 476 9988
www.johansens.com/peterislandresort

CARIBBEAN - ANTIGUA (ST. JOHN'S)

**The Verandah**

Indian Town Road, St. John's

Tel: +1 268 460 5000
www.johansens.com/verandah

CARIBBEAN - BRITISH VIRGIN ISLANDS (PETER ISLAND)

**The Villas at Peter Island**

Peter Island

Tel: +1 770 476 9988
www.johansens.com/villaspeterisland

CARIBBEAN - ANTIGUA (ST. MARY'S)

**Carlisle Bay**

Old Road, St. Mary's

Tel: +1 268 484 0000
www.johansens.com/carlislebay

CARIBBEAN - BRITISH VIRGIN ISLANDS (VIRGIN GORDA)

**Biras Creek Resort**

North Sound, Virgin Gorda

Tel: +1 310 440 4225
www.johansens.com/birascreek

CARIBBEAN - BARBADOS (CHRIST CHURCH)

**Little Arches**

Enterprise Beach Road, Christ Church

Tel: +1 246 420 4689
www.johansens.com/littlearches

CARIBBEAN - CURAÇAO (WILLEMSTAD)

**Avila Hotel on the beach**

Penstraat 130, Willemstad

Tel: +599 9 461 4377
www.johansens.com/avilabeach

CARIBBEAN - BARBADOS (ST. JAMES)

**Coral Reef Club**

St. James

Tel: +1 246 422 2372
www.johansens.com/coralreefclub

CARIBBEAN - DOMINICAN REPUBLIC (PUERTO PLATA)

**Casa Colonial Beach & Spa**

P.O. Box 22, Puerto Plata

Tel: +1 809 320 3232
www.johansens.com/casacolonial

CARIBBEAN - BARBADOS (ST. JAMES)

**The Sandpiper**

Holetown, St. James

Tel: +1 246 422 2251
www.johansens.com/sandpiper

CARIBBEAN - GRENADA (ST. GEORGE'S)

**Spice Island Beach Resort**

Grand Anse Beach, St. George's

Tel: +1 473 444 4423/4258
www.johansens.com/spiceisland

CARIBBEAN - BARBADOS (ST. PETER)

**Cobblers Cove**

Speightstown, St. Peter

Tel: +1 246 422 2291
www.johansens.com/cobblerscove

CARIBBEAN - JAMAICA (MONTEGO BAY)

**Half Moon**

Rose Hall, Montego Bay

Tel: +1 876 953 2211
www.johansens.com/halfmoon

# Hotels - Caribbean

All the properties listed below can be found in our Recommended Hotels, Inns, Resorts & Spas - The Americas, Atlantic, Caribbean & Pacific 2008
Details of this Guide and others in our portfolio can be found on page 343.

CARIBBEAN - JAMAICA (MONTEGO BAY)

**Round Hill Hotel and Villas**

P.O. Box 64, Montego Bay

Tel: +1 876 956 7050
www.johansens.com/roundhill

CARIBBEAN - ST. KITTS & NEVIS (NEVIS)

**Montpelier Plantation Inn**

P.O. Box 474, Nevis

Tel: +1 869 469 3462
www.johansens.com/montpelierplantation

CARIBBEAN - JAMAICA (MONTEGO BAY)

**Tryall Club**

P.O. Box 1206, Montego Bay

Tel: +1 876 956 5660
www.johansens.com/tryallclub

CARIBBEAN - ST. LUCIA (SOUFRIÈRE)

**Anse Chastanet**

Soufrière

Tel: +1 758 459 7000
www.johansens.com/ansechastanet

CARIBBEAN - JAMAICA (OCHO RIOS)

**Royal Plantation**

Main Street , P.O. Box 2, Ocho Rios, St. Ann

Tel: +1 876 974 5601
www.johansens.com/royalplantation

CARIBBEAN - ST. LUCIA (SOUFRIÈRE)

**Jade Mountain at Anse Chastanet**

Soufrière

Tel: +1 758 459 4000
www.johansens.com/jademountain

CARIBBEAN - PUERTO RICO (OLD SAN JUAN)

**Chateau Cervantes**

Recinto Sur, Old San Juan

Tel: +1 787 724 7722
www.johansens.com/cervantes

CARIBBEAN - ST. LUCIA (SOUFRIÈRE)

**Ladera Resort**

Soufrière

Tel: +1 758 459 7323
www.johansens.com/ladera

CARIBBEAN - PUERTO RICO (RINCON)

**Horned Dorset Primavera**

Apartado 1132, Rincón, 00677

Tel: +1 787 823 4030
www.johansens.com/horneddorset

CARIBBEAN - ST. MARTIN (BAIE LONGUE)

**La Samanna**

P.O. Box 4077, 97064

Tel: +590 590 87 64 00
www.johansens.com/lasamanna

CARIBBEAN - SAINT-BARTHÉLEMY (ANSE DE TOINY)

**Le Toiny**

Anse de Toiny, 97133

Tel: +590 590 27 88 88
www.johansens.com/letoiny

CARIBBEAN - THE GRENADINES (MUSTIQUE)

**Firefly**

Mustique Island

Tel: +1 784 488 8414
www.johansens.com/firefly

CARIBBEAN - SAINT-BARTHÉLEMY (GRAND CUL DE SAC)

**Hotel Guanahani & Spa**

Grand Cul de Sac, 97133

Tel: +590 590 27 66 60
www.johansens.com/guanahani

CARIBBEAN - THE GRENADINES (PALM ISLAND)

**Palm Island**

Tel: +1 954 481 8787
www.johansens.com/palmisland

CARIBBEAN - SAINT-BARTHÉLEMY (GRAND CUL DE SAC)

**Le Sereno**

Grand Cul de Sac

Tel: +590 590 298 300
www.johansens.com/lesereno

CARIBBEAN - TURKS & CAICOS (GRACE BAY BEACH)

**Grace Bay Club**

P.O. Box 128, Providenciales

Tel: +1 649 946 5050
www.johansens.com/gracebayclub

# Hotels - Caribbean & Pacific

All the properties listed below can be found in our Recommended Hotels, Inns, Resorts & Spas - The Americas, Atlantic, Caribbean & Pacific 2008
Details of this Guide and others in our portfolio can be found on page 343.

CARIBBEAN - TURKS & CAICOS (PARROT CAY)

**Parrot Cay**

P.O. Box 164, Providenciales

Tel: +1 649 946 7788
www.johansens.com/parrotcay

PACIFIC - FIJI ISLANDS (LAUTOKA)

**Blue Lagoon Cruises**

183 Vitogo Parade, Lautoka

Tel: +679 6661 622
www.johansens.com/bluelagooncruises

CARIBBEAN - TURKS & CAICOS (POINT GRACE)

**Point Grace**

P.O. Box 700, Providenciales

Tel: +1 649 946 5096
www.johansens.com/pointgrace

PACIFIC - FIJI ISLANDS (QAMEA ISLAND)

**Qamea Resort & Spa**

P.A. Matei, Tavenui

Tel: +679 888 0220
www.johansens.com/qamea

CARIBBEAN - TURKS & CAICOS (GRACE BAY BEACH)

**The Somerset on Grace Bay**

Princess Drive, Providenciales

Tel: +1 649 946 5900
www.johansens.com/somersetgracebay

PACIFIC - FIJI ISLANDS (SAVUSAVU)

**Jean-Michel Cousteau Fiji Islands Resort**

Lesiaceva Point, SavuSavu

Tel: +1 415 788 5794
www.johansens.com/jean-michelcousteau

CARIBBEAN - TURKS & CAICOS (WEST GRACE BAY BEACH)

**Turks & Caicos Club**

West Grace Bay Beach, P.O. Box 687, Providenciales

Tel: +1 649 946 5800
www.johansens.com/turksandcaicos

PACIFIC - FIJI ISLANDS (SIGATOKA)

**Myola Plantation**

P.O. Box 638, Sigatoka

Tel: +679 652 1084
www.johansens.com/myola

CARIBBEAN - TURKS & CAICOS (GRACE BAY BEACH)

**The Regent Palms**

P.O. Box 681, Grace Bay, Providenciales

Tel: +1 649 946 8666
www.johansens.com/regentpalms

PACIFIC - FIJI ISLANDS (UGAGA ISLAND)

**Royal Davui**

P.O. Box 3171, Lami

Tel: +679 336 1624
www.johansens.com/royaldavui

## Recommendations in the Pacific

PACIFIC - FIJI ISLANDS (YAQETA ISLAND)

**Navutu Stars Resort**

P.O. Box 1838, Lautoka

Tel: +679 664 0553 and +679 664 0554
www.johansens.com/navutustars

PACIFIC - FIJI ISLANDS (LABASA)

**Nukubati Island, Great Sea Reef, Fiji**

P.O. Box 1928, Labasa

Tel: +61 2 93888 196
www.johansens.com/nukubati

PACIFIC - FIJI ISLANDS (YASAWA ISLAND)

**Yasawa Island Resort**

P.O. Box 10128, Nadi Airport, Nadi

Tel: +679 672 2266
www.johansens.com/yasawaisland

---

## The International Mark of Excellence

For further information, hotel search, gift certificates, online bookshop and special offers visit:

# www.johansens.com

Annually Inspected for the Independent Traveler

# Index by Property

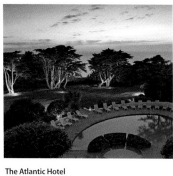

# Index by Property

# Index by Property/Location

## Index by Location

### London

### England

#### A

#### B

#### C

#### D

# Index by Location

# Index by Location

# Index by Location/Consortium

## Index by Consortium

### Pride of Britain members

#### England

#### Scotland

#### Wales

### Leading Hotels of the World

#### England

#### Ireland

### Small Luxury Hotels of the World Members

#### Channel Islands

#### England

#### Ireland

#### Scotland

### Ireland's Blue Book

#### Ireland

### Relais & Châteaux

#### Channel Islands

#### England

#### Ireland

#### Scotland

#### Wales

SCOTLAND

Berwick-Upon-Tweed

Northumberland
National Park

A697

A68

A68

A68

A69

65

Carlisle

A7

A595

A69

A596

61

A595

M6

67

A595

A66

68

A595

71

70  69

A66

A66

64

M6

Lake District
National Park

A591

63

A6

A685

62

72

Windermere

Kendal

221

A595

73

74

A591

Yorkshire Dales
National Park

A595

A590

66

M6

A65

A590

Barrow-in-
Furness

A683

A65

Skipton

Fleetwood

M6

133

131

A59

217

A56

A6068

Blackpool

M55

Preston

A59

M65

A646

Southport

132

A59

M6

M61

M66

M62

A565

M58

A666

Bolton

M60

Manchester

M67

A580

A577

M57

A580

Wigan

M60

Liverpool

Liverpool

M62

M60

M53

A566

49

Manchester

M56

WALES

330

© Lovell Johns Limited, Oxford

Douglas

Isle
of
Man

North East England

Berwick-Upon-Tweed

Alnwick

Newcastle

Middlesbrough

Durham

Thirsk

Skipton

Harrogate

York

Hull

Leeds
Bradford

Halifax

Wakefield

Huddersfield

Doncaster

Sheffield

North York Moors
National Park

Teeside

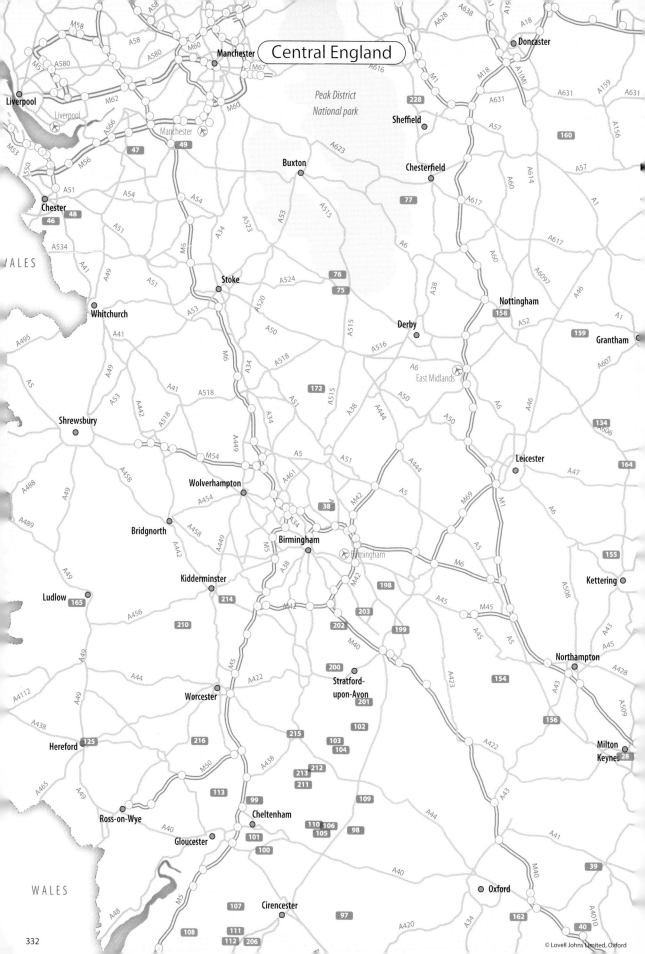

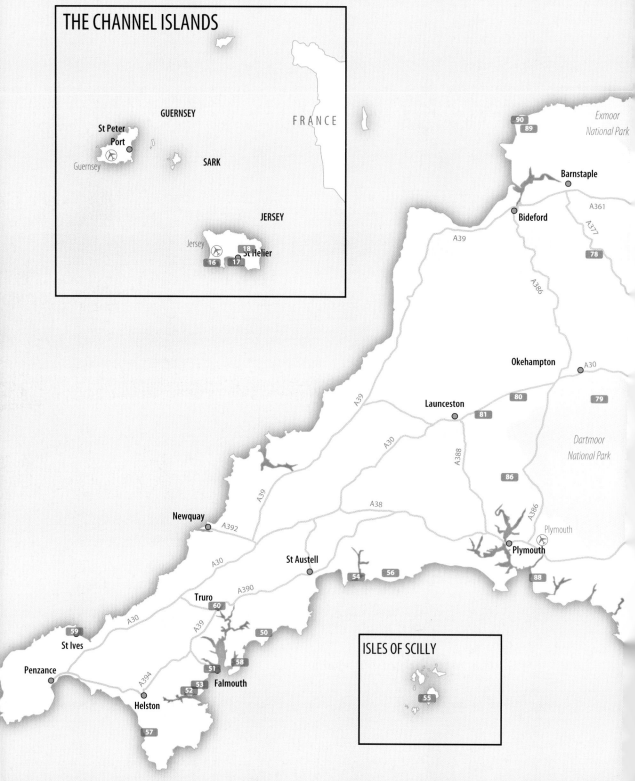

WALES

## THE CHANNEL ISLANDS

FRANCE

GUERNSEY

St Peter Port

Guernsey

SARK

JERSEY

Jersey

18
St Helier

16

17

Exmoor
National Park

90

89

Barnstaple

Bideford

A361

A39

A377

A386

78

Okehampton

A30

Launceston

80

81

79

A39

Dartmoor
National Park

A30

A388

86

A38

Newquay

A392

Plymouth

A386

St Austell

54

56

Plymouth

88

Truro

A390

60

50

A39

St Ives

59

A30

ISLES OF SCILLY

Penzance

A394

51

58

53

Falmouth

52

55

Helston

57

WALES

## South West England

Bristol

Exmoor
National Park

Taunton

Exeter

Torquay

Kingsbridge

Yeovil

Blandford
Forum

Warminster

Bridport

Dorchester

Weymouth

Bournem

Bournem

# Southern England

© Lovell Johns Limited, Oxford

# South East England

# Ireland

SCOTLAND

Coleraine
City of Derry
Londonderry
A37
A2
A26
A44
A6
A29
M2
A36
Larne
N14
A5
A505
M2
Belfast
234
N15
A32
A5
A29
Belfast
N15
A4
A1
A20
N16
A4
Armagh
M1
Sligo
A505
A7
Ballina
N17
251
A28
Newry
N4
A24
A1
249
N5
N2
Dundalk
232
250
Cavan
250
M1
Knock International
N3
Drogheda
238
236
N5
Longford
N1
M1
237
N4
N2
248
Athlone
N6
Dublin
Galway
N17
N6
M4
Dublin
239
235
N7
Dun Laoghaire
246
N7
N18
N7
N11
N9
Shannon
Shannon
253
Limerick
Kilkenny
N8
N24
N10
247
N9
Tralee
N21
N30
245
N20
N9
Wexford
244
243
N8
N24
252
254
242
illarney
N22
233
N25
Waterford
241
Cork
240
Kenmare
Cork
WALES

© Lovell Johns Limited, Oxford

# Scotland

© Lovell Johns Limited, Oxford

Wales

Holyhead

282

277 278
Llandudno

283

A55

A55

A55

A5

Caernarfon

A5

A470

A494

A483

A487

*Snowdonia
National Park*

A5

A494

Wrexham

A525

A5

281

A494

279

A470

Dolgellau

288

280

A487

A458

276

A470

A483

A470

A44

A489

**ENGLAND**

Aberystwyth

A470

A44

A470

A44

A44

A483

275

A483

289

A483

A487

A487

A40

A483

A470

287

Brecon

A438

Fishguard

A40

286

A40

Carmarthen

A40

A40

A470

A40

Brecon Beacons National Park

A479

284

A40

A483

Abergavenny

A477

A48

A483

A465

A449

Pembroke

Swansea

M4

285

274

M4

A470

A40

Cardiff

290

M4

Cardiff

CONDÉ NAST
**JOHANSENS**

GREAT BRITAIN & IRELAND

RECOMMENDED SMALL HOTELS
INNS & RESTAURANTS
2008

# Tell us about your stay

Following your stay in a Condé Nast Johansens Recommendation, please spare a moment to complete this Guest Survey Report. This is an important source of information for Condé Nast Johansens, in order to maintain the highest standards for our Recommendations and to support our team of Inspectors. It is also the prime source of nominations for Condé Nast Johansens Awards for Excellence, which are held annually and include properties from all over the world that represent the finest standards and best value for money in luxury, independent travel.

## 1. Your details

Your name: .................................................

..............................................................

Your address: ............................................

..............................................................

..............................................................

Postcode: .................................................

Country: ...................................................

E-mail: .....................................................

Telephone: ...............................................

Please tick if you would like to receive information or offers from The Condé Nast Publications Ltd by telephone ☐ or SMS ☐ or E-mail ☐. Please tick if you would like to receive information or offers from other selected companies by telephone ☐ or SMS ☐ or E-mail ☐. Please tick this box if you prefer not to receive direct mail from The Condé Nast Publications Ltd ☐ and other reputable companies ☐

## 2. Hotel details

Name of hotel: ..........................................

Country: ...................................................

Date of visit: ....................... Room No: ........

## 3. Reason for your visit

○ Leisure  ○ Business  ○ Meeting  ○ Restaurant

## 4. Any other comments

..............................................................

..............................................................

..............................................................

..............................................................

..............................................................

If you wish to make additional comments, please write separately to the Publisher,
Condé Nast Johansens Ltd, 6-8 Old Bond Street, London W1S 4PH, Great Britain

## 5. Your rating of the hotel

Please tick one box in each category below (as applicable)

| | EXCELLENT | GOOD | DISAPPOINTING | POOR |
|---|---|---|---|---|
| **Bedrooms** | | | | |
| Comfort | ○ | ○ | ○ | ○ |
| Amenities | ○ | ○ | ○ | ○ |
| Bathroom | ○ | ○ | ○ | ○ |
| **Public Areas** | | | | |
| Inside | ○ | ○ | ○ | ○ |
| Outdoor | ○ | ○ | ○ | ○ |
| **Housekeeping** | | | | |
| Cleanliness | ○ | ○ | ○ | ○ |
| Maintenance | ○ | ○ | ○ | ○ |
| **Service** | | | | |
| Check in/out | ○ | ○ | ○ | ○ |
| Professionalism | ○ | ○ | ○ | ○ |
| Friendliness | ○ | ○ | ○ | ○ |
| Dining | ○ | ○ | ○ | ○ |
| **Internet Facilities** | | | | |
| Bedrooms | ○ | ○ | ○ | ○ |
| Public Areas | ○ | ○ | ○ | ○ |
| **Ambience** | ○ | ○ | ○ | ○ |
| **Value for Money** | ○ | ○ | ○ | ○ |
| **Food and drink** | | | | |
| Breakfast | ○ | ○ | ○ | ○ |
| Lunch | ○ | ○ | ○ | ○ |
| Dinner | ○ | ○ | ○ | ○ |
| Choice of dishes | ○ | ○ | ○ | ○ |
| Wine List | ○ | ○ | ○ | ○ |
| **Did The Hotel Meet Your Expectations?** | ○ | ○ | ○ | ○ |

I most liked: ...............................................

I least liked: ..............................................

My favourite member of staff: ....................

**Please fax your completed survey to +44 (0)207 152 3566
or go to www.johansens.com where you can complete the survey online**